Drupal 6 Site Builder Solutions

Build powerful web site features for your business and connect to your customers through blogs, product catalogs, newsletters, and maps

Mark Noble

BIRMINGHAM - MUMBAI

Drupal 6 Site Builder Solutions

First published: December 2008

Production Reference: 1121208

Published by Packt Publishing Ltd.
32 Lincoln Road
Olton
Birmingham, B27 6PA, UK.

ISBN 978-1-847196-40-8

www.packtpub.com

Cover Image by Gabriela y la pintura (Linaza100@hotmail.com)

Credits

Author

Mark Noble

Reviewers

Alan Doucette

Dave Myburgh

Senior Acquisition Editor

David Barnes

Development Editor

Ved Prakash Jha

Technical Editor

Gagandeep Singh

Copy Editor

Sumathi Sridhar

Editorial Team Leader

Akshara Aware

Project Manager

Abhijeet Deobhakta

Project Coordinator

Rajashree Hamine

Indexer

Monica Ajmera

Proofreader

Dirk Manuel

Production Coordinators

Rajni R. Thorat

Shantanu Zagade

Cover Work

Shantanu Zagade

About the Author

Mark Noble has worked in software development and web site design for over 13 years, in a variety of capacities including development, quality assurance, and management. He takes pride in developing software and web sites to make businesses run more effectively, and delights in helping users to get their jobs done more easily.

Mark currently works developing web sites, using a combination of Java and PHP, to help libraries to manage their collections. He also performs contract work for clients in a variety of industries, developing both traditional desktop applications as well as web-based applications, using Drupal and a variety of other technologies. When he isn't working for a client, Mark enjoys building sites using Drupal. His other hobbies include playing with his family, photography, hiking, travel, and geocaching.

I would like to thank my wife, April, and my kids, Zoe and Theo, for their support during the writing of this book. I know that at times when deadlines got short, I did too. I love you all and I'm looking forward to having some downtime and relaxation with everyone.

About the Reviewers

Alan Doucette is a partner at KOI (`koitech.net`), a web development company. He is passionate about PHP and open source software. He is also very active in the web community and is a contributor to Drupal. His constantly-changing blog is kept at `http://alanio.net`.

> Thanks go to the awesome Drupal community for all of their daily hard work creating great open source software. I would also like to thank my business partner, Ben Davis, for his support and for dealing with a Drupal fanatic.

Dave Myburgh was involved with computers even before the web existed. He studied as a molecular biologist, but discovered that he liked working with computers more than bacteria. He had his own computer business in South Africa (where he grew up), doing technical support and sales. He even created a few static web sites for clients during that time.

He went back to science for a few years when he first came to Canada, and then got sucked into the world of Drupal when a friend wanted a site for a local historical society. Since then he has once again started his own company, which now builds web sites exclusively in Drupal (he doesn't "do static" anymore). There is no lack of work in the Drupal world, and he now balances his time between work and family. He has also reviewed several Drupal books, including *Drupal 5 Themes*, and *Drupal 6 Themes*.

> I would like to thank my family for being so supportive of me and what I do. Working from home can be a mixed blessing sometimes, but having the opportunity to watch my son grow up makes it all worthwhile.

Table of Contents

Preface

A high quality web site can be an important part of any business marketing plan. However, many businesses choose not to have a web site because they think it will be too expensive or too difficult to build and maintain.

You can purchase hosting for a web site for as little as US $5 to US $10 per month. You can create your own site using a design program for a few hundred dollars, or you can have a professional web site designer create the site, which can cost several thousands of dollars. After you set up the site you will need to budget for maintenance of your site. Depending on how you have built the site, this can either require a large amount of work or can be very expensive.

Fortunately, there is a solution to help you build a high quality web site that is still affordable. Drupal is an extremely powerful content management system that allows you to easily create web pages and redesign the layout of a web site.

Drupal also offers a powerful plug-in system that allows you to add custom functionality to a web site. There are hundreds of pre-built custom modules that gives you access to a wide variety of functionality available on the Drupal web site. Available functionality includes:

- Creating slideshows of pictures
- Creating events and displaying calendars that include the events
- Incorporating pictures and videos from Flickr and YouTube
- Building maps with Google Maps
- Creating product catalogs and using e-commerce to sell products

In this book, we will use Drupal to build a site for a fictional client from the ground up. We will explore a wide variety of functionality within Drupal so that you can apply these techniques to your own site.

What this book covers

Chapter 1 introduces you to Drupal and the Good Eatin' web site, our fictional client for this book. We will download and install Drupal onto our web server and perform the basic setup of the site.

In *Chapter 2*, we will begin building the content of our web site, and set up the navigation system. Then, we will add images and slideshows to the site. Finally, we will install a custom theme for our site to change the overall appearance of the site.

In *Chapter 3*, we use CCK and views to create the restaurant's menu, showing the items available at each meal. We will also use Taxonomies to categorize the content in the menu.

In *Chapter 4*, we will invite our customers to interact with the site by leaving comments, rating content, filling out polls, and answering surveys.

In *Chapter 5*, we build a company blog so that customers can easily get timely updates from our company. We also integrate content from blogs on other web sites.

In *Chapter 6*, we create a calendar to display current events at the Good Eatin' restaurant. We will also build a newsletter so that we can deliver information straight to our customer's inboxes on a regular basis.

In *Chapter 7*, we integrate content from several popular web services including Flickr, YouTube, and Google Maps, to enhance our site. We will also discuss publishing our site to social networking sites such as Digg and del.ico.us.

In *Chapter 8*, we will add downloadable content to our site, including PDF files and other freebies. We will also discuss ways of automatically generating printable content and PDF files from our pages so that customers can save any content they want for future use.

In *Chapter 9*, we set up a take-out menu for our restaurant and allow customers to place orders online and pay for them at our e-commerce site.

In *Chapter 10*, we will discuss how to maintain your site including backing up files, optimizing your site, and updating the site when new versions of Drupal and custom modules are released.

In *Chapter 11*, we explore ways of adapting the techniques that we have learned in this book to a variety of other types of businesses. We also discuss outsourcing your web site development to a professional, and leveraging the knowledge you gained in this book to ensure that you get the site you want for the best possible price.

What you need for this book

To follow along with the examples in this book, you will need a computer which can run MySQL and PHP, which are prerequisites for Drupal. Luckily, every major operating system can run these applications. You may want to create an account with a web site hosting company to test your work, although, you can also use a regular desktop or laptop computer.

You will also need the Drupal Content Management system which is available from Drupal.org. We will discuss downloading and installing Drupal in Chapter 1.

Who is this book for

This book is designed primarily for business owners who want to create a new web site for their company, or upgrade a company web site to a site that is easier to maintain and has advanced capabilities. However, technical users will also find the book useful, as we will explore a wide variety of modules that are used to build web sites with Drupal.

Previous experience with web site development or programming languages is not required, although it is helpful to have basic computer skills.

Conventions

In this book, you will find a number of styles of text that distinguish between different kinds of information. Here are some examples of these styles, and an explanation of their meaning.

Code words in text are shown as follows: "To create a list, put the list start tag at the beginning of the list, and the list end tag at the end of the list."

A block of code will be set as follows:

```
<div class="GMapEZ GSmallMapControl" style="width: 600px;
                                             height: 480px;">
  <a href="http://maps.google.com/maps?q=111%20Main%20Street,
                                       %20Parker,%20CO"></a>
</div>
```

When we want to draw your attention to a particular part of a code block, the relevant lines or items will be made bold:

```
<a href="#original" class="ZOOM">Original Location</a>
```

New terms and **important words** are introduced in a bold-type font. Words that you see on the screen, in menus or dialog boxes for example, appear in our text like this: "Now, click on the **edit permissions** link to set up the permissions for our moderator role".

Warnings or important notes appear in a box like this.

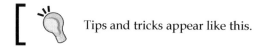

Tips and tricks appear like this.

Reader feedback

Feedback from our readers is always welcome. Let us know what you think about this book, what you liked or may have disliked. Reader feedback is important for us to develop titles that you really get the most out of.

To send us general feedback, simply send an email to feedback@packtpub.com, making sure that you mention the book title in the subject of your message.

If there is a book that you need and would like to see us publish, please send us a note via the **SUGGEST A TITLE** form on www.packtpub.com, or send an email to suggest@packtpub.com.

If there is a topic that you have expertise in and you are interested in either writing or contributing to a book on, see our author guide on www.packtpub.com/authors.

Customer support

Now that you are the proud owner of a Packt book, we have a number of things to help you to get the most from your purchase.

Errata

Although we have taken every care to ensure the accuracy of our contents, mistakes do happen. If you find a mistake in one of our books—maybe a mistake in text or code—we would be grateful if you would report this to us. By doing this you can save other readers from frustration, and help to improve subsequent versions of this book. If you find any errata, please report them by visiting http://www.packtpub.com/support, selecting your book, clicking on the **let us know** link, and entering the details of your errata. Once your errata are verified, your submission will be accepted and the errata added to any list of existing errata. Any existing errata can be viewed by selecting your title from http://www.packtpub.com/support.

Piracy

Piracy of copyright material on the Internet is an ongoing problem across all media. At Packt, we take the protection of our copyright and licenses very seriously. If you come across any illegal copies of our works in any form on the Internet, please provide the location address or website name immediately so that we can pursue a remedy.

Please contact us at copyright@packtpub.com with a link to the suspected pirated material.

We appreciate your help in protecting our authors, and supporting our ability to bring you valuable content.

Questions

You can contact us at questions@packtpub.com if you are having a problem with some aspect of the book, and we will do our best to address it.

1
Introducing Good Eatin'

Although several books have been written about Drupal, most have been written for developers to help them understand how to build sites with Drupal, enhance sites by using custom modules, and change the appearance of Drupal based sites by using themes. In this book, we take a different approach. Throughout the book, we will develop a web site for a (fictional) business, to meet the needs of this business.

We have included an explanation of all of the key features in Drupal that most small-to-medium sized businesses would want to use on their sites. A thorough step-by-step description of how to integrate each piece of functionality into your web site is included, along with an explanation of the business need that is being satisfied by using the functionality.

After reading this book, you will be able to adapt the techniques used in this book to either develop a site for your company on your own, or work with a development firm to create a web site that truly meets the needs of your business.

In this chapter, we will introduce our client, the Good Eatin' Bistro, and discuss their plans to build a web site. We will also introduce Drupal and describe why it is a good fit for our client's web site.

The Good Eatin' Bistro

Chef Wanyama is the owner of the Good Eatin' Bistro, a popular upscale restaurant. The past few years have been very good, and he has expanded from one restaurant to three. Each restaurant is decorated in a safari theme and Chef Wanyama is extremely proud of the decor. The Good Eatin' Bistro serves a wide variety of food, but specializes in creating meals using exotic game meats.

Chef Wanyama has recently added both take out and delivery to his menu and would like to do additional promotion for this aspect of his business, which he feels will bring in additional revenue. He also gives cooking classes, and would also like to promote these.

Plans for a Good Eatin' web site

Chef Wanyama had a web site designed for him several years ago, but it has proven to be difficult to maintain, and is therefore several years out of date. Chef Wanyama would like to build a new web site for his businesses to highlight the new specials at his restaurant. He would like to provide a destination for his customers where they can visit his restaurant online, learn more about the restaurant, find out about specials, and receive discounts if they are loyal customers.

Chef Wanyama has several key goals for his site:

1. The site must be easy to update so that it is always current.
2. Chef Wanyama should be able to make updates to the site without having to pay a consultant to do so.
3. He should be able to delegate simple tasks without compromising on site security.
4. The overall site should be secure and easy to maintain.
5. It should possible to add new functionality to the web site without requiring a complete start over.

After Chef Wanyama came to us expressing his desire to have a new web site built, we sat down with him to determine what pages and sections should be added to the web site, so that we can plan our development. Based on these discussions, we decided on the following structure for the site:

1. **Home Page**: This includes links to other areas in the site, current events, and sample menu items. Chef Wanyama may want the home page to have a look different from the rest of the site.
2. **Menu Pages**: This includes food, wine, and cocktails. There will be two methods for creating menu pages: a simple method where each page is developed independently, and a second method where editors can fill in a template for each menu. Each menu item will be categorized, so that customers can search the menu more easily.
3. **Menu Search**: This allows visitors to search the menu for foods, based on a variety of criteria.
4. **Menu item rating**: This allows visitors to rate items on a scale of 1-5.
5. **About Us Page**: This page provides contact information.
6. **Guest Book**: This allows visitors to comment on the restaurant and give feedback. Chef Wanyama can see when new comments are added, and he can optionally remove comments if they do not meet the site's standards.

7. **Map**: This helps the visitor find all of the Good Eatin' restaurants, using Google Maps.

8. **Polls and Surveys**: From time to time, the restaurant will have polls to see what items patrons want added to the menu, and what they think of the new items on the menu.

9. **Picture Gallery**: This shows the pictures of the food on the menu as well as pictures of the restaurants.

10. **Monthly Newsletter**: This is a newsletter that visitors can subscribe to. Chef Wanyama will be able to create the newsletter content on the site. Customers can also view the previous editions of the newsletter.

11. **Event Calendar**: This showcases musical events and other events occurring at the Good Eatin' restaurants.

12. A **Member Rewards site**: This gives details of the free meals for members who have visited the restaurant a specified number of times.

13. **Online ordering**: This will allow visitors to order take out and delivery.

14. **Forum**: This is a forum to solicit suggestions and ideas for improvement, to discuss policies, and so on.

15. **Blog**: This will be used by Chef Wanyama and his employees for discussing topics important to them, including information on new menu recipes, running a restaurant, and more.

16. **Administration Area**: This helps Chef Wanyama optimize his site so that the visitors can make the most out of the web site.

Selecting a foundation for the Good Eatin' site

In this section, we will explore a range of possible technologies that could be used to build the Good Eatin' site. The pros and cons of each method will be discussed, and we will choose the final technology that will be be used to build the site.

Simple static web pages

Most web sites are created by simply creating standalone HTML pages that do not change. These pages can be created with a dedicated web site design program or with a simple text editor such as Microsoft Notepad. These pages are then uploaded to the web server using an FTP client, or another transfer client provided by the web host.

Key advantages

There are several advantages to using this method of web development:

1. Custom editors can make creating web sites as easy as writing a letter.
2. Web site editors may provide pre-built themes to make the web site appealing without graphical design experience.
3. It is a very easy way to get started.
4. For simple sites, simple techniques are sometimes appropriate.
5. A web site can be created relatively quickly.
6. Sites can be built for free, or for the cost of a web site design program.
7. The hardware requirements are very low, so the web site will run on nearly any host.

Key disadvantages

Although static web pages can be easy to develop, there are a number of disadvantages that appear after you deploy the site and try to make revisions to it later.

1. Adding a new page to the site may require changes to all of the existing pages on the site.
2. Changing elements that are common to all pages, such as the header or the footer, may require changes to every page on the site.
3. When major changes are needed to the web site, it may be easier to start over than to rebuild the site.
4. It is easy to have errors within the web site, leading to pages that cannot be reached, or errors that the visitor may encounter.
5. Advanced functionality cannot be added without custom programming.
6. Created code can be inefficient or incorrect leading to web sites that do not display properly in all browsers.
7. Security and optimization techniques created by other developers are not automatically applied to your site.

Fully-customized site with PHP and MySQL

At the other extreme of simple static pages is a fully-customized web site built entirely from scratch using a programming language such as PHP and a database such as MySQL. In this type of system, all of the functionality for the web site is built by one or more programmers specifically for your web site. Some common libraries may be used to speed up development, but the majority of the site will be custom-created.

Key advantages

There are several advantages to developing a completely custom web site for your company.

1. The final site will be fully customized to meet the exact needs of your company.
2. New functionality can be added by another programmer at a later date.
3. Complex functionality may be easier to develop when starting from a clean slate.
4. Complex functionality may be impossible to build without custom programming.
5. The site may be much more efficient than a site built on a predefined framework or content management system.

Key disadvantages

Unfortunately, developing a completely custom web site is a difficult, time-consuming process and has several disadvantages. They are:

1. Relatively low-skilled programmers may create a web site that is difficult to maintain and enhance.
2. Changing the look and feel of the site may require significant rework unless the site is designed to allow customization.
3. The site may requires a great deal of work by programmers to create and maintain.
4. Security flaws may be inadvertently introduced, which could compromise the overall server or private data of your customers.
5. The site may require more hardware resources than simpler sites, and may require significant resources to run at acceptable speeds.
6. Creating all of the functionality from scratch can prove to be very costly.

Drupal content management system

Drupal is a content management system based on PHP and MySQL. To use Drupal, you need to install it onto your web server. After it is installed, you use Drupal to create and edit pages. Drupal handles most of the common functionality that is needed to build web sites of any size, including:

- User management
- Categorization of content
- Building menus
- Creating a consistent look for all pages
- Adding pictures to pages
- Creating and maintaining blogs
- Creating and maintaining forums
- Contact forms
- Translation and internationalization
- And much more

Although these features alone are sufficient to handle many sites, Drupal also offers a powerful module system that allows developers to create modules that plug in to the core Drupal framework to seamlessly provide new capabilities. Many modules have been created by the Drupal community and released for use by other users, free of charge. Modules are available for nearly every conceivable task, but if you don't find what you are looking for, a custom module can always be created to handle your exact needs.

Drupal also provides a powerful theme system that allows you to change the look and feel of your web site and have all of the pages changed throughout the entire web site, instantly. Several free themes are available on the Drupal web site, and these can be customized to fit your needs. Alternatively, you could develop a custom theme for your own site. Commercial themes can also be purchased from a variety of web sites.

Benefits of building with Drupal

Drupal offers a number of benefits not found with the other methods of building a web site. Many of these are related to the ease of maintenance and the ability to concentrate on business functionality rather than building common, repetitive functionality.

1. You are free to concentrate on building content and functionality to support your business rather than creating basic functionality already provided by Drupal.
2. The look and feel of the site can be easily changed without rewriting the entire site or changing all of the pages.
3. All changes to the site take effect immediately, so you can ensure that the changes are correct.
4. Changes can be previewed prior to the web site being updated, to make sure that they work properly.
5. Revisions to pages can be tracked, and you can require pages to go through an approval process prior to being made viewable.
6. You do not have to use FTP or other methods to deploy pages to your site.
7. Development costs are low as Drupal is available free of charge.
8. There is an active community that can help to answer any questions that you may have.
9. Drupal is actively maintained and enhanced, which helps to ensure that potential security issues are rapidly found and fixed.
10. Drupal can be used effectively by a wide range of people, even if they do not have any programming experience.
11. Site management can be delegated to a team of people who can share responsibility for the entire site between them, or take individual responsibility for specific areas within the site.
12. As Drupal is constantly being maintained and updated, you can gain access to new technologies more rapidly than would otherwise be possible.

Disadvantages of Drupal

Although Drupal is a very powerful tool, its very power causes a few disadvantages:

1. A short learning curve is needed to get started and use the system effectively.
2. It is more hardware-intensive than basic static pages.
3. Additional programming may be needed to customize Drupal modules to do exactly what you want. Alternatively, you may have to compromise on desired functionality, based on what is actually available.

4.   Hackers may try to target Drupal sites as there are a large number of sites that use Drupal.

5.   There may be limitations to the framework, which could make building custom functionality more difficult.

Deciding on Drupal

As you may have guessed from the title of the book, we are picking Drupal for the Good Eatin' site. Drupal gives us the best combination of functionality, flexibility, security, and ease of use for our web site. In fact, Drupal is an appropriate choice for a range of web sites from small sites to large sites and everything in between. The chances are, if you are planning to build a site, that Drupal will fulfill all of your needs.

Extending the Good Eatin' site to other businesses

Although this book will concentrate on using Drupal to build a web site for a restaurant, most of the techniques discussed can be used to build sites for other types of businesses as well.

In Chapter 2, we discuss common functionality that is applicable to nearly all web sites.

In Chapter 3, we build a restaurant menu using techniques that could also be used to create a product catalog for other businesses.

In Chapter 4, we discuss interacting with customers by using polls, surveys, comments, and more. All of these would be useful to a great majority of businesses.

In Chapter 5, we build a company blog. For some companies, a blog is their only online presence. For others, a company blog is essential for keeping their customers up-to-date on current events.

In Chapter 6, we create a newsletter, as well as a calendar of events. Newsletters are a fantastic way of reminding customers about your products and services, and a calendar can help you to publicize special events relating to your business.

In Chapter 7, we integrate content from third-party web sites such as YouTube and Flickr.

In Chapter 8, we offer free content to those customer giving them an additional reason to come to your web site and continue visiting it.

In Chapter 9, we discuss online ordering and payments. E-commerce is used by many online sites to provide a revenue stream.

Getting started with Drupal

In this book, we will jump straight into using Drupal to build a practical web site, and not spend a lot of time talking about basic functionality, the design of Drupal, or theoretical aspects related to Drupal. We will use Drupal 6 the most recent active version of Drupal throughout this book. Drupal 7 is currently in development, while Drupal 5 is also available for use on sites.

If you have not installed Drupal yet, you can use the following steps to install it:

1. Navigate to `http://drupal.org` in your web browser. You can either download Drupal from the home page, or you can navigate to `http://drupal.org/project/Drupal+project` and download it from there.

2. After you download the Drupal installation, you will need to unpack it. The installation is delivered in `tar.gz` format, for which you may need a specialized tool to unpack such as 7-Zip. 7-Zip is a freely-available program designed to work with a wide variety of compressed file formats.

3. After you unpack the installation, upload it to your web host. If you have not selected a host yet, skip ahead to Chapter 11, where we talk about recommendations for site hosting.

4. You can now browse to the location where you have installed Drupal in a web browser, to begin the installation process. You should see a screen similar to the following:

Drupal

▶ Choose language
Verify requirements
Set up database
Install site
Configure site
Finished

Choose language
○ Install Drupal in English
○ Learn how to install Drupal in other languages

5. Click on the **Install Drupal in English** link to proceed with the installation.

6. Drupal will now validate that all requirements for Drupal have been met. If any errors are displayed, they will need to be corrected before proceeding. On a default installation, you will need to create a `settings.php` file based on the `default.settings.php` file, which can be modified during the install process, as shown in the following screenshot:

Requirements problem

The following error must be resolved before you can continue the installation process:

The Drupal installer requires that you create a settings file as part of the installation process.

1. Copy the ./sites/default/default.settings.php file to ./sites/default /settings.php.

2. Change file permissions so that it is writable by the web server. If you are unsure how to grant file permissions, please consult the on-line handbook.

More details about installing Drupal are available in INSTALL.txt.

Please check the error messages and try again.

After you fix any errors that are reported, you can click **try again**, and repeat this step until no errors are reported.

7. You will now need to create a database for your site. The exact method of creating a MySQL database will depend on the host that you have chosen for your site. If you are unsure of how to create a database on your host, contact your provider for additional help.

8. After your database has been created, you will need to enter the name of the database, as well as the username and password for the database.

Database configuration

Basic options

To set up your Drupal database, enter the following information.

Database type: *

◉ mysqli

○ pgsql

The type of database your Drupal data will be stored in.

Database name: *

    yoursite_db

The name of the database your Drupal data will be stored in. It must exist on your server before Drupal can be installed.

Database username: *

    youruser

Database password:

    ●●●●●●●●●●●●

These will either be provided for you when your database was created by your hosting company, or you would have specified them yourself if you built the database from scratch.

9. After you have entered the database information, click **Save** and continue with the installation. Drupal will automatically build all of the necessary tables for you, and update the configuration for your site. You will now need to enter some basic information for your site. First, enter the name of the site and a contact email address that will be used to send emails from the site.

Configure site

All necessary changes to *./sites/default* and *./sites/default/settings.php* have been made. They have been set to read-only for security.

To configure your website, please provide the following information.

Site information

Site name: *

Your Site Name

Site e-mail address: *

admin@yoursite.com

The *From* address in automated e-mails sent during registration and new password requests, and other notifications. (Use an address ending in your site's domain to help prevent this e-mail being flagged as spam.)

---

10. Next, you will need to add an administrator account. This account will be used for site administration, and has abilities which the other accounts will not. You should try to make the password for this account as difficult to guess as possible, to reduce the possibility of having your site compromised by malicious users.

Administrator account

The administrator account has complete access to the site; it will automatically be granted all permissions and can perform any administrative activity. This will be the only account that can perform certain activities, so keep its credentials safe.

Username: *

```
YourSiteAdmin
```

Spaces are allowed; punctuation is not allowed except for periods, hyphens, and underscores.

E-mail address: *

```
admin@yoursite.com
```

All e-mails from the system will be sent to this address. The e-mail address is not made public and will only be used if you wish to receive a new password or wish to receive certain news or notifications by e-mail.

Password: *

```
•••••••••
```           Password strength: Low

**Confirm password:** *

```
•••••••••
```           Passwords match: Yes

The password does not include enough variation to be secure. Try:

○ Adding both upper and lowercase letters.

○ Adding numbers.

○ Adding punctuation.

If you enter a password that is not very difficult to guess, Drupal will warn you and provide suggestions for a more robust password.

11. Finally, you will need to define some basic server configuration options. In most cases, Drupal sets these items correctly for you, but you may need to review the time zone setting to ensure that this is correct.

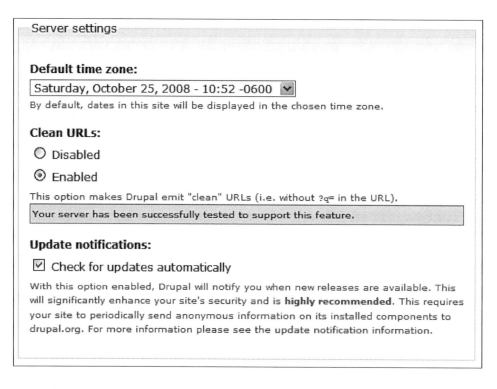

12. When you are satisfied with all of the information, click **Save** to complete the installation process.

13. Once the installation is complete, you can return to the main page, where you can login and begin the additional configuration of your web site. We will start building the Good Eatin' site from this stage, starting from Chapter 2.

If you want a more thorough introduction to Drupal, with explanations of some of the more theoretical aspects of Drupal, check out *Building Powerful and Robust Websites with Drupal 6* by David Mercer, also published by Packt Publishing.

# Jumping straight to dessert—Good Eatin' on the web

If you want to see an example of the techniques used in this book, as well as a live example of the complete web site, you can visit `goodeatin.drupalbyexample.com`. This site contains all of the examples developed throughout the course of this book. If you have questions about how to use Drupal, please post them on `drupalbyexample.com`, and I will try to answer your questions as quickly as possible. Alternatively, you can visit the Drupal forums at `drupal.org/forum`, to see if you can find an answer to your question; if not, you can post the question to the community.

# Summary

In this chapter, we developed the requirements for Chef Wanyama's Good Eatin' website. We also looked at some of the possible methods of building the web site, before deciding that Drupal is perfectly suited to this web site.

Now that we have our requirements for the web site and have decided to build it using Drupal, it's time to get our hands dirty and begin building the web site. We will start with the basic functionality that 99% of the web sites need and then gradually move on to more complex tasks. We will use a step-by-step approach to building the site, so that you can follow along with the examples.

# 2

# Creating Good Eatin's Online Presence

In this chapter, we will set up the fundamental parts of the Good Eatin' web site using the Drupal Content Management System. We will start by building a few pages, including the **About** page and the **Home** page. We will also discuss how to delete and edit pages. After we get comfortable managing content, we will add your pages to the navigation system so that customers can easily find all of the information that they need. After the navigation has been completed, we will make your site look more visually appealing by adding images and slideshows. Finally, we will add a theme to your site, based on one of the many themes available on the Drupal web site.

At each step in this chapter, we will point out ways to ensure that your site is secure so that hackers and other malicious visitors can't interfere with your business.

Before we start making any changes, let's have a look at the default site provided by Drupal.

At the end of this chapter, you will understand the techniques used by the vast majority of web sites on the Internet, and your site will look as shown in the following screenshot:

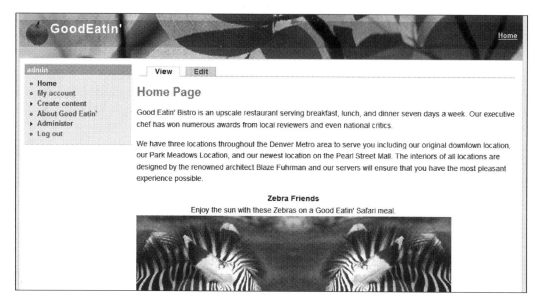

# About Good Eatin': Adding static pages

This section will describe how to set up an informational page that has static text. For our client, this will cover adding the **About Good Eatin'** page. We will also create a basic **menu** page which will be changed later.

## Adding a page

At the core of every site are pages that don't change or rarely change. Drupal makes it extremely easy to add these types of pages to a web site without having any programming knowledge. We will demonstrate these techniques on the **Good Eatin'** site by creating a simple home page and an about page.

To add a new static page, select the **Create Content** link from the menu on the left most side of the site. You will now be presented with a list of content types that Drupal knows how to create. By default, Drupal knows about the **Page** type and the **Story** type. Most static pages, including our About Good Eatin' page, will use the **Page** type. However, if you want visitors to be able to comment on your pages, or if you are creating a blog-style site, the **Story** type may be a better choice, because comments are turned on by default for this type. We will discuss comments in detail in the next chapter.

To create our About Good Eatin' page, click on the **Page** link. Drupal will now present you with a form on which you can enter information about the Page. You can enter a title that is displayed in the title of the web browser and above the content when it is displayed on the site. We used **About Good Eatin'** as the title of our page.

A typical about page will contain the name of the company, the address of the company, and a brief history of what the company does. We will use this as a guideline when we create our About Good Eatin' page.

You can enter information exactly as you do in the word processor of your choice, using the enter key to separate paragraphs. Drupal will automatically convert the text you enter into correct HTML for display in a web browser. You don't need to worry about learning HTML. However, if you do know HTML, you can use tags to format your pages. Refer to the HTML primer sidebar for information on the basic tags that Drupal allows the pages to include.

The text we used for the About Good Eatin' page is shown below:

```
<em>Good Eatin' Bistro</em> is a full service restaurant serving
breakfast, lunch, and dinner daily. Good Eatin' Bistro was founded in
2008 by <cite>Mark Noble</cite> to serve as an example website for the
<strong>Drupal 6 Site Builder Solutions</strong>.

<dl>
<dt>Address:</dt>
<dd>1500 Main Street<bar>
Anytown, CO<bar>
United States of America</dd>

<dt>Phone:</dt>
<dd>303-555-5555</dd>
</dl>
Hours of operation
<ul>
<li>M-F: 8AM - 10PM</li>
<li>Sat: 7AM - 12PM</li>
<li>Sun: 8AM - 8PM</li>
</ul>
```

Spicin up your site with simple HTML

Drupal allows you to use several simple HTML tags to improve the formatting of a page. Although HTML can be intimidating at first, it is really quite easy to learn and use.

Basic formatting

These tags allow you to change the appearance of the text when it is displayed on your web site. To use one of these tags, simply place the starting tag before the text whose style you want to change, and the ending tag when you want to return to the previous style. For example, to set the text `hello` in bold, you would enter `<strong>hello</strong>`. You can nest tags to apply more than one style to a piece of text. For example, to bold and italicize the text `hello`, you enter `<em><strong>hello</strong></em>`. When you apply more than one tag to a piece of text, make sure the pairs of open and close tags are correctly nested, and do not overlap.

Start Tag	End Tag	Purpose
`<em>`	`</em>`	Provide emphasis to a piece of text; this is done by italicizing the text. You should use this tag when you want to draw the reader's attention to a particular piece of text.
`<strong>`	`</strong>`	Make a piece of text stand out from the rest of the text; this is done by bolding the text when it is displayed in a browser. Setting text in bold can help readers to quickly scan your page to determine if they want to read it in more detail. You should use this tag when a piece of text is more important than the remainder of the text.
`<cite>`	`</cite>`	This tag is used to indicate a citation from another source; this is typically rendered as italicized text.
`<code>`	`</code>`	The code tag displays the text using fixed-width characters, which allows characters to line up. This greatly aids readability for text where the position of characters on subsequent lines is important.

Creating lists

There are three styles of list that you can create using HTML tags: **ordered lists**, **unordered lists**, and **definition lists**. The ordered list, precedes each element in the list with a number. The unordered list precedes each element in the list with a bullet. The definition list first displays the definition term and then indents the definition under the term. To create a list, put the list start tag at the beginning of the list, the list end tag at the end of the list, and surround each item in the list with list `item` tags.

List Type	Start Tag	End Tag	Element Tag	Example Code	Example List
Unordered List	\<ul\>	\</ul\>	\<li\>*element* \</li\>	\<ul\> \<li\>Item 1\</li\> \<li\>Item 2\</li\> \<li\>Item 3\</li\> \</ul\>	• Item 1 • Item 2 • Item 3
Ordered List	\<ol\>	\</ol\>	\<li\>*element* \</li\>	\<ol\> \<li\>Item 1\</li\> \<li\>Item 2\</li\> \<li\>Item 3\</li\> \</ol\>	1. Item 1 2. Item 2 3. Item 3
Definition List	\<dl\>	\</dl\>	\<dt\>*term name* \</dt\> \<dd\>*description* \</dd\>	\<dl\> \<dt\>Address \</dt\> \<dd\> 2500 Main St. Anytown, CO USA \</dd\> \<dt\>Phone \</dt\> \<dd\> 303-555-5555 \</dd\> \</dl\>	Address 2500 Main St. Anytown, CO USA Phone 303-555-5555

Linking to other pages

You can use the \<a\> tag to create a link to another part of your site or to another web site. This tag is slightly more complicated than the other tags because you must specify the destination that you would like the user to be taken to when the link is clicked.

The link tag has the following format: `<a href="destination">Link Text</a>`. For example, to link to the Good Eatin' home page, we would use the following tag:

```
<a href="http://goodeatin.drupalbyexample.com">Good Eatin'
Bistro</a>
```

Editing a page

After you have created a page, you can change the text on the page at any time by editing the page. To edit a page, first open the page in your browser, and then select the **Edit** link that appears next to the title of the page.

Drupal displays a form that is similar to the form we used when adding the page to the site.

Security considerations

You can control who is allowed to add pages to your web site by using permissions. By default, only the administrator is allowed to create pages and stories. If you are working on the site with a team, it is a good idea to create new roles which give team members access to only the functionality that they need to do their jobs.

Let's create an editor role so that other people in our team can add pages to our site. To create a new role, click on **User Management** and then **Roles**, within the **Administer** menu. Type **editor** as the name of the role and click the **Add role** button. Now that we have a new role, we can assign permissions to it by selecting the **edit permissions** link. The permissions you set will depend on what the user needs to do to perform his or her job and how much you trust the user. In most cases, it is best to give users fewer permissions in the beginning, and then give them additional privileges as they become more familiar with the site.

For our site, we will give the editor the following permissions, which are located below the **node module** heading:

- **Create page content**: Allows the user to create pages for the site
- **Edit own page content**: Allows the user to edit pages they have created, but not pages created by other users

A full list of permissions for creating and editing content is shown here:

Permission	anonymous user	authenticated user
node module		
access content	☑	☑
administer content types	☐	☐
administer nodes	☐	☐
create event content	☐	☐
delete any event content	☐	☐
delete own event content	☐	☐
delete revisions	☐	☐
edit any event content	☐	☐
edit own event content	☐	☐
revert revisions	☐	☐
view revisions	☐	☐

If you trust the users who will become editors, you could also give them the privilege to edit any page content, which would give them the ability to edit pages created by other users. If you are using Drupal 5, be careful when deciding which pages a user can edit because allowing a user to edit a page will also allow them to delete it.

If you choose to use other content types such as the **Story** type, you will need to assign permissions to these as well.

We will discuss additional permissions in future sections, so don't worry if you don't know what they all mean now.

Creating Clean URLs

Due to technical issues with how Drupal creates and displays pages, the default path for a page looks like this:

```
http://www.yoursite.com?q=node/1
```

This format can be confusing to visitors because it is more difficult to type and because it is not as familiar. Some search engines will also not index anything that comes after a question mark in a URL. This effectively makes your site have only one page in the eyes of some search engines. You can convert these to standard URLs by using Clean URLs. This will make the same page's path as follows:

```
http://www.yoursite.com/node/1
```

In Drupal 6 and later versions, you can set up Clean URLs during the installation process. If you are still using Drupal 5 or if you did not configure Clean URLs during installation, you can access this setting by clicking on **Site Configuration** and then selecting **Clean URLs** from the **Administer** menu.

To enable Clean URLs, your site must first pass an automated test. In Drupal 6 and later versions, this is done during installation and when the Clean URLs configuration page is loaded. In Drupal 5, you must click on the **Run the clean URL test** link on the **Clean URLs test** page. If your setup meets the requirements, you can click on the **enabled** link to correct the URLs.

If your setup does not meet the requirements, there is a wealth of information on the Drupal site at: `http://drupal.org/node/15365` that will help you determine why, and correct any issues. If you continue to have trouble setting up Clean URLs, you may need to contact your site host.

Street presence, setting up the home page

In this section, we will create the home page for the Good Eatin' web site. We will cover two possible styles of home pages. The first displays short snippets of text called **teasers** from other portions of the web site. This type of page is typically used on news sites and blog sites. The other type of home page is a more static page which contains its own unique content. This type of page is typical of most web sites.

Blog style home pages

The first page that most visitors to your site will see is the home page. Drupal makes it very easy to control the appearance and content of the home page.

By default, Drupal uses a blog style format, in which a portion of several other pages are displayed on the home page. Drupal calls the part of each page that is displayed a **teaser**.

The teaser is automatically created by Drupal according to the **Post Settings**, which can be accessed from the **Administer** menu by clicking first on **Content management** and then on **Post Settings**. From this page, you can easily control how many posts will be displayed on the home page, and also how long the teasers will be.

In Drupal 6 and later, you can easily control how much of the page is used for the teaser. First, open the page in the editor, position the cursor where you want the teaser to be separated from the rest of the content and click the **Split summary at cursor** button. To accomplish the same functionality in Drupal 5, you need to add a comment with the text `<!-break-->` as follows:

This is a sample page with a teaser break

```
<!--break-->
```

More information after the teaser.

To add content to the home page, you must select the **Promoted to front page** checkbox in the **Publishing options** section when saving the page.

Creating a traditional home page

Although a blog style home page is appropriate for some sites, for the Good Eatin' web site, we want a more traditional page which will allow us to direct visitors to the most important parts of our site.

The first step in creating a traditional home page is to create a static page that will serve as the foundation for our home page. We will create the page in exactly the same way as we created the about page.

When you create a home page, you should introduce the visitors to the products or services that you offer and make it easy for them to find their way around the remainder of the site. A typical visitor will spend only 20-30 seconds on a page before deciding if he or she wants to explore the site further or move on to another site. So a clear presentation of what differentiates you from your competitors is imperative.

For the initial home page, we enter the text as shown here:

Create Page

Title: *

Home Page

▷ Menu settings

Split summary at cursor

Body:

Good Eatin' Bistro is an upscale restaurant serving breakfast, lunch, and dinner seven days a week. Our executive chef has won numerous awards from local reviewers and even national critics.

We have three locations throughout the Denver Metro area to serve you including our original downtown location, our Park Meadows Location, and our newest location on the Pearl Street Mall. The interiors of all locations are designed by the renowned architect Blaze Fuhrman and our servers will ensure that you have the most pleasant experience possible.

We also offer cooking classes on a regular basis where we teach you to replicate our finest dishes.

After you have created the home page, you need to tell Drupal that you want to use this page, rather than the default page, as the home page when visitors come to your web site. First, make note of the path in the address bar when you are viewing the new home page. This will be in the format `yoursite.com/node/#`, assuming that you are using Clean URLs. If you are not using Clean URLs, the URL will be in the format `yoursite.com/?q=node/2`. For the Good Eatin' site, the home page is located at `http://goodeatin.drupalbyexample.com/node/2`. The number for your site may be different and will depend on the number of pages that you have already added to your site. Now, open the **Site information** page in the **Administration** interface. This page is accessed by clicking on **Site configuration** and then **Site information**, within the **Administration** menu. The page appears as follows:

Site information

[more help...]

Name: *

GoodEatin'

The name of this website.

E-mail address: *

admin@drupalbyexample.com

The *From* address in automated e-mails sent during registration and new password requests, and other notifications. (Use an address ending in your site's domain to help prevent this e-mail being flagged as spam.)

Slogan:

Your site's motto, tag line, or catchphrase (often displayed alongside the title of the site).

Mission:

Your site's mission or focus statement (often prominently displayed on the front page).

Footer message:

This text will be displayed at the bottom of each page. Useful for adding a copyright notice to your pages.

Anonymous user: *

Anonymous

The name used to indicate anonymous users.

Default front page: *

http://goodeatin.local/ node/2

The home page displays content from this relative URL. If unsure, specify "node".

Save configuration   Reset to defaults

Change the **Default front page** to make it the path of the page you have created and, then click **Save configuration** to complete the changes. You can also add a site slogan, site mission, and a message that will be displayed at the bottom of all of the pages on the site.

Other home page ideas

Another type of home page that is used occasionally is a Flash-based home page which displays a short video to visitors before they access the actual site. Although this technique can be great for certain sites where the use of video or music is the key to the web site, it is normally not a good idea for informational sites to use this option, because some visitors may turn off Flash, and some search engines may have a hard time indexing Flash-based pages.

If you want to use a Flash-based home page, the **Front Page** module allows you to create custom home pages. The Front Page module is described in detail on the Drupal web site at: `http://drupal.org/project/front`.

The **Splash** module will also allow you to display a different page prior to displaying your main web site. More information on the Splash menu can be found on the Drupal web site at: `http://drupal.org/project/splash`.

Getting around: Setting up navigation

As your site gets larger and more complex, you will need to ensure that visitors can easily find what they are looking for. With traditional web site development, managing navigation is among the most difficult, time consuming, and error prone tasks. Fortunately, Drupal handles the details of maintaining the navigation system for us, so we can concentrate on making sure that the navigation structure makes sense and is easy for the user to understand.

Building menus

The primary way to organize content in Drupal is by using menus. The Drupal menu system organizes content in a simple outline, where a page can be nested under another page. Drupal handles the expansion and collapsing of menus to hide menus that aren't immediately relevant to the user. This helps to keep the menu short and also ensures that the visitor can easily understand your site layout. You can also create multiple menus for the site. For example, many sites will have a main menu that is displayed on the left-hand side of the screen, and a smaller menu that is displayed at the top of the page and that lets the visitor jump to a specific section of the web site.

Types of menus

Drupal offers three different built-in menus. The **Navigation** menu, the **Primary links** menu, and the **Secondary links** menu. Although you can use these menus for any purpose you want, the standard uses are as follows:

The **Navigation** menu typically lists all pages that you want to be publicly displayed. On most sites, this menu is displayed on the left-hand side of the screen, and allows the user to quickly navigate to any page on the web site. The Navigation menu may have multiple levels, which can be expanded or collapsed.

The **Primary links menu** will list only the most important pages of the site. This helps your visitors by quickly pointing out the pages that you feel are the most important ones, and allowing the visitors to quickly jump to these sections. The items in the Primary links menu will normally be duplicated in the Navigation menu. However, the Primary links menu will only have one level. By default, the Primary links menu is displayed in the upper-right corner of the screen.

The **Secondary links menu** can be used for items that need to be available on each page, but that are not as important as the Primary links. You could use the Secondary links for privacy notices, contact information, search, or links to subsections within your site. For example, our Good Eatin' site could use the Secondary links menu to provide links to the breakfast, lunch, dinner, and drinks menus. Most sites display the Secondary links menu below the Primary links menu.

Designing your menus

Before you start building your menus, it is a good idea to build an outline in your word processor so that you have a plan to work from. By planning ahead, you can ensure that the menu will make sense to your visitors.

Our final main menu structure for the Good Eatin' site will be as follows:

1. Home Page
2. Food
    a) Breakfast
    b) Lunch
    c) Dinner
    d) Drinks
    e) Menu Search

3. Fun Stuff
   a) Music nights at Good Eatin' Bistro
   b) Good Eatin' Gallery
   c) Good Eatin' Newsletter
   d) Polls and Surveys

4. Take Good Eatin' Home
   a) Order Takeout
   b) Cooking Classes
   c) Recipes
   d) Guest Book

5. Company Information
   a) About Good Eatin'
   b) Employment
   c) Press

The primary menu that will be displayed at the top of the site will contain the following items:

1. Home
2. Food
3. Fun
4. Company

Adding a page to a menu

Although it makes sense to outline the menu structure when you are planning the web site, it is a good idea to build the menu as you add each page to the site. This will help you to ensure that all of the site's pages are added to the the menu correctly.

There are two methods of adding pages to a menu. The first method is by editing a page and then updating the menu settings. To create a menu link for the **Home Page**, first edit the **Home Page** and then expand the **Menu settings** section.

The **Menu settings** section allows you to control the text that will be displayed for this page when visitors view the menu, the Parent under which this page will be displayed, and a weight that controls the position of this page in the list.

Home Page	View	**Edit**

Title: *

Home Page

▽ Menu settings

Menu link title:

The link text corresponding to this item that should appear in the menu. Leave blank if you do not wish to add this post to the menu.

Parent item:

<Navigation>	▼

The maximum depth for an item and all its children is fixed at 9. Some menu items may not be available as parents if selecting them would exceed this limit.

Weight:

0	▼

Optional. In the menu, the heavier items will sink and the lighter items will be positioned nearer the top.

For the **Home Page**, set the **Menu link title** to **Home**, the **Parent item** to **** and the **weight** to **-7**. Click **save** to update the menu and you will be able to see the **new** menu in the side navigation. Repeat the process for the **About Page**, and this time set the **Menu link title** to **About Good Eatin'**, the **Parent item** to **** and the **weight** to **7**.

The parent item controls which menu item this page will be shown beneath. **Children** are independent underneath the parent items. If we look back to the first section of the menu we want to ultimately create, the parents and children as follows:

1. **Home Page: Parent** is **<Navigation>,** no children.

2. **Food: Parent** is **<Navigation>,** children are Breakfast, Lunch, and Dinner.

    a) Breakfast: Parent is Food, no children

    b) Lunch: Parent is Food, no children

    c) Dinner: Parent is Food, no children

You should now be able to see both the **Home** and **About Good Eatin'** pages in the **Navigation** menu. If you log out and then view the site, or view the site in a different browser, you will see only the **Home** and **About Good Eatin'** items in the **Navigation** menu.

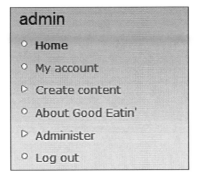

Creating custom menu items

To create custom menu items, you will need to use the Menu manager. This can be accessed by clicking on the **Administer** link, then the **Site building** link and finally the **Menus** link. You can also access the page directly by navigating to **admin/build/menu**. The **Menu manager** is shown in the following screenshot:

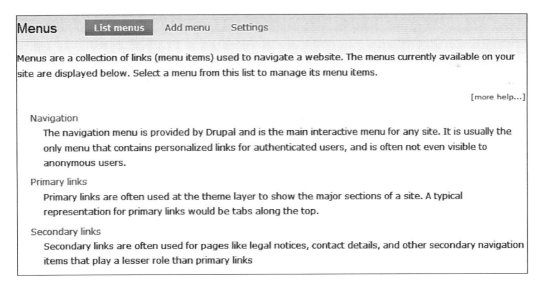

Once the **Menu manager** has opened, select the menu you want to edit. Because we have already done the **Navigation** menu, we will work on the **Primary Links** menu and add our home page and the **About Good Eatin'** page. By default, the **Primary Links** page appears as follows, because we have not created any menu items yet:

Primary links   **List items**   Add item   Edit menu

To rearrange menu items, grab a drag-and-drop handle under the *Menu item* column and drag the items (or group of items) to a new location in the list. (Grab a handle by clicking and holding the mouse while hovering over a handle icon.) Remember that your changes will not be saved until you click the *Save configuration* button at the bottom of the page.

There are no menu items yet.

To add a custom menu item, click on the **Add item** menu. Drupal will present you with a form where you can enter information about the menu item. This information includes:

- **Path**: This indicates the path which will be loaded when the user clicks on the menu item
- **Menu link title**: This is the text that will be displayed when the visitor views the menu
- **Description**: This allows you to give the visitor additional information when the visitor hovers over the menu item about what will happen if the visitor clicks on the item
- **Enabled**: This indicates whether or not the visitor can access the menu item; you can disable the menu item rather than delete it if a page is temporarily removed from the site
- **Expanded**: The expanded option controls whether or not a visitor can automatically see items that are contained within this one
- **Parent item**: This works exactly like adding a page to a menu and defines the link that this menu item will be displayed under
- **Weight**: This is used to control how the menu items are sorted when they are displayed by Drupal

We will create custom menu items in both the Primary links and Secondary links menus. The Primary links menu will contain a menu item for the Home page and the Secondary links menu will contain a menu item for the About Good Eatin' page.

To create the **Home page** menu item, open the **Menu manager**, click on the **Primary links** item, and then click on the **Add item** link. Enter **node/2** for the **Path**, **Home** for the **Menu link title**, and **Return to the home page** for the **Description**. The remaining settings can be left with their default settings. When you click the **Save** button, Drupal will automatically create and display the **Home** link.

To create the **About Good Eatin'** menu item, you will follow a procedure similar to the home page, except that you will select the **Secondary links** link before clicking the **Add item** link. Enter **node/1** for the **Path**, **About Good Eatin'** for the **Menu link title**, and **Learn more about Good Eatin'** for the **Description**. All other settings can be left with their default values again. When you save the menu item, you will immediately be able to see the new menu item.

Setting the order of menu items

Drupal 6 and newer versions allow you to control the order of links within a menu with a graphical drag–and–drop interface as shown below:

To use the editor, click down on the 4-pointed arrow icon to the left of the menu item name and , still holding down the mouse button, move the item to the required position in the list. The display of the menu will automatically change as you move the item up or down. By using the graphical editor, you do not need to worry about the relative weights of the menu items and when you move an item, the remaining items are automatically renumbered as necessary. You can also change the nesting of menu links by dragging the item to the left or the right. This allows you to easily and intuitively change the parent of the menu item.

If you are using Drupal 5, you will need to manually control the order of items within the menu by assigning a relative weight to each item within the menu. Although the concept of weights is used frequently within Drupal, it may not be familiar to you. When items are displayed in a list, Drupal sorts them according to their specified weight weight prior to displaying them. This causes the items with a negative weight to be closer to the top of the list, and items with a high weight will to be closer to the bottom of the list. If two items have the same weight, they may be displayed alphabetically, chronologically, or randomly depending on the list being displayed. Each level of a menu contains separate weights, so you don't need to worry about using a limited number of weights for a potentially unlimited number of menu items. However, if you find yourself running out of weights, take another look at your design to see if there is a better way of organizing the content. Most visitors will have a hard time in quickly understanding the various options, so simplifying your content will also help your customers.

When you manually define weights for items in a list, it is a good idea to leave gaps between the numbering, so that you can easily insert new items without having to re-order all of the existing items. For example, if you have four items to sort, you could use the numbers **-6**, **-2**, **2**, and **6** for the weights of each item. When you want to insert a new item between items **2** and **3**, you could use a weight of **0** and won't need to reorder any of the other items.

Deleting a page from the menu

Deleting a page from the menu is extremely easy. If you added the menu while editing the page, simply re-edit the page, select the **Delete this menu item** checkbox and **save** the page.

If you created the menu item using the Menu manager, you will also need to delete it using the Menu manager. Simply find the menu item that you want to delete in the Menu manager and click the **delete** link. You cannot delete **system menu** items. However, you can disable **system menu items** to prevent them from being displayed, by deselecting the **Enabled** checkbox for the menu within the Menu manager.

Security considerations

Drupal handles the security aspects of menus and ensures that a menu item is only shown to a visitor if they have the permission to visit the page to which the menu item points.

It is important that you test your menus in the same way as each type of user can access the site. Because our site is new, this simply means that we need to test it by logging in once as administrator and again as an unregistered user. An easy way of doing this is to open the web site in two different web browsers, for example Firefox and Internet Explorer. You can use one web browser to develop the site as an administrator, and the other to test the site as it will be accessed by other types of users.

Version differences

If you are still using Drupal 5, the Menu manager is slightly different to the Menu manager in Drupal 6, although the core functionality is still the same. In Drupal 5, the Menu manager displays all of the menus with their menu items on a single page. Drupal 6 and later presents each menu on its own page, which makes managing the menu much more intuitive.

Drupal 5 also has fewer weights available for ordering menus. In Drupal 6 and 7, the weights range from -50 to +50, but in Drupal 5 the weights range from -10 to +10.

Drupal 6 also introduced drag-and-drop ordering of the menus, which is a fantastic time-saver especially if you have a large menu.

Enabling modules

The functionality that we have used so far is included in the default installation of Drupal and you don't need to do anything special to use it. However, the real power of Drupal is unleashed when you begin enabling the optional modules that are included with Drupal, and when you install custom modules.

The Drupal installation includes over 20 modules, some of which are not enabled by default. These modules may be disabled by default for several reasons. Some are disabled because they are not needed by every Drupal installation, or they may require extra configuration, or they may have an impact on performance. There are also several optional modules that are enabled by default because they are used by a majority of sites. However, if your site doesn't need the functionality they provide, you can disable them.

You can view a complete list of modules that are available on your site by selecting **Site building** and then **Modules** from the **Administer** menu. This page gives you a list of all of the currently-installed modules, and allows you to enable or disable them. The listing for each module includes a short description of the module, along with information about what other modules are required. If you try to enable a module that depends on disabled modules, Drupal will prompt you to see if you want to enable the required modules that are currently disabled.

If you want more information on a specific module, the Drupal site contains a lot of information on each module. Information on all of the core modules is available at `http://drupal.org/handbook/modules`.

To enable a module, select the **Enabled** checkbox next to the module, and then click the **Save Configuration** button. If you enable multiple modules at the same time, Drupal will take care of enabling the modules in the correct order and checking any dependencies for you.

After a module has been enabled, the **Administer** menu will be updated with **new configuration options** for the module. There may also be new permissions for the new module. Check the documentation for the module to learn more about how to configure the module.

A page by any other name: Using aliases

When visitors return to your site, it will help them to have a meaningful path for each page. This will help them to be able to type in the URL for the page. A clear path can also help search engines understand what your page is about.

Unfortunately, the default paths that are created for each page are in the format **node/#**, where # is a unique identifier for the page. This can be confusing for visitors and certainly won't help you with the search engines. However, Drupal offers a solution through the use of **page aliases**. A page alias allows you to access a page using a different URL. There is no limit to the number of aliases you can assign to a page, but in most cases, you will want only one additional path for any given page.

To create an alias, you must enable the **Path module**. After the Path module is enabled, Drupal will add a new section called **URL path settings** to the edit form when you edit a page. For example, edit the **About Good Eatin'** page and then open the **URL path settings** section. Enter **about-good-eatin** for the **new path**. When creating paths, it is good practice not to use spaces in the path and to separate words with either hyphens (-) or underscores (_). The hyphen may be better for search engines as some search engines may treat words separated with underscores as a single word. You should not use spaces because they are not technically allowed in URLs. Most browsers will translate any spaces to %20, but you may run into compatibility issues.

After you have created an alias, you can use the alias to create menus and build other links.

Creating multiple aliases for a page

Sometimes a single path for a page is not enough. For example, if you are migrating to Drupal from an old site, you will probably want to alias the old pages to use the new paths, so that visitors and search engines using the old paths can still find your information. This is possible for any page on your old site which is accessed with simple URLs that do not have extra query information. For example, the URL `www.oldsite.com/home_page.html` can be aliased, while the URL `www.oldsite.com/home_page.html?a=Helllo` cannot be.

If you want to create more than one alias, you need to click on **Site Building** and then on **URL aliases**, in the **Administer** menu. You can create a new alias by selecting the **Add alias** link. Drupal will open a form where you can enter the "real" path and the alias of the path. The "real path" is the existing system path on the site. For our home page, this is **node/2**. The path alias is another name that you would like to use to access the page. For the home page, we can use **home**.

Automatically creating page aliases

If your find yourself creating new aliases for pages that follow a defined format, you can use the **Pathauto** module to automatically build aliases for you. More information on this is available at: `http://drupal.org/project/pathauto`.

Deleting a page

If you decide that a page is no longer relevant to your site, you can remove it from your web site. There are two ways of doing this. You can either **unpublish** the page or completely delete the page.

Unpublishing the page will prevent the visitors from viewing the page, but the page will still be stored within Drupal, so it can be republished later if the content becomes relevant again. To unpublish a page, edit the page and then click on the **Publishing options** link. This will expand the **Publishing options** section. Simply deselect the **Published** checkbox and then save the page. Drupal will ensure that the page is removed from all of the menus so that unauthorized visitors can't view it.

If you want to return to the page later, you will either need to type in the URL for the page or you can find the page via the content manager, which can be accessed at `yoursite.com/admin/content/node`. This page can also be reached from the **Administer** menu by selecting **Content Management** and then **Content**.

The other method of removing a page from your site is by deleting it. If you delete a page, it will be completely removed from the site and cannot be recovered. To delete a page, edit the page and then click the **Delete** button at the bottom of the page. You will be asked to confirm that you really want to delete the page. If you click on the **Delete** button again, the page will be completely removed from your site. If you change your mind in between clicking the two Delete buttons, you can select the **Cancel** link.

Leveraging the help of others: Installing custom modules

We have already discussed enabling core modules to add functionality to your site. In addition to the optional core modules, many developers from across the globe have contributed modules with custom functionality to Drupal. Custom modules add support for a wide range of functionalities, including:

- Integration with third-party websites such as YouTube, Amazon, and Flickr
- Administration assistance, including backing up your site, maintaining your database, and tracking site usage
- Creation and display of custom content
- Product sales and advertising

If you want to add a specific piece of functionality to your site, the chances are that there is already a module available that does just what you need. A complete list of modules can be found at: http://drupal.org/project/Modules.

The modules that are available depend on the version of Drupal you are using. The Drupal site tells you which versions of Drupal each module is compatible with, and also allows you to filter the available modules based on your version of Drupal.

Custom module development typically lags Drupal development by a few months, and many modules will not be ported to the very latest version until it is generally released. For that reason, you may want to wait to migrate to the latest version of Drupal until all of the modules that you use have been ported to the latest version. Although most custom modules are actively maintained by developers, you may find some modules that are not being actively maintained by the original developer. If this is the case for a module you want to use, you can take over the development process yourself, have a developer modify the custom module for you, or sponsor additional development of the module. The Drupal site offers a forum dedicated exclusively to companies who want custom development done. You can find the forum at: http://drupal.org/paid-services.

To install a custom module, you will need to carry out the following steps:

1. Find the module you want to install, on the Drupal web site. As an example, we will download the Image Module, which is available at `http://drupal.org/project/image`.

2. Download the version of the module that corresponds to the version of Drupal you are using. As you can see from the following image, a module may have multiple releases. The official releases should be used for production web sites. Development snapshots can be used for test purposes. You should use the version that is recommended for your version of Drupal. We are using Drupal 6 for the Good Eatin' site, so we will download that version by clicking on the **Download** link.

Releases				
Official releases	**Date**	**Size**	**Links**	**Status**
6.x-1.0-alpha1	2008-Apr-13	35.77 KB	Download · Release notes	Recommended for 6.x ✓
5.x-2.0-alpha1	2008-Apr-13	40.2 KB	Download · Release notes	Supported for 5.x ⚠
5.x-1.8	2008-Apr-13	133.95 KB	Download · Release notes	Recommended for 5.x ✓
Development snapshots	**Date**	**Size**	**Links**	**Status**
6.x-1.x-dev	2008-Apr-18	136.5 KB	Download · Release notes	Development snapshot ⊗
5.x-2.x-dev	2008-Apr-22	137.82 KB	Download · Release notes	Development snapshot ⊗
5.x-1.x-dev	2008-Apr-22	134.01 KB	Download · Release notes	Development snapshot ⊗

3. After you have downloaded the module, you need to expand it. Drupal modules are stored as `gzipped .tar` files. If you are using the Windows operating system, you probably don't have a program to open these files and you need to download one. 7-Zip is a freely-available program that will allow you to open these files. You can download 7-Zip from `http://www.7-zip.org/`.

4. If you use 7-Zip, you will need to first extract the `.tar` file and then extract the files from it. After you have done this, you will have a group of files that make up the module. For the image module, these files will be located in a folder named `image`.

5. Now that you have the module expanded, you will need to upload it to your web site using FTP. This is similar to uploading the installation files for Drupal. When you upload the module, you should upload the entire folder to `sites/all/modules`. If this is the first module that you have added, you will need to create the `modules` directory.

6. The next step is to `enable` the module. To do this, open the **Module manager** in your site. This is accessed by clicking on **Site building** and then **Modules**, from the **Administer** menu. As you can see from the following image, a single module installation may provide more than one module.

Enabled	Name	Version	Description
☐	**Image**	6.x-1.0-alpha1	Allows uploading, resizing and viewing of images. Required by: Image Attach (disabled), Image Gallery (disabled), Image Import (disabled)
☐	**Image Attach**	6.x-1.0-alpha1	Allows easy attaching of image nodes to other content types. Depends on: Image (disabled)
☐	**Image Gallery**	6.x-1.0-alpha1	Allows sorting and displaying of image galleries based on categories. Depends on: Image (disabled), Taxonomy (enabled)
☐	**Image Import**	6.x-1.0-alpha1	Allows batches of images to be imported from a directory on the server. Depends on: Image (disabled)
☐	**ImageMagick Advanced Options**	6.x-1.0-alpha1	Adds advanced options to the ImageMagick image toolkit.

▽ Image

Each module can be enabled independently as long as all requirements are met. As you can see, the **Image module** is required by many of the other modules, which cannot be enabled until the **Image module** is enabled. We will enable only the **Image module**, by selecting the **Enabled** button next to the **Image module** and then clicking on the **Save Configuration** button.

7. After the module has been enabled, you should check the permissions for the module to determine if any changes are necessary. This is done on the **Permissions** page, which can be accessed by clicking on **User management** and then **Permissions**, from the **Administer** menu. As you can see, there are several permissions available for the **Image module**.

Permission	anonymous user	authenticated user
image module		
create images	☐	☐
edit images	☐	☐
edit own images	☐	☐
view original images	☐	☐

We will allow authenticated users to create images and edit their own images. Simply select the checkboxes for these options and then click the **Save permissions** button.

8. Depending on the module that you install, there may be settings specific to the module. You should check for these by clicking on the **Administer** menu and looking for new settings. The majority of the new settings will appear in the **Site Configuration** submenu. However, some settings may appear in other areas. The documentation that came with the module will typically describe where to find the any required or available settings. In the case of the **Image module**, there are two new sets of settings: the **Images** settings and the **Image toolkit** settings. Both of these are located in the **Site Configuration** menu within the **Administer** menu.

Now that the custom module has been installed, you can use the module to enhance your site.

Security considerations

When you add a custom module to your site, you do expose yourself to possible security risks. However, the Drupal community does an incredible job of reviewing each module for possible security issues, and Drupal core does an excellent job of protecting you from potential problems.

You can further protect yourself by registering on the Drupal web site and subscribing to the security alerts newsletter.

Whetting their appetites: Adding images

Pictures are a crucial part of any web site because, as the old saying goes, *a picture is worth a thousand words*. Pictures also help to draw users into the site and give them a reason to explore further. Studies have shown that you only have a few seconds to gain a visitor's interest before he or she navigates away from your web site. Stunning images will encourage users to look at the site in more detail.

Drupal offers several methods for inserting images into your web site, ranging from the basic use of HTML to using custom modules.

Inserting images with simple HTML

HTML provides the `img` tag to allow web sites to include images on their pages. You can use the `img` tag as follows: `<img src="http://yoursite.com/imagepath/ imagename'" />`. For example, a link to an image on the Good Eatin' site could be:

```
<img src="http://goodeatin.drupalbyexample.com/images/zebra.jpg" />
```

You can either use double quotes or single quotes around the source, but I found that using single quotes typically integrates better with Drupal. You can also add size information to the image if you want, by adding `width` and `height` attributes to the tag. A tooltip can be added to the image by including a `title` attribute. If you need to include a double quote within the title, you should use `&quot;` in place of the double quote. If you need to include a single quote in the title, you should use `&rsquo;` in place of the single quote.

If you try editing the home page or the About Good Eatin' page, and add an image to the page, you will notice that it doesn't show up after you save it. This is because Drupal applies filters to your content in order to prevent your site from security attacks. These filters are combined into **Input formats**, which are applied to the content. Using input formats also helps to simplify content management when you have multiple editors with various levels of experience. This is because you can give each editor access to different input formats depending on their experience.

To make your image tag visible, you will either need to change the input format you are using or create a new format for the page that allows the image tag to be displayed.

If you trust all of your editors not to abuse the formats, the easiest solution is to simply change from the **Filtered HTML** format to the **Full HTML** format. However, it is much more secure to add a new format that allows images.

Changing the selected format

The active format is set in the **Input format** section, as shown below:

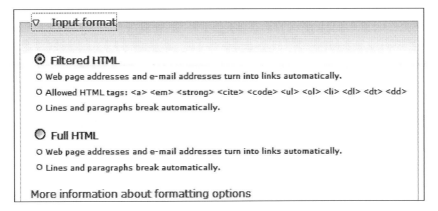

By default, there are two possible active formats, the **Filtered HTML** format and the **Full HTML** format. The **Filtered HTML** format allows access to only a subset of HTML tags. The tags you can use are listed in the description. The **Full HTML** format has no such restrictions. To change the selected **Input format**, simply edit the page, expand the **Input format** section, and then click the **Save** button.

Creating and editing input formats

To manage the available input formats, click on the **Site Configuration** link and then the **Input Formats** link within the **Administer** menu.

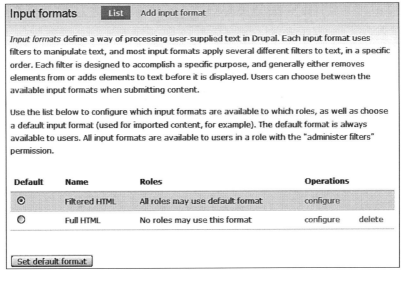

To create a new **Input format**, select the **Add input format** link. Drupal will now open a form to create a new input format. You will need to enter a name for the format, and you can also decide which users should be allowed to use this input format. This allows you to provide more functionality to users that have more experience, or are more trusted. The settings for our new image filter are as follows:

Add input format
List **Add input format**

Name: *
Image Format
Specify a unique name for this filter format.

Roles
Choose which roles may use this filter format. Note that roles with the "administer filters" permission can always use all the filter formats.

☐ anonymous user

☑ authenticated user

Filters
Choose the filters that will be used in this filter format.

☑ HTML corrector
Corrects faulty and chopped off HTML in postings.

☑ HTML filter
Allows you to restrict whether users can post HTML and which tags to filter out. It will also remove harmful content such as JavaScript events, JavaScript URLs and CSS styles from those tags that are not removed.

☑ Line break converter
Converts line breaks into HTML (i.e.
 and <p> tags).

☐ URL filter
Turns web and e-mail addresses into clickable links.

After saving the input format, you need to configure the filters so that the image tag is allowed. Click on the **Configure** link and Drupal will display the settings for the filters.

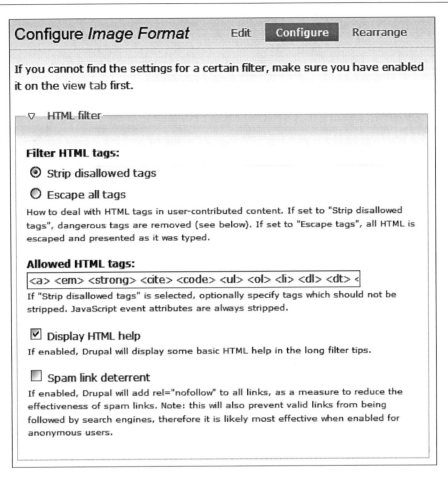

To provide better support for adding images to our input format, change the **Allowed HTML tags** to add `<img>` at the beginning of the text.

You can now use the input format anywhere, to enter images. To insert the image, you will need to:

1. Create a directory on your web server to store the images. To simplify site administration and backup, Drupal creates a subdirectory called `sites` under the directory where Drupal is installed. In this directory, there are two subdirectories named `all` and `default`. This structure is designed to allow multiple sites to utilize the same Drupal installation.

Any file contained in the `all` directory is accessible to all web sites running in the installation. Files that relate to a single site should be placed in a folder based on the domain of the web site, for example, `example.com` or `goodeatin.drupalbyexample.com`. If a site-specific folder cannot be found, Drupal will look in the default folder.

For more information about the sites directory, see the article at: `http://drupal.org/node/53705`.

2. Upload the image to your server via FTP.

3. Verify that the image is accessible by opening a web browser and entering `http://yoursite.com/sites/yoursite.com/files/images/imagename.jpg` as the address.

4. Update your web page to include the `img` tag with the `src set` to the address you used in step 3.

5. Change the input format to a format that allows the `img` tag.

6. Save the content and view the page to ensure that your changes are correct.

If you want to display the image in different sizes depending on where it is installed, you will need to manually resize each image to the desired size.

If you have multiple editors for your site, you will need to provide each editor that will enter images images the permissions to send image files to your server. This can pose a security risk to your site as the user could update other files in addition to the image files.

Inserting images using the image module

Because inserting images manually can be a security risk, as well as a time-consuming and error-prone process, the Drupal team created the **Image module** which allows images to be easily added to any page. We have already installed the Image module in a previous section, so we can now jump straight into adding images.

Creating images

To create a new image, select the **Image link** from the **Create content** menu. Drupal will display a form where you can select the image to be added to the site, give the picture a **Title**, and add a description to it.

Create Image

Title: *

    Safari Elephant

Image:

    tore\disk0021\2007 08 11\Elephant Smile.jpg [Browse...]

Click "Browse..." to select an image to upload.

▷ Menu settings

☐ Rebuild derivative images.

Check this to rebuild the derivative images for this node.

[Split summary at cursor]

Body:

    This elephant is one of the many animals you might see on a Good Eatin' Safari!

After you have saved the image, it will automatically be added to the web site. You can also insert the image into other pages on the web site by using the `img` tag. To refer a picture that you created with the image module using an `img` tag, you will use a tag that looks like:

```
<img src='http://www.yoursite.com/image/view/##/size'/>.
```

Replace the `##` with the node ID of the image you inserted, and replace `size` with the image size that you want to use. By default, you can use `thumbnail`, `preview`, and `_original` as image sizes, and you can also add additional sizes by customizing the image module.

All pictures that were created with the image module will be promoted to the front page automatically. If you don't want an image to be promoted to the front page, you can turn off the **Promoted to front page** option in the **Publishing options** for the image. If you want to insert a large number of images, you may want to disable this option in the **Image content type**.

Automatically resizing images

The image module will automatically resize images for you so that you can use them in a variety of situations. By resizing the images, your pictures will look their absolute best no matter where you use them.

By default, the image module stores an image in its original size. It also creates a thumbnail that is a maximum of 100 pixels on any axis, and a preview image which is a maximum of 640 pixels on any axis. When both of these images are created, by default the image is scaled proportionally, so the smaller side will be less than the maximum. Therefore the final image won't be square unless the original image is square.

You can create up to three additional image sizes. To create new image sizes, select the **Site Configuration** link and then the **Images** link, from the **Administer** menu. We will create two new image sizes: a **Menu Item List** and a **Menu Item Large**. The settings for these new image sizes are as follows:

Image sizes

The *Scale image* operation resizes images so that they fit with in the given dimensions. If only one dimension is specified the other dimension will be computed based on the image's aspect ratio. The *Scale and crop image* operation resizes images to be exactly the given dimensions. If only one dimension is specified the image will not be cropped, making this is equivalent to *Scale image*.

Note: 'Original' dimensions will only be used to resize images when they are first uploaded. Existing originals will not be modified.

Label	Operation	Width	Height	Link
Original	Scale image			Same window
Thumbnail	Scale image	100	100	Same window
Preview	Scale image	640	640	Same window
Menu Item List	Scale and crop image	150	150	Same window
Menu Item Large	Scale image	300	300	Same window
	Scale image			Same window

We will use the first image size to display pictures of food on our menu when more than one item is displayed on a page. We will use the second one to display pictures of food when only one item is displayed on a page. The **Menu Item** list will also crop the image so that it is square.

After you have created the new sizes, the images will be automatically regenerated when you view them. You can also regenerate the images manually by editing them, selecting the **Rebuild derivate images** checkbox and then finally saving the image.

Deleting images

Deleting an image is exactly the same as deleting a page. Simply edit the image, and click on the **Delete** button. Deleting an image will permanently remove the image from your site. If you want to remove it temporarily, you can **unpublish** the image.

Dinner and a show: Adding slideshows to the site

If you have a large number of pictures, you can display them in a slideshow format, where pictures are displayed one after another in a specific order. Pictures in a slideshow typically use a fade transition from one to the other. Drupal has at least two custom modules that allow you to easily build slideshows—the **Slideshow Creator** module and the **Lightbox** module.

Showing images on the page using Slideshow Creator

The Slideshow Creator module can be downloaded from `http://drupal.org/ project/slideshow_creator`. It also requires the **JQuery Plugin** module, which is available at `http://drupal.org/project/jquery_plugin`. Download these two modules, install them on your site, and then enable them using the Module Manager.

The Slideshow Creator module does not have any additional permissions that you need to worry about. However, there are a few configuration settings:

Slideshow Creator

Height:

400

The slideshow height, in pixels.

Width:

400

The slideshow width, in pixels.

Layout:

Default ▾

The slideshow layout

Current Slide String:

Slide

The text to be displayed on the Current Slide part.

[Save these settings]

These options allow you to control the size of the slideshow that will be embedded in the page, as well as specify some basic options related to the display.

Slideshow Creator works by creating a new filter that you can add to any input format, similarly to how we enabled the use of img tags on a page.

To enable this filter:

1. Click on the **Site Configuration** link and then the **Input formats** link, from the **Administer** menu.

2. Click on the **configure** link for the input format that you want to add slideshows to. We will add slideshow capabilities to our **image format**.

3. Select the checkbox next to the **Slideshow Creator filter**.

4. Save the input format.

You can use **Slideshow Creator** to either display specific pictures or to display all of the pictures that are stored within a specified folder on your web server. Displaying specific pictures gives you much more control and allows you to give each image a title, description, and the page to be displayed when the image is clicked (if any). Displaying all images in a folder is much easier to manage as you do not need to add each image to the slideshow individually.

Basic steps for inserting a slideshow

To insert a new slideshow, use the following steps:

1. Upload the pictures that you want to display in the slideshow to your site by using either FTP or the Image module.

2. Edit the page that you want to add the slideshow to.

3. Create the slideshow using a filter tag (see the following sections for details).

4. Save the page.

Setting up a slideshow with individual images

A slideshow with individual images uses the following format for the filter tag.

```
[slideshow:VERSION, img=|IMAGE_URL|LINK|TITLE|DESCRIPTION|TARGET|,
img=|IMAGE_URL|LINK|TITLE|DESCRIPTION|TARGET|]
```

- The VERSION should be set to 2 for the current version of Slideshow Creator.

- The IMAGE_URL should be set to the full path to the image that you want to display.

- The LINK is the destination you want the visitor to be taken to if they click on the picture. You can leave this blank if you do not want the user to be able to click on the image.

- The TITLE will be displayed above both the picture and the description. It can be left blank if you do not want to display a title.

- The DESCRIPTION is displayed immediately below the title but above the picture. This can also be omitted if it is not required.

- The TARGET is used in conjunction with the LINK and describes how the new page will be opened when the image is clicked. Valid values are: _blank, _parent, _top, and _self. The _blank option, which is the default, will open the link in a new window or tab, depending on the browser. The _self option will open the link in the same window that the slideshow is being displayed in (and will therefore replace the slideshow). The _parent and _top values are only used by sites that use frames.

Multiple images can be inserted by separating each img section from the previous one with a comma.

The following filter tag is used on the Good Eatin' home page to display a few pictures for the restaurant.

```
[slideshow:2, img=|http://goodeatin.drupalbyexample.com/image/view/3/
preview||Elephant Smile|This Elephant is one of the many animals you
may see as you take a Safari through the Good Eatin' restaurant.|,
img=|http://goodeatin.drupalbyexample.com/image/view/4/preview||Zebra
Friends|Enjoy the sun with these Zebras on a Good Eatin' Safari meal. ]
```

Setting up a slideshow to display all images in a folder

Although creating a slideshow with individual images gives you an enormous amount of control over how the slideshow is displayed, it can be very convenient to create a slideshow that simply displays all of the pictures in a folder. This type of slideshow uses the following filter tag format:

```
[slideshow:VERSION, dir=|DIR_IMAGE|DIR_RECURSIVE|DIR_LINK|TITLE|DESCR
IPTION|TARGET|]
```

The VERSION, TITLE, DESCRIPTION, DIR_LINK, and TARGET have the same usage as the individual img version, with the exception that the values will be applied to each image in the folder. The folder-specific settings are as follows:

- DIR_IMAGE is the folder where the files are located on your web server. This path will be relative to the folder where Drupal is installed. Slideshow Creator will include all PNG, GIF, JPEG, JPG, and BMP pictures found within this folder in the slideshow.

- `DIR_RECURSIVE` can be set to either **yes** to include images that are within the subfolders of the specified image folder or left blank to include only the specified folder. In most cases you will leave this blank because it is more convenient to organize the pictures for each slideshow in a single folder.

You can combine `img` groups and `dir` groups within a single slideshow to leverage the power of each method to meet your needs.

When you display all of the images within a folder, the images are displayed in random order, and it is not possible to reliably control the order of the display.

Additional configuration options

Slideshow Creator also contains several undocumented features that you can use to further customize your slideshows. Some of these allow you to override the default settings that are configured via the **Administration** menu, so that you have more precise control over the layout of the slideshows, and you can have slideshows with different sizes and layouts on different pages. You can even have multiple slideshows on one page, each with different options. The following options are available:

- `width`: This allows you to control the width of the slideshow. If an image within the slideshow is wider than the specified width, it will be cropped.

- `height`: This allows you to control the height of the slideshow. If an image within the slideshow is taller than the specified height, it will be cropped.

- `layout`: This allows you to control the order of the elements (Title, Description, Picture, and Controls) in the slideshow. Valid values are `Default`, `Reverse`, `Top`, `Bottom`, and `None`. These result in the following configurations (elements listed as they appear, from top to bottom):
  - `Default`: Controls, Title, Picture, Description
  - `Reverse`: Title, Picture, Description, Controls
  - `Top`: Picture, Title, Description, Controls
  - `Bottom`: Controls, Title, Description, Picture
  - `None`: Picture, Title, Description

- `blend`: This controls the speed of transition between images. It should be set in milliseconds, so to specify 2 seconds you would enter 2000.

- `timeout`: This controls how long each image is displayed for, before the next image starts loading. This is also set in milliseconds.

- `fx`: This controls what type of effect is used to transition between slides. Some of the available transitions are **shuffle, zoom, fade, turnDown, curtainX, scrollRight, blindX, blindY, blindZ, cover**, and **uncover**.

Any of these additional options used should be added before the list of images begins. For example, the following code adds a zoom transition effect to the slideshow and places the controls for the slideshow, under the pictures.

```
[slideshow:2,width=450,height=650, layout=top, fx=zoom, img=|http://
goodeatin.drupalbyexample.com/image/view/3/preview||Elephant
Smile|This Elephant is one of the many animals you may see as you take
a Safari through the Good Eatin' restaurant.|, img=|http://goodeatin.
drupalbyexample.com/image/view/4/preview||Zebra Friends|Enjoy the sun
with these Zebras on a Good Eatin' Safari meal. ]
```

Additional documentation for the Slideshow Creator Module is available at: `http://drupal.org/node/237049`.

Additional documentation for the JQuery Cycle module, which is used to build the slideshow, is available at: `http://www.malsup.com/jquery/cycle/`.

Version-specific issues

The author of Slideshow Creator is currently providing the module only to the users of the current version of Drupal (version 6 at the time of writing). If you are using another version, you may be able to find a download that is compatible with your version, but support may not be available through the original author.

Showing images over the page with Lightbox2

The Slideshow Creator module allows you to view slideshows within a page. However, sometimes it looks better to display images in a new window that floats over the main page. This is especially true for pictures on a photography or art web site, where the pictures are the main focus of the page.

Showing the slideshow over the main page also improves the appearance of the slideshow when all of the pictures are not the same size.

A sample **lightbox** looks like the following picture:

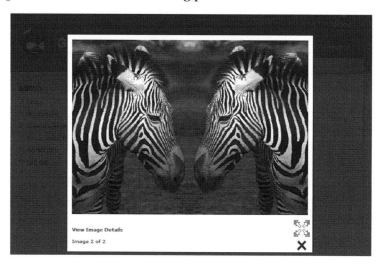

To use the Lightbox2 module:

1. Download the module from the Drupal web site. The project page is located at http://drupal.org/project/lightbox2.
2. Copy the module to your web site and enable it in the Module manager.
3. Configure Lightbox2 by selecting **Site Configuration** and then **Lightbox 2**, from the **Administer** menu. Lightbox2 has a large number of settings, divided into four sections. Let's explore each of these.

General settings

The **general settings** page contains a variety of settings used to control the display of the Lightbox. These settings are:

- **Use Lightbox2 Lite:** Enabling this setting will greatly limit the functionality of Lightbox2. All controls will be removed, so the visitor will not be able to navigate from image to image. This may be desirable if your site gets a large amount of traffic, or if you want to ensure that only one image is displayed at a time.

- **Use Alternative Layout:** In the normal Lightbox layout, the **next** and **previous** buttons are overlaid on the image and display only when the mouse passes over the link. When the alternative layout is active, the links are always displayed and they are placed below the image, alongside the caption. I personally prefer to have this option enabled because it is much more user friendly to always show the navigation to the user rather than make them search for the controls.

- **Force visibility of navigation links:** Enabling this setting causes Lightbox 2 to always display navigation controls.

- **Image Count Text and Page Count Text:** These settings allow you to customize the text that is displayed in the caption.

- **Disable Zoom Feature**: This setting will prevent the user from resizing the image if the image is larger than the page. Disabling the zoom may make for a cleaner Lightbox.

- **Video Settings**: This setting allows you to display videos within the Lightbox.

- **Page Specific Lightbox2 Settings:** This setting gives you the ability to prevent specific pages from displaying a Lightbox. This is useful if you are using custom modules that the Lightbox module detects and automatically attempts to display a Lightbox.

Advanced settings

The **Advanced settings** section offers a variety of settings that allow you to fine-tune how the Lightbox is displayed on the page. Using these options, you can control colors of the Lightbox, how long each transition between images lasts, and whether or not the user can see your web site beneath the Lightbox.

Slideshow settings

The **Slideshow settings** page provides various settings that control the functionality of the slideshow. This includes how long each picture is displayed, what should happen when the slideshow finishes, and what happens when the user clicks on the **Next** or **Previous Image** buttons. These options are all well-documented on the settings page itself.

HTML content settings

The **HTML Content settings** control how large the Lightbox will be if it is displaying HTML content. These settings also control whether or not a border is displayed on the Lightbox.

Automatic image handling settings

The **Automatic image handling settings** are used to control how Lightbox2 automatically inserts itself into the images within your site. If used correctly, this functionality will save you a great deal of time because you don't need to manually add links to each image and ensure that you have all the settings correct.

In most cases, you can leave these settings with their default values as they are all set to sensible values. However, there are a few settings that you should take note of:

- **Image trigger size** (in **Image node settings**): This setting controls which sizes of images will trigger the Lightbox to be displayed. If you have added new custom sizes, you should review this setting to ensure that each new size is set correctly. For example, we will add the **Menu Item List** as a trigger for the Lightbox.

- **Custom image trigger classes** (in **Custom Class Images**): If you are using img tags, you can also use the custom image trigger classes to automatically display the Lightbox, which simplifies your page creation and maintenance.

Viewing the slideshow

There are several ways of adding the slideshow to your page. If you are using simple img tags, you must surround the image with a link that tells the Lightbox to open. For example, the following code will display a thumbnail image on the page.

```
<a href="image/view/3/preview" rel="lightbox" title="Elephant"><img
src="http://goodeatin.drupalbyexample.com/image/view/3/thumbnail"
class="thumbnail"/></a>
```

When the user clicks on the image, the preview image will be displayed in the Lightbox. Any other images on the page that contain the rel="lightbox" attribute will also be displayed in the Lightbox.

Version-specific issues

The latest versions of the Lightbox 2 module (from version 5.x-2.0 and later) do not support Internet Explorer version 5.5 or earlier, due to the use of jQuery. If you need to support a large number of users who are still using this very old version of Internet Explorer, you may need to find an alternative solution.

Additional topics

The Lightbox2 module provides a lot of power, and displaying slideshows is just the beginning of what it can do. You can use Lightbox2 to display nearly any type of content, including HTML pages, video, Flickr photos, and much more.

The Drupal site contains a wealth of information about the Lightbox2 module. The documentation begins at: `http://drupal.org/node/144469`.

Personalizing the restaurant: Adding themes to the site

One of the great things about Drupal is that it allows you to thoroughly customize the appearance of your web site, rather than force you to build each aspect of your design from scratch. Drupal provides several custom themes that can be used as-is. You can also use the custom themes as a starting point, and build on them to create your own unique theme. A theme is used to give your site a consistent look and feel across all pages. Using themes, you can easily change the look of your site without changing the actual content of your site. This makes redesigning your site much easier (and cheaper) because you only have to modify the theme, and you don't have to edit each individual page.

You can even have multiple themes set up on your site and allow your users to choose to view your site using their favorite theme.

Selecting and installing a ready-made theme

You can find a large list of themes that have been contributed to Drupal at `http://drupal.org/project/Themes`. You can use these themes as inspiration for your own site design, or you can use a theme as-is.

Most themes are shown with a preview image so that you can get an idea of what your site will look like using the theme.

After you have found a theme that you want to try, you can install it on your site by carrying out the following steps:

1. Download the theme by clicking on the **Download** link for the theme.
2. Unpack the gzipped `.tar` file using the same techniques you have already used for unpacking modules.
3. Upload the new theme to your web site by using FTP. The theme should be placed in the `sites/all/themes` directory. If you haven't added a custom theme yet, you will need to create the `themes` directory.

4. Open the **Theme manager** by selecting the **Site building** link and then the **Themes** link, from the **Administer** menu. If the theme has been added correctly, you will see it in the list of themes shown in the **Theme manager**.

5. To enable the theme on the site, select the **Enabled** checkbox for the theme. After enabling the theme, you can set it to be active for a specific user, or you can make it the default theme for the entire site. As shown in the following image, we will enable the custom Foliage and Marinelli Themes.

6. The Foliage Theme can be downloaded from `http://drupal.org/project/foliage` and the Marinelli theme can be `downloaded from http://drupal.org/project/Marinelli`. The Marinelli theme also contains two subthemes that control where each column is placed.

Screenshot	Name	Version	Enabled	Default	Operations
	Chameleon Minimalist tabled theme with light colors.	6.2	☑	○	configure
	Foliage Table-less, source-ordered and multi-column theme.	6.x-1.3	☑	○	
	Garland Tableless, recolorable, multi-column, fluid width theme (default).	6.2	☑	○	configure
	Marinelli A fresh 3-column layout for Drupal. Still usable over 4000m!	6.x-1.7	☑	◉	

7. After the theme has been enabled, you can configure it by selecting the **configure** link.

Once you have enabled a theme, you can easily switch back and forth between themes to decide which theme you like best. If you decide that you don't like a theme, you can remove it by simply deleting the theme files from your web server.

Configuring a theme

The configuration options for a theme will vary depending on the actual theme. However, all themes allow you to determine if the following elements are displayed or not: logo, site name, site slogan, mission statement, user pictures in posts, user pictures in comments, search box, shortcut icon, primary links, and secondary links.

You can also configure the logo that should be used on the site. You can either use a default logo or add your own custom logo. If you choose to use your own custom logo, you can either specify a path to an existing file on your web server, or you can upload a new image.

You can also configure the shortcut icon that is displayed in the address bar when customers visit the web site. Again, you can either use the default icon or use a custom icon. This icon is also called the **favicon**, and is also displayed alongside the site name in the user's favorites, if they add it as a favorite.

If you select the **Global settings** option when you configure the themes, the changes will be applied to all of the themes you have installed.

Creating themes

When you create a custom theme, you should carefully consider the structure of your site and the content that you intend to display on your site. You should also think about the custom modules that you plan to add to your site. By considering these items at the beginning, you can plan ahead and ensure that your design is flexible enough to accommodate all of your plans.

After you have planned your theme, you will need to create a graphical design. Depending on your budget, you may do this yourself, have a graphic designer do it for you, or even hire a large design firm that can create several designs and test-market them to find out what your target audience likes best. If you choose to outsource your theme creation, you can find a qualified professional via the Drupal we bsite at `http://drupal.org/paid-services`.

After the design is complete, you will need to break the design down into individual images and ensure that any dynamic content can be placed over the background images. If there are any page-specific images, these will need to be created as well.

You can now build the css file for your theme, which will control the overall look of the page.

Finally, create your page template, which is typically called `page.tpl.php`. You can also change the appearance of other types of content by creating a template file for that content type. For example, a template file named `comment.tpl.php` will control the appearance of all comments within the site.

For a more complete discussion on creating your own themes, pick up a copy of *Drupal 6 Themes* or *Drupal 5 Themes*, both by Ric Shreves and both published by **Packt Publishing**. You can find more information about these books at:

```
http://www.packtpub.com/drupal-6-themes/book
```

```
http://www.packtpub.com/drupal-5-themes/book
```

Version-specific issues

A theme that is created in one version of Drupal is not guaranteed to work in future versions of Drupal, because the developers of Drupal have elected not to force backwards compatibility to be a constraint on development. This allows new development to use best practices to ensure that the latest version of Drupal is the best it can technically be. Although this is a fantastic strategy for Drupal as a whole, it does mean that you may have to make some modifications to your theme after each new release.

Playing in the kitchen: Topics to research on your own

In this chapter, we have covered a lot of ground and thoroughly explored a number of topics that are used in several other chapters in this book. As you continue to enhance your site, there are a number of areas that you may want to explore on your own.

Using Image Assist to easily insert images

The **Image Assist module** allows you to insert images while you are editing the page. This makes adding images much easier. The Image Assist module also works automatically with Lightbox2 to create a slideshow of all of the images on a page.

Book style pages

Drupal provides the **Book module** that is designed for the online editing of books that are created by groups of people in a collaborative environment.

Setting up a graphical editor

There are several graphical editors, also called **wysiwyg (what-you-see-is-what-you-get)** editors that can automatically be opened whenever you create a new page. These editors are similar to a word processor embedded in your web site. You can change the font of the text by clicking on buttons rather than inserting HTML tags. There are several modules that you may want to explore to provide this functionality, including:

- **TinyMCE**: `http://drupal.org/project/tinymce`
- **Tiny Tiny MCE**: `http://drupal.org/project/tinytinymce`
- **HTMLBox**: `http://drupal.org/project/htmlbox`

Timing the publication of content

If you have time-sensitive information, you can schedule the content for automatic publishing on a specific date and/or at a specific time. You can do this by using the **Rules module** for Drupal 6, which is available at `http://drupal.org/project/rules` or the **Workflow-ng module**, for Drupal 5, which is available at `http://drupal.org/project/workflow_ng`.

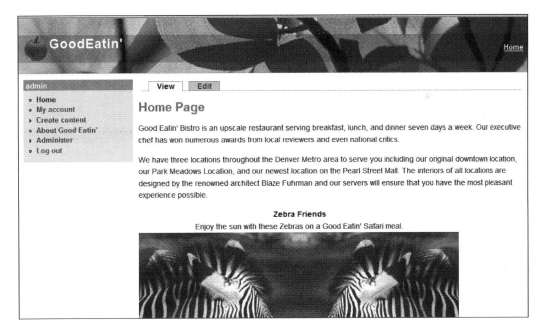

Summary

Congratulations! We have covered a lot of ground in this chapter, but we now know how to leverage the power of Drupal to create the core pages of your web site. The techniques that you have learned in this chapter can be applied to a wide range of web sites and will probably be used in every web site that you create with Drupal.

In the forthcoming chapters, we will continue to enhance the Good Eatin' web site with new functionality. Although we will be using more advanced techniques in the future chapters, we will continue to refer back to many of the techniques you have learned in this chapter, especially:

- Installing and configuring custom modules
- Creating new pages
- Creating menus

As you have seen in this chapter, Drupal makes creating and maintaining a site fun, and frees you from complex programming or detailed coding.

3
Adding Products and Services

In the previous chapter, we laid the groundwork for our site and added a few pages that are common to nearly all sites on the web. In this chapter, we will use Drupal to build a custom content type to store individual items that appear on the Good Eatin' menu. We will also explore different ways of displaying the content, to make the menu look its best.

At the end of this chapter, you will understand how to use CCK to build new content types, and how to theme CCK content types to customize the display.

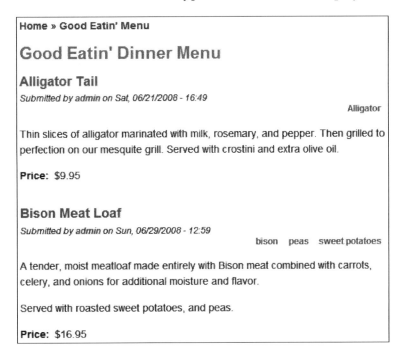

Home » Good Eatin' Menu

Good Eatin' Dinner Menu

Alligator Tail

Submitted by admin on Sat, 06/21/2008 - 16:49

Alligator

Thin slices of alligator marinated with milk, rosemary, and pepper. Then grilled to perfection on our mesquite grill. Served with crostini and extra olive oil.

Price: $9.95

Bison Meat Loaf

Submitted by admin on Sun, 06/29/2008 - 12:59

bison   peas   sweet potatoes

A tender, moist meatloaf made entirely with Bison meat combined with carrots, celery, and onions for additional moisture and flavor.

Served with roasted sweet potatoes, and peas.

Price: $16.95

Building the good eatin' menu with a custom content type

In this section we will set up a Menu item content type for the Good Eatin' web site. Our menu will contain the name of the dish, a description of the dish, the price of the dish, and a picture of the dish.

Introduction to the CCK module

Good Eatin' Goal: Learn about what the CCK Module offers, and install CCK on our site.

Additional modules needed: CCK (`http://drupal.org/project/cck`).

The **Content Creation Kit,** which is often abbreviated to, CCK is used to develop new types of content that can be used throughout a web site. This is a fantastic method of building content that fits nicely into a template, and of ensuring that all of the content has the same format and all the required fields are filled out correctly. Some examples of good content for use with CCK, along with examples of possible fields, are:

- **Movie:** Title, Director, Production Company, Year Released, Rating, and so on

- **Meeting:** Subject, Start Time, End Time, Organizer, Topic, Location, and so on

- **Book:** Title, Author, Year Published, Age Group, and so on

- **Home Listing**: Address, Price, Number of Bedrooms, Number of Bathrooms, Garage Type, Lot Size, and so on

- **Shirt:** Manufacturer, Style, Price, Color, and so on

The CCK module has a large number of field types that can be used to build custom content types. Some of these types include: **Date, Duration, Email, Fivestar ratings, Images, Ratings**, and **Slideshows**. Using specific field types when you build your new types helps to ensure that the information that is entered is valid. It will also help you to view and filter the display as content is added to your site.

Installing CCK and CCK field modules

The CCK module is available for download at: `http://drupal.org/project/ cck`. You can download and install the module just like any other module. The base installation of CCK includes a wide range of modules that can be individually enabled, as shown in the next screenshot:

▾ CCK			
Enabled	**Name**	**Version**	**Description**
☐	**Content**	6.x-2.0-beta	Allows administrators to define new content types. Required by: Content Copy (disabled), Content Permissions (disabled), Fieldgroup (disabled), Node Reference (disabled), Number (disabled), Option Widgets (disabled), Text (disabled), User Reference (disabled)
☐	**Content Copy**	6.x-2.0-beta	Enables ability to import/export field definitions. Depends on: Content (disabled)
☐	**Content Permissions**	6.x-2.0-beta	Set field-level permissions for CCK fields. Depends on: Content (disabled)
☐	**Fieldgroup**	6.x-2.0-beta	Create field groups for CCK fields. Depends on: Content (disabled)
☐	**Node Reference**	6.x-2.0-beta	Defines a field type for referencing one node from another. Depends on: Content (disabled), Text (disabled), Option Widgets (disabled)
☐	**Number**	6.x-2.0-beta	Defines numeric field types. Depends on: Content (disabled)
☐	**Option Widgets**	6.x-2.0-beta	Defines selection, check box and radio button widgets for text and numeric fields. Depends on: Content (disabled) Required by: Node Reference (disabled), User Reference (disabled)
☐	**Text**	6.x-2.0-beta	Defines simple text field types. Depends on: Content (disabled) Required by: Node Reference (disabled), User Reference (disabled)
☐	**User Reference**	6.x-2.0-beta	Defines a field type for referencing a user from a node. Depends on: Content (disabled), Text (disabled), Option Widgets (disabled)

To use CCK, you will need to enable the Content module, which will allow you to create new content types and add custom fields to the new type. You will also need to enable the modules that provide the various field types. In the default installation, these are:

- **Text**: This allows free form text to be entered
- **Number**: This allows numeric values to be entered
- **Node Reference**: This allows links to other nodes (pages, content types, and so on) to be inserted in a type
- **User Reference**: This allows links to users who are registered on the web site

There are also several additional modules, which provide more content types that you can install. These can be found on the Drupal site at: `http://drupal.org/project/Modules/category/88`.

The following modules, which are part of the default CCK module, provide different methods of viewing, editing, and administering fields:

- **Option Widget:** This provides checkboxes and option buttons for various fields. These can be very helpful if your content fields need to be restricted to specific values.

- **Field Group:** This allows you to group fields into logical sections. This is especially useful when your content types have a large number of fields.

- **Content Copy:** This allows you to duplicate content easily. This is useful if you want to add several items that are similar.

- **Content Permissions:** This gives you fine-grained control over which fields can be viewed and edited based, on a user's role. This is especially important for sites on which several different types of users work.

We will enable the **Content, Number, Text,** and **Option Widgets** modules to aid us in creating our menu item type.

Designing the menu item

Good Eatin' Goal: Design a content type to represent meals and drinks which are available at the restaurant.

Additional modules needed: CCK (`http://drupal.org/project/cck`).

Basic steps

When you start designing your site it is a good idea to think about what types you will need, and design the types before building them. It is relatively easy to add new fields to a type, but if you do so you may need to modify all of the existing content, which can be extremely time-consuming.

Even seemingly simple types, such as an address, require some thought—depending on what addresses will be used. For example, if the addresses entered are only from the United States, typical fields are Street 1, Street 2, City, State, and Zip Code. If the address has to include international addresses, typical fields are Street 1, Street 2, City, State/Province, Zip/Postal Code, and Country. If the address is only for a single country, state, or city, you can eliminate or automatically fill out some of the fields, to make entering information more convenient for your editors and users. The types of validation that you do will also depend on what expected values can be entered. For example, for truly international sites, it is impractical to include every state or province in a drop-down list for users to select from. On the other hand, if you know that addresses are only within a specific country, giving a list of states or provinces is very easy.

Step 1: Determine how the content type will be used

The first step in creating a new content type is deciding how the type will be used. You need to think about whether there will be a large or small number of entries, whether the information will be entered by experienced users, inexperienced users, or the general public. You also need to consider where the information will be displayed on the site, and in what format.

By collecting this information at the beginning, you can use it to guide future steps.

Step 2: Determine what fields need to be included

Think about what fields need to be included in the content type. You can do this in a number of ways:

- Use the fields from an existing paper form
- Use the fields from an existing back end system that the site will interface with
- Create fields based on the business process that you are adding to the site
- Brainstorm the possible values with a group of co-workers
- Look at example data to find commonalities, and then create a new field for each piece of common data

If you have tried several methods and still can't determine what the fields should be, you may want to try breaking the type into several separate but related types, or hiring a consultant to help you. Alternatively, you may have simply found a type that is not a good candidate to be created using CCK.

Each content type in Drupal automatically contains a field for a title, which is a single line of text, and a field for the description, which is a block of text. These fields can be renamed or hidden from view depending on your requirements. You will find that most content types that you create will use these two fields.

For our menu item, we will include the following fields:

- The name of the menu item (using the default **title** field)
- A description of the item (using the default **body** field)
- The price of the item
- A rating for the item
- Information for with dietary concerns or allergies (gluten free, vegan, vegetarian, and so on)
- What meals the item is available for

- The course type of the item (appetizer, first course, second course, dinner, dessert, drink, and so on)
- Whether the menu item is available only seasonally
- When the menu item is available, if it is only available seasonally

Step 3: Determine what type each field should use and what validation should be done

After you have a list of the fields that you want to include in your new content type, you need to think about what information the field will contain, so that you can select an appropriate type for the field. You will want to consider whether the field contains basic textual information, numeric information, references to other content, dates, or some other type of information.

As you decide what types should be used, you should also consider how long each field should be, and whether it should be restricted to specific values, or if editors can enter anything they want in the field.

For our menu item, the fields will use the following types:

Field	Type	Validation
Name	Text (single line)	Must be provided, no length requirements
Description	Text (multiple lines)	Must be provided, text should be at least 10 words long
Price	Numeric (decimal)	Must be a number greater than 0
Ingredients	Text free form list	This will be a free form list of key ingredients that visitors can search or select on.
Dietary Concerns	Text (free form list)	This will be a free-form list of possibilities that editors can add to as new allergens are added; it can be left blank if there are no allergens for the food
Meals	Text (simple list)	Must be filled out; possible values are Breakfast, Lunch, Dinner, Dessert, and Drinks. Multiple items can be included if it is available at more than one meal

Field	Type	Validation
Course Type	Text (simple list)	Must be filled out; new values can be added by the editor. Default values are: appetizer, first course, second course, soup, salad, dessert, and drink
Seasonal	Numeric (true/false)	Must be filled out; default value is false
Seasonal Start	Date	Can be left blank if Seasonal is false; can include month, date, and year
Seasonal End	Date	Can be left blank if Seasonal is false; can include month, date, and year

Step 4: Determine how the fields should be displayed when the user edits them

When an editor creates or edits your new content type, you can make things easier for them by selecting a meaningful control that they use to edit the field. By default, CCK only gives you a simple text field that you can use to enter information. By enabling the **Option Widgets** module, you get a selection list, option buttons, and checkboxes. Using these optional controls makes selection faster, and easier to validate.

Step 5: Determine who will be viewing and editing the content type

In this final step, you need to consider who will enter the content and who will view it. This will help you to determine which permissions are to be added for each field. If you find that there are several different permissions needed, you may need to explore the **Content Permissions** module which is included in the **Core CCK** installation. This module allows you to set permissions for each individual field independently.

Our menu item type does not need specific permissions for each field.

Creating the menu item type

Good Eatin' Goal: Build the Menu Item Content Type.

Additional modules needed: CCK (`http://drupal.org/project/cck`).

Now that our Menu item content type has been fully designed, we can begin implementing the menu item for the Good Eatin' web site.

Basic steps

To create a new content type, we begin at the **Content Type Manager**, which is available by selecting **Content management** and then **Content types**, from the **Administer** menu. The **Content Type Manager** is shown in the following screenshot:

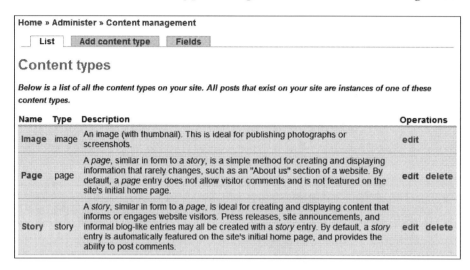

Next, click on the **Add content type** tab at the top of the screen. Drupal will then display a form that asks for the **Name**, **Type**, and **Description** of the new type. We will use the following values:

- **Name**: **Menu Item**
- **Type**: **Menu_item**
- **Description:** A Menu item that is included on the restaurant's menu contains information needed to display the item as well as to categorize it for use throughout the web site.
- The **Add Content** screen also contains additional options for **Submission** requirements, **Workflow** settings, and **Comment** settings.
- The **Submission form settings** section is shown in the following screenshot. This section allows you to customize the labels for the **Title** and **Body** fields, which we will rename to **Name** and **Description,** respectively. You can also control how many words can be entered in the description. If the editor enters fewer words, Drupal will display an error and the editor will have to enter more words before they can save the entry. By requiring at least 10 words, we will help to ensure that our menu items contain complete descriptions, which will help our search engine rankings.

▾ Submission form settings

Title field label: *

Name

Body field label:

Description

To omit the body field for this content type, remove any text and leave this field blank.

Minimum number of words:

10 ▾

The minimum number of words for the body field to be considered valid for this content type. This can be useful to rule out submissions that do not meet the site's standards, such as short test posts.

Explanation or submission guidelines:

The menu item represents a single item on the menu including drinks and food. The menu item includes various information about the dish so it can be correctly categorized and displayed to customers. Please provide a meaningful description about each item (at least 10 words) which will make a customer want to come into the restaurant for tasting!

This text will be displayed at the top of the submission form for this content type. It is useful for helping or instructing your users.

- The **Comment settings** section allows you to control whether or not visitors to your site can comment on this type of content. We would like to get feedback on our food so we will enable comments for the **Menu Item** type. Most of the default settings are perfect for our needs, but we will make some changes to improve the display when multiple visitors comment on the same menu item. Change the **Default display mode** to **Flat list—expanded**. As we do not expect to have discussions between users, there is no reason to group comments based on replies.

- The **Workflow settings** section controls what happens after new content has been submitted to the site. As our home page is not automatically created from recent postings, we will disable the **Promoted to front page** setting and leave all other settings as their defaults. If you want to explicitly approve all of the new content, you can disable the **Published** setting. This will cause new content to go into a review queue before it is published to the web site.

Adding a price to the menu item

Good Eatin' Goal: To add a field which will store the price of the menu item.

Additional modules needed: CCK (`http://drupal.org/project/cck`).

Basic steps

Now that we have created the **Menu Item** content type, we can set up the custom fields for our type based on the design we did earlier.

1. To create a new field, edit the **Menu Item** by clicking on the **Edit** link in the **Content Type Manager**.

---

2. Next, click on the **Add field** link. Drupal will then display a form where you can define the basics of the new field.

```
┌─────────────────────────────────────────────────────────────────────────────┐
│   ▓ Edit ▓    ▓ Manage fields ▓   ▓ Display fields ▓   │ Add field │          │
│                                                                               │
│ Menu Item                                                                     │
│ ┌─ Create new field ──────────────────────────────────────────────────────┐  │
│ │                                                                           │  │
│ │  Field name: *                                                            │  │
│ │  field_ [                                               ]                  │  │
│ │  The machine-readable name of the field. This name cannot be changed later! The name will be prefixed with 'field_' and can │  │
│ │  include lowercase unaccented letters, numbers, and underscores. The length of the name, including the prefix, is limited to no │  │
│ │  more than 32 letters.                                                    │  │
│ │                                                                           │  │
│ │  Label: *                                                                 │  │
│ │  [                                                        ]                │  │
│ │  A human-readable name to be used as the label for this field in the *Menu Item* content type. │  │
│ │                                                                           │  │
│ │  Field type: *                                                            │  │
│ │  [ Date                      ▼]                                           │  │
│ │  The type of data you would like to store in the database with this field. │  │
│ └───────────────────────────────────────────────────────────────────────────┘  │
│                                                                               │
│ [ Continue ]                                                                  │
└─────────────────────────────────────────────────────────────────────────────┘
```

3. For the price field, set the **Field name** to **Price**, the **Label** to **Price**, and the **Field type** to **Decimal**. Then click **Continue**.

4. After you click the **Continue** button, Drupal will prompt you for the **Widget type** that is used to edit the field. For the price field, the **Text field** is the most appropriate Widget.

5. Click **Continue** again, and Drupal will display a new form that contains some standard settings, as well as some settings that vary depending on the **Field type** you select.

6. For the price field, we will update the **Help text** and the **Default Price** as shown in the following screenshot:

```
┌─ Menu Item settings ──────────────────────────────────────────────────────┐
│ These settings apply only to the *Price* field as it appears in the *Menu Item* content type. │
│                                                                            │
│ Help text:                                                                 │
│ [The price of the dish or drink as it should appear on the menu.  This should not be discounted for specials │
│ or coupons.                                                              ] │
│ Instructions to present to the user below this field on the editing form.  │
│                                                                            │
│ ┌─ ▾ Default value ──────────────────────────────────────────────────────┐ │
│ │                                                                         │ │
│ │  Price:                                                                 │ │
│ │  [0.00          ]                                                       │ │
│ │                                                                         │ │
│ │  ┌─ ▸ PHP code ──────────────────────────────────────────────────────┐ │ │
│ └─────────────────────────────────────────────────────────────────────────┘ │
└────────────────────────────────────────────────────────────────────────────┘
```

7. There are also a number of values specific to the Decimal field type. These settings allow you to customize the allowable values and various formatting options. We will use the following values for our price field:

Global settings

These settings apply to the *Price* field in every content type in which it appears.

☑ Required

Number of values:

| 1 ▾ |

Select a specific number of values for this field, or 'Unlimited' to provide an 'Add more' button so the users can add as many values as they like.
Warning! Changing this setting after data has been created could result in the loss of data!

Minimum:

| 0.00 |

Maximum:

| 50.00 |

Precision:

| 10 ▾ |

The total number of digits to store in the database, including those to the right of the decimal.

Scale:

| 2 ▾ |

The number of digits to the right of the decimal.

Decimal marker:

| decimal point ▾ |

The character users will input to mark the decimal point in forms.

Prefix:

| $ |

Define a string that should be prefixed to the value, like $ or €. Leave blank for none. Separate singular and plural values with a pipe (pound|pounds).

Suffix:

| |

Define a string that should suffixed to the value, like m², m/s², kb/s. Leave blank for none. Separate singular and plural values with a pipe (pound|pounds).

— ▸ **Allowed values**

Adding seasonal information to the menu item

Good Eatin' Goal: Create fields that store information on whether or not a menu item is seasonal, and if it is seasonal what dates the menu item will be available on.

Additional modules needed: CCK (`http://drupal.org/project/cck`), Date (`http://drupal.org/project/date`).

Chef Wanyama likes to rotate his menu seasonally to ensure that he is always including the freshest ingredients in his dishes. To support this, we will allow him to specify whether each item is seasonal or not, and if it is seasonal what dates the menu should be available on. The display of the menu will take these dates into account, to display only those menu items that are currently available.

Basic steps

1. We will begin by adding the **Seasonal** field, which is a text field, using the **Select list** widget. This field is added just like the Price field, except that we will use **Select list** for the **Widget type**. We will ensure that the valid values are only **Yes** and **No** by setting the **Allowed values list**, as shown in the following screenshot:

2. To add the start and end dates, you will need to add a second field, using a **Date field**.

3. In order to access the **Date** field, you must first download the Date Module from the Drupal site and install it on your site. As a minimum, you will need to make sure that you activate the **Date API**, **Date**, **Date Timezone**, **Date Popup**, and **Calendar** modules.

Enabled	Name	Version	Description
☑	**Date**	6.x-2.0-rc4	Defines CCK date/time fields and widgets. Depends on: Content (disabled), Date API (disabled), Date Timezone (disabled) Required by: Date Copy (disabled)
☑	**Date API**	6.x-2.0-rc4	A Date API that can be used by other modules. Required by: Date (disabled), Date PHP4 (disabled), Date Popup (disabled), Date Repeat API (disabled), Date Timezone (disabled), Date Copy (disabled)
☐	**Date Copy**	6.x-2.0-rc4	Import and export CCK date data. Depends on: Content (disabled), Date (disabled), Date API (disabled), Date Timezone (disabled)
☐	**Date PHP4**	6.x-2.0-rc4	Emulate PHP 5.2 date functions in PHP 4.x, PHP 5.0, and PHP 5.1. Required when using the Date API with PHP versions less than PHP 5.2. Depends on: Date API (disabled)
☑	**Date Popup**	6.x-2.0-rc4	Enables jquery popup calendars and time entry widgets for selecting dates and times. Depends on: Date API (disabled), Date Timezone (disabled)
☐	**Date Repeat API**	6.x-2.0-rc4	A Date Repeat API to calculate repeating dates and times from iCal rules. Depends on: Date API (disabled)
☑	**Date Timezone**	6.x-2.0-rc4	Needed when using Date API. Overrides site and user timezone handling to set timezone names instead of offsets. Depends on: Date API (disabled) Required by: Date (disabled), Date Popup (disabled), Date Copy (disabled)

4. Now that the appropriate Date modules have been enabled, we can add our new field. The start and end dates are implemented as single **Date** fields using the *jQuery pop-up* calendar, with the ending date being required if a starting date is entered.

5. Begin as we did for adding the Price field and seasonal fields, by clicking on the **Add field** link. This time, we will name the field **Seasonal Dates** and set the **Widget type** to **Text Field** with *Date Pop-up calendar*. Click **continue** to add the field and enter the advanced information.

6. We can now enter the basic information for our date field. The basic options that you need to select are as follows:

Menu Item settings

These settings apply only to the *Seasonal Dates* field as it appears in the *Menu Item* content type.

Default value:

○ Blank

◉ Now

○ Relative

A default value to use for this field. If you select 'Relative', add details below.

-- ▸ **Customize Default Value**

Input format:

`06/19/2008 10:55:05PM` ▾

Set the order and format for the date parts in the input form. The format will be adapted to remove values not in the granularity for this field.

Years back and forward:

`-1:+3`

Number of years to go back and forward in the year selection list, default is -3:+3.

Time increment:

`1` ▾

Increment the minute and second fields by this amount.

-- ▸ **Customize Date Parts**

Help text:

If the menu item is seasonal, enter the dates the item is available here. The item will automatically appear on the menu at the correct times of the year.

Instructions to present to the user below this field on the editing form.

---

7. We can now enter the advanced information for the seasonal dates. Because the hour and minutes are not important in this case, we will remove them from the display. We will also make sure that the fields are not required, because not all dishes will be seasonal. The advanced options are set as follows:

Global settings

These settings apply to the *Seasonal Dates* field in every content type in which it appears.

☐ Required

Number of values:

[1   ▼]

Select a specific number of values for this field, or 'Unlimited' to provide an 'Add more' button so the users can add as many values as they like.

Warning! Changing this setting after data has been created could result in the loss of data!

To Date:

○ Never

○ Optional

◉ Required

Display a matching second date field as a 'To date'. If marked 'Optional' field will be presented but not required. If marked 'Required' the 'To date' will be required if the 'From date' is required or filled in.

Granularity:

☑ Year

☑ Month

☑ Day

☐ Hour

☐ Minute

☐ Second

Set the date elements to be stored (at least a year is required).

Default Display

Date display:

[June 19, 2008   ▼]

*Custom display format:

[   ]

▸ **Additional Display Settings**

Time zone handling:

[No time zone conversion ▼]

Select the timezone handling method to be used for this date field.

Adding which meals the menu item is available for

Good Eatin' Goal: Add fields to determine at which meals an item is available. This will be used to build menus for each meal.

Additional modules needed: CCK (`http://drupal.org/project/cck`).

The Meals field is similar to the Seasonal field because it is a text field with a selection list widget. However, we will allow the editor to select multiple options from our list.

Basic steps

1. Edit the **Menu Item** content type.
2. Add a new text field with the name set to **meals** and the label set to **Available at these meals**, with widget of **Select List**.
3. Set the **Allowed values** list to:
   ```
   Breakfast
   Lunch
   Dinner
   Dessert
   ```
4. Select the **Required** checkbox and set the **Number of values** to **Unlimited**.
5. Save the new field.

Adding an image for the menu item

Good Eatin' Goal: Allow Chef Wanyama to optionally add picture of the item for display in the menu.

Additional modules needed: CCK (`http://drupal.org/project/cck`), IMCE (`http://drupal.org/project/imce`), IMCE CCK Image (`http://drupal.org/project/imceimage`).

Basic steps

1. Begin by downloading and installing the IMCE and IMCE CCK Image modules.
2. Create a new field, by clicking on the **Add field** link. Name the field **Picture** and set the **label** to **Picture**. The type will be an IMCE image with an IMCE image widget.

3. After you click **continue** to create the field, you can enter the settings for the field. These settings allow you to control what types of pictures can be inserted, as well as whether or not a picture has to be entered.

Picture

[more help...]

┌─ *Menu Item* settings ──────────────────────────────────
These settings apply only to the *Picture* field as it appears in the *Menu Item* content type.

Valid File Types: *

`png,gif,jpg,jpeg`

Help text:

`Enter a picture of the item for sale.`

Instructions to present to the user below this field on the editing form.
Allowed HTML tags: <a> <b> <big> <code> <del> <em> <i> <ins> <pre> <q> <small> <span> <strong> <sub> <sup> <tt> <ol> <ul> <li> <p>
 <img>

── ▸ **Default value** ─────────────────────────────────

┌─ Global settings ──────────────────────────────────
These settings apply to the *Picture* field in every content type in which it appears.

☑ Required

Number of values:

`1`

Maximum number of values users can enter for this field.
'Unlimited' will provide an 'Add more' button so the users can add as many values as they like.
Warning! Changing this setting after data has been created could result in the loss of data!

`Save field settings`

---

4. If you want to ensure that each item has a picture, you may want to expand the **Default value** section and specify a default picture to be used. A default image will typically be a generic image with a graphic showing that an image was not found or is not available.

5. We can now save the field settings by clicking **Save field settings**.

6. When the editor clicks the link to add a picture to the content type, he or she will be presented with a dialog box similar to the following one:

7. To add a new file, he or she simply clicks on the **Upload** link, which will open the panel shown below. This gives the editor the opportunity to select a file to upload and indicate which sizes of image should be created on the web site.

8. After the editor selects an image to insert, he or she simply clicks the **Add image to imceimage** link and the picture will be automatically inserted.

Alternative solutions

Another possible solution for attaching images to content types created with CCK is the **Image Field Module** (`http://drupal.org/project/imagefield`) which adds CCK support to the Image module. To use the Image Field module, you must also install the Filefield (`http://drupal.org/project/filefield`) and ImageAPI(`http://drupal.org/project/imageapi`) modules. The Image Field Module gives you some additional options for controlling the allowable sizes of files, as well as letting editors configure the title text and alt text that will be used to display a tooltip, and the alternative text if images display has been disabled by the visitor, respectively. However, the editor cannot easily select images that have already been uploaded to the site. The input form for the Image Field Module will appear like this:

Controlling access to the content type

Good Eatin' Goal: Modify the permissions of our editor role so that editors can create new Menu Items.

Additional modules needed: None.

Basic steps

1. We can easily control who can create Menu Items by editing the permissions for each role. Begin by opening the **Permissions Manager** by selecting **User management** and then **Permissions** from the **Administer menu**.

2. The **Permissions Manager** contains detailed permissions for each content type that you have created. These nodes are listed in the **node module** section. We will allow the user to perform any type of action with the menu item type, as shown here:

Permission	anonymous user	authenticated user	editor
node module			
access content	☑	☑	☑
administer content types	☐	☐	☐
administer nodes	☐	☐	☐
create menu_item content	☐	☐	☑
create page content	☐	☐	☐
delete any menu_item content	☐	☐	☑
delete any page content	☐	☐	☐
delete own menu_item content	☐	☐	☑
delete own page content	☐	☐	☐
delete revisions	☐	☐	☐
edit any menu_item content	☐	☐	☑
edit any page content	☐	☐	☐
edit own menu_item content	☐	☐	☑
edit own page content	☐	☐	☐
revert revisions	☐	☐	☐
view revisions	☐	☐	☐

Using taxonomy to categorize content

Taxonomy is a powerful way of classifying the content on your site. After the content has been classified, you can group or filter the content based on the categories that have been set for the content type.

If you only have a few pages of content, or if you are grouping based on only one category, the taxonomy module is probably overkill for your needs. But the power of taxonomy is readily apparent if you have hundreds of pages of content and complex categorization needs, or when you are classifying content based on multiple categories.

When you define a taxonomy, you can decide whether the terms in the category are predefined, or if the editors can add new categories as they add new content. It is best to use predefined terms if the terms are well-defined and are not likely to change. For example, the Good Eatin' site will use predefined values for the Meal category. Allowing terms to be dynamically added would be very useful if the terms change frequently, if new categories can be created, or if the initial list of terms is too large for pre-entry to be practical.

You can also create a hierarchy of terms by relating taxonomy categories to each other. For example, if you are categorizing animals by their scientific name, you could create categories for Kingdom, Phylum, Class, Order, Family, Genus, and Species. Each would relate to the category above it. This allows you to easily categorize animals without needing to repeatedly enter the links between the higher level categories.

Drupal uses the following terms to describe its classification system:

- Taxonomy: The highest level of the classification system.
- Vocabulary: A group or category of terms that are used to describe the one aspect of a piece of content. Some example categories are: color, size, and genre.
- Term: A specific identifier within a vocabulary. Red, blue, green, small, medium, large, action, comedy, and romance are all possible terms.

Create a vocabulary for course type

Good Eatin' Goal: Build a Taxonomy to store information about what meals an item is available for.

Additional modules needed: Taxonomy (Core).

Basic steps

To create a new taxonomy, you need to ensure that the taxonomy module has been enabled in the **Module Manager**.

After enabling the taxonomy module, you can create a new taxonomy by using the **Taxonomy Manager**, which can be accessed by selecting **Content management** and then **Taxonomy**, the **Administer** menu. Let's create the vocabularies for our menu item content starting with the **Course Type** vocabulary.

First, click on the **Add Vocabulary** link at the top of the **Taxonomy Manager** screen. Drupal will display a form allowing you to enter information about your new vocabulary. The information we will enter for the **Course Type** is shown in the following screenshot:

Taxonomy

Define how your vocabulary will be presented to administrators and users, and which content types to categorize with it. Tags allows users to create terms when submitting posts by typing a comma separated list. Otherwise terms are chosen from a select list and can only be created by users with the "administer taxonomy" permission.

[more help...]

▾ Identification

Vocabulary name: *

```
Course Type
```
The name for this vocabulary, e.g., *"Tags"*.

Description:
```
The course type identifies the suggested course for the menu item.  If more than one course is selected,
you should describe any differences in the menu item's description.
```
Description of the vocabulary; can be used by modules.

Help text:
```
You must select at least one course for the menu item.
```
Instructions to present to the user when selecting terms, e.g., *"Enter a comma separated list of words"*.

▾ Content types

Content types:

☐ Image

☑ Menu Item

☐ Page

☐ Story

Select content types to categorize using this vocabulary.

▾ Settings

☐ Tags
Terms are created by users when submitting posts by typing a comma separated list.

☑ Multiple select
Allows posts to have more than one term from this vocabulary (always true for tags).

☑ Required
At least one term in this vocabulary must be selected when submitting a post.

Weight:
```
0
```
Vocabularies are displayed in ascending order by weight.

After you save your new vocabulary, you will be returned to the **Taxonomy Manager**, which will now include your new category, as shown here:

```
Taxonomy

The taxonomy module allows you to categorize your content using both tags and administrator defined terms. It is a
flexible tool for classifying content with many advanced features. To begin, create a 'Vocabulary' to hold one set of
terms or tags. You can create one free-tagging vocabulary for everything, or separate controlled vocabularies to
define the various properties of your content, for example 'Countries' or 'Colors'.

Use the list below to configure and review the vocabularies defined on your site, or to list and manage the terms
(tags) they contain. A vocabulary may (optionally) be tied to specific content types as shown in the Type column and,
if so, will be displayed when creating or editing posts of that type. Multiple vocabularies tied to the same content type
will be displayed in the order shown below. To change the order of a vocabulary, grab a drag-and-drop handle under
the Name column and drag it to a new location in the list. (Grab a handle by clicking and holding the mouse while
hovering over a handle icon.) Remember that your changes will not be saved until you click the Save button at the
bottom of the page.

                                                                                        [more help....]

Created new vocabulary Course Type.

Name         Type        Operations
Course Type  Menu Item   edit vocabulary  list terms  add terms
```

Adding terms to the course type vocabulary

Good Eatin' Goal: Create the Terms that will be used in the Course Type Vocabulary.

Additional modules needed: Taxonomy (Core).

Basic steps

Now that our vocabulary has been created, we can define the terms that can be used within this vocabulary by clicking on the **add terms** link. A single term includes the name of the term and the description of the term. You can also use the advanced options to define a hierarchy of terms, or to define synonyms for the term. Synonyms are especially useful when you want to allow editors to enter their own terms, because it allows you to link terms with the same meaning to each other, even if two editors used different words.

The information for our appetizer term is shown here:

Add term to *Course Type*

▾ Identification

Term name: *

```
Appetizer
```

The name of this term.

Description:

```
Delicious tidbits to whet your appetite.  All appetizers are sized for two people to share.
```

A description of the term. To be displayed on taxonomy/term pages and RSS feeds.

▸ Advanced options

Our remaining terms are added in the same way. Our final list of terms for our
Course Type is shown in the following screenshot:

Terms in *Course Type*

*Course Type is a flat vocabulary. You may organize the terms in the Course Type vocabulary by using the handles on
the left side of the table. To change the name or description of a term, click the edit link next to the term.*

[more help...]

[more help...]

Name	Operations
✛ Appetizer	edit
✛ Soups	edit
✛ Salads	edit
✛ First Course	edit
✛ Second Course	edit
✛ Desserts	edit
✛ Non-alcoholic Drinks	edit
✛ Alcoholic Drinks	edit

[Save] [Reset to alphabetical]

These terms can be sorted manually or displayed in alphabetical order. Manually sorting terms can make an entry more efficient if some terms are much more common than the others, or if the terms can be naturally ordered by time, size, or relative importance.

Adding the ingredients list vocabulary

Good Eatin' Goal: Add a vocabulary that will store some of the key ingredients in menu items, so that customers can easily find meals that feature specialty foods or ingredients that they prefer.

Additional modules needed: Taxonomy (Core).

Basic steps

Building the Ingredients List vocabulary follows a similar process to the one used for building the Course Type vocabulary. However, we will modify the settings so that the editor doesn't need to enter a value, and he or she she can enter new terms when they enter a new menu item. These settings are as follows:

Adding vocabularies as CCK fields

Good Eatin' Goal: Modify the Menu Item type to allow the editor to enter the taxonomy using standard CCK widgets. This will also make the display of the taxonomy easier.

Additional modules needed: Taxonomy (Core), Content Taxonomy (`http://drupal.org/project/content_taxonomy`).

Basic steps

1. Install the Content Taxonomy Module and activate it.

2. Open the **Content Type Manager** and edit the Menu Item type.

3. Click on the **Add Field** link at the top of the screen.

4. Enter the basic information about the new field type including the **Field name** and **Label**. Set the **Field type** to **Content Taxonomy Fields**, as shown here:

Menu Item

┌─ Create new field ───

Field name: *

field_ | ingredients |

The machine-readable name of the field. This name cannot be changed later! The name will be prefixed with 'field_' and can include lowercase unaccented letters, numbers, and underscores. The length of the name, including the prefix, is limited to no more than 32 letters.

Label: *

| Key Ingredients |

A human-readable name to be used as the label for this field in the *Menu Item* content type.

Field type: *

| Content Taxonomy Fields ▼ |

The type of data you would like to store in the database with this field.

└───

[Continue]

---

5. Click **Continue** to save the basic information, and Drupal will prompt you for the type of Widget to be displayed. Because we will be entering from a large list of possible values, the **Autocomplete** widget is the most appropriate.

6. **Select Continue** and Drupal will display a form with field-specific information. We will use the values shown in the following screenshot:

```
┌─ Global settings ──────────────────────────────────────────────────────────┐
│  These settings apply to the Key Ingredients field in every content type in which it appears. │
│                                                                              │
│  ☑ Required                                                                  │
│  Number of values:                                                           │
│  [ Unlimited ▼]                                                              │
│  Select a specific number of values for this field, or 'Unlimited' to provide an 'Add more' button so the users can add as many │
│  values as they like.                                                        │
│  Warning! Changing this setting after data has been created could result in the loss of data! │
│                                                                              │
│  ☑ Save values additionally in the term_node table.                          │
│  If this option is set, saving of terms is additionally handled by the taxonomy module. So saved terms from Content Taxonomy │
│  fields will appear as any other terms saved by the core taxonomy module. Set this option if you are using any other taxonomy │
│  application, like tagadelic. Otherwise terms are only saved in the cck tables and can only be accessed via the node or a view │
│                                                                              │
│    ┌─ ▼ Specify terms to show ──────────────────────────────────────────┐    │
│    │  Vocabulary:                                                         │    │
│    │  [ Key Ingredients ▼]                                                │    │
│    │                                                                      │    │
│    │  Terms:                                                              │    │
│    │  [ — ▼]                                                              │    │
│    │  If any term is selected here, only child terms of the selected are going to be shown in the field. Otherwise the whole │    │
│    │  vocabulary selected above                                           │    │
│    │                                                                      │    │
│    │  Depth of taxonomy tree:                                             │    │
│    │  [                                                      ]             │    │
│    │  leave blank for unlimited depth                                     │    │
│    │                                                                      │    │
│    │  ☐ Indent child terms with ' - ' signs                               │    │
│    └──────────────────────────────────────────────────────────────────┘    │
└──────────────────────────────────────────────────────────────────────────┘
```

By selecting the **Save values additionally in the term_node table** checkbox, we will be able to use the taxonomy in a variety of other situations.

7. The final step is to ensure that the **Key Ingredients** vocabulary is not associated with the Menu Item Content Type. This is important because if the two are associated, the edit form will have duplicate edit areas for the taxonomy.

Adding content with the menu item type

Now that we have built our Menu Item Content Type, we can begin to use this type to build that content that will comprise the Good Eatin' menu.

Creating a new menu item

Good Eatin' Goal: Build Menu Items using our new content type, for display on the web site.

Additional modules needed: None.

Basic steps

1. We will start by clicking on the **Create content menu**. Drupal will now open the same list of possible content types that we saw when we built our static pages in Chapter 2. However, now our new Menu Item type is also available.

2. Click on **Menu Item** and Drupal will present you with a form based on the custom fields that we have created.

3. Complete all of the fields for the new content type, and then click the **Save** button.

4. Once the Menu item has been created, the default display will look like this:

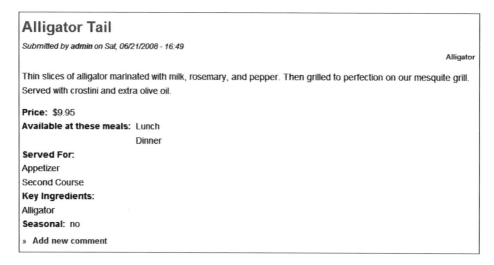

Customizing the display of the menu item

Although the default view works for some content types, most of the time you will want to customize the look of your content type so that it is clear and appealing to visitors.

We can improve the display of this menu item to make it more compact and remove information that is not relevant to most visitors, such as who submitted the content, and when it was created. We will discuss various ways of doing this in this section.

Modifying the order of fields and the titles of the menu item

Good Eatin' Goal: Customize how the fields of our menu item content type are displayed, to maximize usability for our visitors.

Additional modules needed: CCK.

Basic steps

The most basic customization you can do is provided by the CCK module. This module allows you to control how each field is labeled, and the format used to display it.

To use the basic display customization, edit your content type and then click on the **Display fields** link at the top of the screen. Drupal will then display a screen similar to the one shown below:

```
Home » Administer » Content management » Menu Item

    Edit      Manage fields     Display fields     Add field

    General   |   Advanced   |

Menu Item
Configure how this content type's fields and field labels should be displayed when it's viewed in teaser and full-page
mode.

Field                        Label         Teaser           Full node
Price                        Above         9999             9999
Available at these meals     Above         Default          Default
Seasonal                     Above         Default          Default
Seasonal Dates               Above         Default          Default

  Save
```

You can customize whether labels are above the value, on the same line as the value, or not displayed at all. You can also customize how the content is formatted in the **Teaser** and **Full node**. The **Teaser** display is used when multiple items are displayed on the same page, and the **Full node** is used when the item is displayed on its own.

If you need additional customization for your content type, you can theme the content or use content templates.

Advanced customization with content templates

Good Eatin' Goal: Discuss the possibilities that are offered by Content Templates.

Additional modules needed: Content Templates (`http://drupal.org/project/contemplate`).

Basic steps

The content template module, also called **ConTemplate**, is available for download at: `http://drupal.org/project/contemplate`. This module provides an easy method of customizing the display of your content. The content template module has a few settings that are related to performance-tuning when templates are created. If you experience any performance issues, you may need to modify these settings.

Download, install, and enable the ConTemplate module. After you have enabled the content template module, you can create a new template by selecting **Content Management** and then **Content templates**, from the **Administer** menu. You can also simply edit the content type and then click on the **template** tab at the top of the screen.

The content template module requires you to use the PHP programming language to modify the content. If you use this method, you have complete control over the display. But with power comes responsibility, and you must make sure that you include all of the fields that you want to display, and must make sure that you update the template if you add new fields to the type.

A full discussion of PHP is beyond the scope of this book. For more information on theming with PHP, check out the *Drupal 6 Themes* or *Drupal 5 Themes* books, both of which are also available from Packt Publishing. For more information about programming with PHP, you can visit the official PHP web site at `www.php.net`.

Displaying groups of menu items with Views

Now that we have created some content, we need to organize the menu so that our visitors can easily browse it. We will demonstrate several techniques for making Chef Wanyama's site as easy as possible for visitors to navigate.

Based on our discussion with Chef Wanyama, we have identified three ways in which the site will display the menu items. The first method of presentation will be a single page with all menu items for a specific meal. This will be linked into the main navigation menu. The second method will allow the user to search the menu according to several fields, including the description, price, allergens, and course. The final method will show an index of allergens so that the visitor can easily find which items they can safely eat.

We will use a combination of views and taxonomy to create each of these displays. Before we dive into creating each display, let's look at the Views module.

Introducing the Views module

Good Eatin' Goal: Introduce the Views module, and activate it on the Good Eatin' web site so we can build our views.

Additional modules needed: Views (`http://drupal.org/project/views`).

Basic steps

The **Views** module is used to group content according to information in the content. The **Views** module is available for download at: `http://drupal.org/project/views`. Download the module and install it onto your site. After you have added the **Views** module to your site, there are several other modules that you will require in order to be able to activate the **Views** module and the **Views UI** module, as shown in the screenshot:

Enabled	Name	Version	Description
☑	**Views**	6.x-2.0-beta4	Create customized lists and queries from your database. Required by: Views exporter (disabled), Views UI (disabled)
☐	**Views exporter**	6.x-2.0-beta4	Allows exporting multiple views at once. Depends on: Views (disabled)
☑	**Views UI**	6.x-2.0-beta4	Administrative interface to views. Without this module, you cannot create or edit your views. Depends on: Views (disabled)

The **Views** module handles the core tasks of managing and presenting each view. The **Views UI** module is used to create and edit the views. You may also want to download and install the **Advanced Help** module, which improves the help system for some modules—including the Views module. The **Advanced Help** module is available at: `http://drupal.org/project/advanced_help`.

After enabling these modules, you can review the predefined views and create new views by selecting the **Site building** and then the **views** link, from the **Administer** menu.

As you can see, there are a number of predefined views that you can choose from, or you can create on your own:

List	**Add**	**Import**	**Tools**

Views

Not sure what to do? Try the **"Getting started"** page.

Tag: `<All>`   **Displays:** `<All>`   **Type:** `<All>`   **Storage:** `<All>`

Sort by: `Name`   **Order:** `Up`   `Apply`

Default Node view: **archive** (default) **Enable**	
Path: archive *Block, Page*	Display a list of months that link to content for that month.
Default Comment view: **comments_recent** (default) **Enable**	
Title: Recent comments Path: comments/recent *Block, Page*	Contains a block and a page to list recent comments; the block will automatically link to the page, which displays the comment body as well as a link to the node.
Default Node view: **date_browser** (Date) **Enable**	
Path: date_browser *Date browser, Page*	Browse through nodes by year, month, day, or week. Date browser attachment adds back/next navigation to the top of the page.
Default Node view: **frontpage** (default) **Enable**	
Path: frontpage *Feed, Page*	Emulates the default Drupal front page; you may set the default home page path to this view to make it your front page.
Default Node view: **glossary** (default) **Enable**	
Path: glossary *Page*	A list of all content, by letter.
Default Node view: **taxonomy_term** (default) **Enable**	
Path: taxonomy/term/% *Feed, Page*	A view to emulate Drupal core's handling of taxonomy/term; it also emulates Views 1's handling by having two possible feeds.
Default Node view: **tracker** (default) **Enable**	
Title: Recent posts Path: tracker *Page*	Shows all new activity on system.

As you can see, these default views offer solutions to several common problems and you can test enabling them to determine if they are suitable for your site.

Creating the menu items by meal view

Good Eatin' Goal: Temp.

Additional modules needed: Views (`http://drupal.org/project/views`).

The first custom view that we will create will be used to display our menu items based on the meal. This view most closely resembles the traditional menu that you receive when you sit down at a restaurant.

Basic steps

1. To create this view, we start by clicking on **Add** at the top of the **Views Manager** screen. Drupal will then display a form in which you can enter basic information about your new view as shown in the following screenshot:

Views

View name: *

menu_by_meal

This is the unique name of the view. It must contain only alphanumeric characters and underscores; it is used to identify the view internally and to generate unique theming template names for this view. If overriding a module provided view, the name must not be changed or instead a new view will be created.

View description:

This view will display a list of all items that are available for the

This description will appear on the Views administrative UI to tell you what the view is about.

View tag:

menu items by meal   ○

Enter an optional tag for this view; it is used only to help sort views on the administrative page.

View type:

◉ Node
Nodes are a Drupal site's primary content.

○ Comment
Comments are responses to node content.

○ File
Files maintained by Drupal and various modules.

○ Node revision
Node revisions are a history of changes to nodes.

○ Term
Taxonomy terms are attached to nodes.

○ User
Users who have created accounts on your site.

The view type is the primary table for which information is being retrieved. The view type controls what arguments, fields, sort criteria and filters are available, so once this is set it **cannot be changed**.

[Next]

2. After clicking the **Next** button, Drupal displays a form that summarizes the current settings for the view:

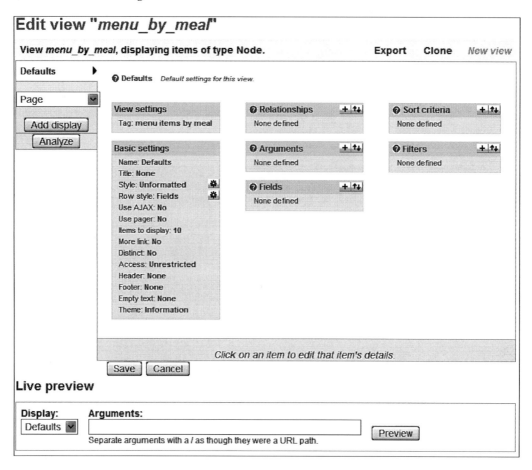

Now that the basis of our view has been created, we can customize the view according to our needs.

Filtering based on the content type

We will now modify the view to display only the menu item content.

1. Click on the **+** symbol next to the **Filters** label.

2. Drupal will display a form just above the **Live Preview** section, which has options for the Filter to be added, as shown in the following screenshot:

Defaults: Add filters

Groups:

Node ▾

☐ Node: Sticky
    Whether or not the node is sticky.
☐ Node: Teaser
    The stored teaser field. This may not be valid or useful data on all node types.
☐ Node: Title
    The title of the node.
☑ Node: Type
    The type of a node (for example, "blog entry", "forum post", "story", etc).
☐ Node: Updated date
    The date the node was last updated.
☐ Node: Updated/commented date
    The most recent of last comment posted or node updated time.

[Add] [Cancel]

The **Groups** list option allows you to easily filter the list of available groups to reduce the number of available options.

3.   Select the **Node: Type** checkbox and click **Add**. Drupal will display a new form that contains the actual values to be filtered, as shown below:

Defaults: Configure filter "Node: Type"

This item is currently not exposed. If you **expose** it, users will be able to change the filter as they view it.

[Expose]

Operator:

◉ Is one of
○ Is not one of

Node type:

☐ Poll
☐ Image
☑ Menu Item
☐ Page
☐ Story

[Update] [Cancel] [Remove]

After you make your selections, click the **Update** button to save your changes. If you want the user to be able to modify this filter, you can click the **Expose** button. This is a great way of adding an **Advanced Search**.

Basic settings

Now that we have defined which content types will be displayed, we can set up various items that control the display of the view in the **Basic Settings** section.

1. We will begin by modifying the title of the view, by first clicking on the link next to the title label. Change the title to **Good Eatin' Menu**.

2. Next, we will modify the display method by clicking the link next to the **Row Style** within the **Basic settings**.

3. The **Fields** option will only display selected fields in a table style format. The **Node** option will display either an entire node or just the teaser for the node. For our view, the **Node** option is a better choice. Select **Node** and click **Update** to save your changes.

4. The **Use pager** and **Items to display** settings control whether the items are displayed on a single page, or whether they are broken up into multiple pages. Because most people expect a menu to be displayed on a single page, we will leave these settings as their defaults.

5. Some additional settings that you may want to set for your view are the Header, Footer, and Empty text settings, which allow you to add text before and after the main content, and to substitute text if no content is shown in the view, respectively.

Adding an argument to control meal display

In order to display menus for each meal independently, we will add an argument to the view. This will allow us to specify a specific meal that is to be displayed on each page.

1. Click on the + symbol next to the **Arguments** link, and Drupal will display a list of all of the available arguments, as shown in the screenshot:

2. We will change the **Groups** field to **Content**, select **Content: Text:
   Available at these meals (field_meals)**, and then click **Add**. Drupal will
   then display a form that allows us to configure the **Argument**, as shown in
   the following screenshot:

**Defaults: Configure Argument "Content: Text: Available at these meals
(field_meals)"**

Title:

The title to use when this argument is present; it will override the title of the view and titles from previous
arguments. You can use percent substitution here to replace with argument titles. Use "%1" for the first
argument, "%2" for the second, etc.

**Action to take if argument is not
present:**

- ⦿ Display all values
- ○ Hide view / Page not found (404)
- ○ Display empty text
- ○ Summary, sorted ascending
- ○ Summary, sorted descending
- ○ Provide default argument

Wildcard:

all

If this value is received as an argument, the
argument will be ignored; i.e, "all values"

Wildcard title:

All

The title to use for the wildcard in substitutions
elsewhere.

Validator:

<Basic validation>

Action to take if argument does not validate:

Hide view / Page not found (404)

- ☐ Glossary mode

Glossary mode applies a limit to the number of characters used in the argument, which allows the
summary view to act as a glossary.

Case:

No transform

When printing the argument result, how to transform the case.

Case in path:

No transform

When printing url paths, how to transform the of the argument. Do not use this unless with Postgres as it
uses case sensitive comparisons.

- ☐ Transform spaces to dashes in URL

[Update] [Cancel] [Remove]

3. We will set the title to **Good Eatin' %1 Menu**, which will display **Good Eatin' Dinner Menu** if the argument is **Dinner** and **Good Eatin' Lunch Menu** if the argument is **Lunch**.

4. If no argument is present, we will display a summary, with values sorted in ascending order.

5. The only other modifications that we will make is to set the **Case** to **Capitalize Each Word** and the **Case in path** to **Lower Case**, and to turn on **Transform spaces to dashes in URL**. These changes will make the title and paths easier to read.

6. Click **Update** to save your changes.

7. The final configuration option that Drupal gives us is the style to be used in the display. In our case, the default **List** is most appropriate, as shown below.

Change summary style for Argument "Content: Text: Available at these meals (field_meals)"

◉ List
○ Unformatted

[Update] [Cancel]

Adding sorting based on course

The final customization that we need to do for our View is to add sorting based on the Course. This will allow our Dinner menu to have separate sections for Appetizers, Soups, Salads, and so on. We will implement this by adding to the Sort Criteria.

1. Click the + symbol next to the **Sort criteria** label, and Drupal will display a form prompting you for the sort criteria, as shown in the following screenshot:

Defaults: Add sort criteria

Groups:
[Content ▾]

☐ Content: Decimal: Price (field_price)
   Decimal - Appears in : Menu Item
☐ Content: Seasonal Dates (field_seasonal_date value)
   Date - Appears in : Menu Item
☐ Content: Seasonal Dates (field_seasonal_date value2)
   Date - Appears in : Menu Item
☑ Content: Text: Available at these meals (field_meals)
   Text - Appears in : Menu Item
☐ Content: Text: Seasonal (field_seasonal)
   Text - Appears in : Menu Item

[Add] [Cancel]

2. We will Change the **Groups** to **Content**, and select the **Content: Text: Available at these meals** checkbox.

3. Click **Add,** and Drupal will prompt you for the order to sort the items on. In our case, the default sort order of **Ascending** is fine, so we can simply click **Update**.

Creating a page and menu to display the View

The final step in creating our View is to give our customers a place to see the View. We do this by building a new display from our defaults.

1. Begin by selecting **Page** from the drop-down list under the **Defaults** label, as shown in the following screenshot:

```
Defaults         ▶

Page             ▾

  Add display
   Analyze
```

2. Then, click the **Add display** button, and Drupal will create a second display for us. Because we selected the Page display type, Drupal has added several additional settings that we can use, as shown in the screenshot:

```
Page settings
  Path: None
  Menu: No menu
```

3. We will begin by customizing the path, by clicking on the link next to the **Path** label. Drupal will then display a form where you can enter the path that the visitor can use to see this page. We will set the path to **menu**, as shown in the following screenshot:

```
❷ Page: The menu path or URL of this view

http://goodeatin.drupalbyexample.com/
menu

This view will be displayed by visiting this path on your site. You may use "%" in your URL to represent
values that will be used for arguments: For example, "node/%/feed".

[Update]  [Cancel]
```

This will display a list of all of the possible menus that the user can access on the menu page, and select a specific page using menu/dinner, menu/lunch, and so on.

4. Next we need to modify the menu information by clicking on the link next to the **Menu** label. Drupal will display a form that allows us to enter information about the menu, as shown in the following screenshot:

This menu will link to a list of all possible menus for the Good Eatin' site.

Advanced search using Views

Good Eatin' Goal: Create a view that customers can use to search the Menu Items with, to find food based on any criteria they set.

Additional modules needed: Views (`http://drupal.org/project/views`).

The Advanced Search will be very similar to the Menu Items by Meal View, except that we will add additional filtering options that will be exposed so that the visitor can control them.

Because we have already created a view with many of the same features that this view will need, we will start by cloning our Menu Items by Meal View.

Creating the View

1. Open the **Views Manager** by selecting **Site Building** and then **Views**, from the **Administer menu**.

2. Click the **Clone** link next to the **menu_by_meal** view. Drupal will then display a form in which we can enter a name and description for our new view, as shown below:

Clone view menu_by_meal

View name: *
```
menu_item_search
```
This is the unique name of the view. It must contain only alphanumeric characters and underscores; it is used to identify the view internally and to generate unique theming template names for this view. If overriding a module provided view, the name must not be changed or instead a new view will be created.

View description:
```
This view will allow visitors to easily search menu items
```
This description will appear on the Views administrative UI to tell you what the view is about.

View tag:
```
menu items search                              ○
```
Enter an optional tag for this view; it is used only to help sort views on the administrative page.

3. Click **Next**, and Drupal will create the new view. You can now modify the basic settings just as you did earlier. Use the following values:
   - **Title: Menu Search**
   - **Style: Table**
   - **Use Pager: Full Pager**

4. Next, we need to delete the Argument that we provided earlier, because this view should display all values. To do this, click on the link for the argument and then click on the **Remove** button at the bottom of the screen.

Adding fields

1. Now we need to add the fields that will be displayed in our table to the View. Start by clicking on the + symbol next to the **Fields** label. Drupal will then display a form that allows you to select the fields that are to be added, as shown in the following screenshot:

Defaults: Add fields

Groups:
```
Node          ▼
```

☐ Node: Published
  The published status of the node.
☐ Node: Sticky
  Whether or not the node is sticky.
☐ Node: Teaser
  The stored teaser field. This may not be valid or useful data on all node types.
☑ Node: Title
  The title of the node.
☐ Node: Type
  The type of a node (for example, "blog entry", "forum post", "story", etc).
☐ Node: Updated date
  The date the node was last updated.

[Add] [Cancel]

2. Select the fields that you want to be displayed, and click the **Add** button. Drupal will then display a new form on which you can customize how the field is displayed.

Defaults: Configure field "Node: Title"

Label:

Title

The label for this field that will be displayed to end users if the style requires it.

☐ Exclude from display

Check this box to not display this field, but still load it in the view. Use this option to not show a grouping field in each record, or when doing advanced theming.

☐ Link this field to its node

[Update] [Cancel] [Remove]

---

3. Click the **Update** button to finish adding the new field.

4. Repeat these steps to include the Node Title, Node Body, Meals, Course Type, and the Ingredients list fields.

Adding filters

Next, we will create an exposed filter for each page so that our visitors can easily search the menu. This process is similar to the process that we followed when we added the filter for Node Type.

1. Click on the + symbol next to the **Filters** label.

2. Drupal will then display a selection from which you can select the fields that can be filtered on. Select all of the fields that you want to display, and then click **Add**. For the taxonomy-based fields, make sure that you select the field prefixed with Taxonomy.

3. Drupal will then display a form where you can set the options for the filter. The options form for the Meals field is as shown in the following screenshot:

Defaults: Configure filter "Content: Available at these meals"

This item is currently not exposed. If you **expose** it, users will be able to change the filter as they view it.   [Expose]

Operator: **Available at these meals:**

◉ Is one of   Breakfast

○ Is all of   Lunch

○ Is none of   Dinner

                   Dessert

☐ Reduce duplicates

This filter can cause items that have more than one of the selected options to appear as duplicate results. If this filter causes duplicate results to occur, this checkbox can reduce those duplicates; however, the more terms it has to search for, the less performant the query will be, so use this with caution.

[Update] [Cancel] [Remove]

---

4. Because we are building a search form, we want to expose the field so that the user can modify the values. When you click on the **Expose** button, the following options are added:

☐ Unlock operator
When checked, the operator will be exposed to the user

Filter identifier:
meals

This will appear in the URL after the ? to identify this filter. Cannot be blank.

Label:
Meals Served

☑ Optional
This exposed filter is optional and will have added options to allow it not to be set.

☐ Force single
Force this exposed filter to accept only one option.

☑ Remember
Remember the last setting the user gave this filter.

☐ Limit list to selected items
If checked, the selected items presented to the user will be the only ones selected here.

5. Once you are satisfied with the options, click **Update** to save the filter.

Creating a page and menu

Now that the view has been fully set up, we can create a Page and Menu for the View. Because we cloned this content type, we can simply modify the existing values.

1. Click on the **Page link** link for the view.

2. Click on the link next to the **Path** label in the **Page Settings** group. Change this value to **search_menu**, and update the setting.

3. Click on the link next to the **Menu** label and change this value to **Search the Menu**.

Using the search form

Now that the Search View is complete, we can use it by clicking on the **Search the Menu** link in the Main Menu. A sample view of the search form is shown in the following screenshot:

Building an index for our vocabularies

Good Eatin' Goal: Create an index of the meals that Good Eatin' serves, based on the key ingredients in each meal.

Additional modules needed: Taxonomy VTN (`http://drupal.org/project/ taxonomy_vtn`).

Basic steps

1. Install and enable the **Taxonomy VTN** module.

2. There are a variety of options available for the Taxonomy VTN module, which can be accessed by selecting **Site configuration** and then **Taxonomy VTN settings**, from the **Administer** menu. For the Good Eatin' web site, the defaults are all correct.

3. Once you enable the Taxonomy VTN module, you will have a new menu item called **Vocabularies**. When you select this menu item, Drupal will automatically display a page similar to the following, which contains one entry for each vocabulary that you have created.

Vocabularies

Show / Hide descriptions

A

- **Allergens** (1)
  A list of any allergens that may be in the dish so our patrons can make informed decisions about what which items to order to avoid becoming sick.

K

- **Key Ingredients** (4)
  A list of the key ingredients which make up this meal which will help customers to select foods which select their interests and diets.

C

- **Course Type** (8)
  The course type identifies the suggested course for the menu item. If more than one course is selected, you should describe any differences in the menu item's description.

---

4. When you select a vocabulary, the terms within the vocabulary will be as shown in the following screenshot:

Terms in Course Type

The course type identifies the suggested course for the menu item. If more than one course is selected, you should describe any differences in the menu item's description.
<< **Back to vocabularies** | **Show / Hide descriptions**

A

- **Alcoholic Drinks** (0)
  Not for kids, but these beverages are delicious
- **Appetizer** (0)
  Delicious tidbits to whet your appetite. All appetizers are sized for two people to share.

N

- **Non-alcoholic Drinks** (0)
  Delicious concoctions and some traditional staples for to satisfy your thirst.

S

- **Salads** (0)
  From lettuce to pasta, these salads are a great accompaniment to any meal.
- **Second Course** (0)
  Our second courses are meat based dishes which are flavorful and filling
- **Soups** (0)
  Delicious soups are a great way to start your meal or make a meal of your own

D

- **Desserts** (0)
  A perfect way to end your meal with something sweet.

F

- **First Course** (0)
  First courses are more filling pasta, potato, and rice dishes.

---

5. If you would like to change the name or position of the menu item, you can do so from the **Menu Manager** which is available by selecting **Site Building** and then **Menus**, from the **Administer** menu.

Summary

Now that you have finished this chapter, you should understand how to use CCK to build a new content type and use that content type on your web site. By using custom types for your content, you can make adding content easy for editors, and make the look of your content consistent for users.

In the next chapter, we will make the web site more interactive by allowing guests to interact with the site through comments, ratings, polls, and user surveys. This type of functionality is very popular with web users because it allows them to become a part of the site. It is also a fantastic way to learn more about your customers so that you can continue to provide better services to them.

4

Interacting With Customers and Visitors

Chef Wanyama thinks that his food is the best in the city and to make sure that his food stays on the top, he is always seeking feedback from his customers both when they are in the restaurant, and when they are visiting the Good Eatin' web site.

In this chapter, we will create a variety of functionalities that will allow the site's users to interact with the web site and help them feel that they are a part of the community, in addition to giving valuable feedback to Chef Wanyama. We will allow users to register on the web site, comment on content, respond to polls, and answer surveys.

Working with users

In this series of tasks, we will explore Drupal's user functionality, which allows you to add users to your site and specify the functionality that they can use. We will also discuss the concept of roles, which allow you to create a group of permissions that can easily be assigned to users. Finally, we will discuss how to assign roles to the users.

Allowing user registration

Good Eatin' Goal: Allow users to register on the web site so that they can access additional content that is not available to unregistered visitors.

Additional modules needed: None.

Drupal contains a sophisticated system of user management and permissions that allows you to easily control who can access your web site and what they can do on the web site.

Basic steps

1. Settings related to user registration are controlled from the **User Settings** page, which is available by selecting **User management** and then **User settings**, from the **Administer** menu. The first section, shown below, controls the registration process that a new visitor must go through to sign up at the web site.

User registration settings

Public registrations:

○ Only site administrators can create new user accounts.

◉ Visitors can create accounts and no administrator approval is required.

○ Visitors can create accounts but administrator approval is required.

☑ Require e-mail verification when a visitor creates an account
If this box is checked, new users will be required to validate their e-mail address prior to logging into the site, and will be assigned a system-generated password. With it unchecked, users will be logged in immediately upon registering, and may select their own passwords during registration.

User registration guidelines:

This text is displayed at the top of the user registration form and is useful for helping or instructing your users.

---

2. The default settings will allow anyone to register for your web site without any interaction from a site administrator. Chef Wanyama is interested in controlling access to the site and wants to approve user registration requests before they are activated. This will help him recognize special customers to include in his VIP club and make sure that only the customers living near his restaurant are registered.

3. Change the **Public registrations** option to **Visitors can create accounts but administrator approval is required**. You can also enter some guidelines to help the user understand the process.

4. The next section controls the format of emails that are sent to the users at various stages of the registration process.

5. Finally, you can control whether or not users can add signatures and pictures when they submit comments and forum posts. Users of a social site may wish to provide a signature to give other users information about themselves. However, on the Good Eatin' site, signatures and pictures aren't necessary.

Create a VIP role

Good Eatin' Goal: Create a VIP role that will be used to give special customers enhanced privileges that normal customers do not have. Customers must be granted VIP access; they cannot sign up for it.

Additional modules needed: None.

Basic steps

1. Drupal allows you to manage roles for the web site on the **Roles Manager** page, which can be accessed by selecting **User Management** and then **Roles**, from the **Administer** menu.

2. After you open the **Roles Manager**, Drupal will display a list of the roles currently available on your site, and also provide you with the ability to add a new role, as shown below:

Roles

Roles allow you to fine tune the security and administration of Drupal. A role defines a group of users that have certain privileges as defined in user permissions. Examples of roles include: anonymous user, authenticated user, moderator, administrator and so on. In this area you will define the role names of the various roles. To delete a role choose "edit".

By default, Drupal comes with two user roles:

- *Anonymous user: this role is used for users that don't have a user account or that are not authenticated.*
- *Authenticated user: this role is automatically granted to all logged in users.*

Name	Operations
anonymous user	locked edit permissions
authenticated user	locked edit permissions
	Add role

---

3. Enter **VIP** user for the name and then press **Add role**. Drupal will now add the role to the **Roles Manager** as shown below:

VIP user	edit role edit permissions

4. From the manager, you can edit the role, which will allow you to modify the name for the role, or delete the role.

5. Once the role has been created, you need to update the permissions for the role so that the user can perform the tasks that they need to. To modify the permissions, click on the **edit permissions** link for the role.

6. Drupal will then display a list of all of the available permissions, arranged by category. By default, all permissions are disabled. This prevents new user roles from gaining unwanted access. When a user is assigned to more than one role, their actual permissions will be a combination of the permissions of each role. This means that you should give each role as few permissions as possible, and assign multiple roles to a user in order to fully define each user.

7. For our VIP role, we will only add the **post comments without approval** permission, and then click the **Save permissions** button to finish the changes.

Assign users to the VIP role

Good Eatin' Goal: Change a registered customer to a VIP customer and let them know that they have been given additional privileges.

Additional modules needed: None.

Basic steps

Now that we have built the new VIP role, we can assign users to the role. Chef Wanyama wants to assign his VIPs manually, but you can also allow visitors to request a different role, or assign roles at sign-up.

1. To create a new user with a VIP role, we will start at the **User Manager**, which is accessed by selecting **User management** and then **Users**, from the **Administer** menu.

2. Next, click on the **Add user** link. Drupal will display a form where you can enter information about the user who is to be added, as shown in the following screenshot:

Users

This web page allows administrators to register new users. Users' e-mail addresses and usernames must be unique.

[more help...]

Username: *

Spaces are allowed; punctuation is not allowed except for periods, hyphens, and underscores.

E-mail address: *

A valid e-mail address. All e-mails from the system will be sent to this address. The e-mail address is not made public and will only be used if you wish to receive a new password or wish to receive certain news or notifications by e-mail.

Password: *

Confirm password: *

Provide a password for the new account in both fields.

Status:

○ Blocked
◉ Active

Roles:

☑ authenticated user
☐ VIP user

☐ Notify user of new account

[Create new account]

3. Enter the required information about the new user, including a password. To make the user a VIP user, select the **VIP user** checkbox in the **Roles** section.

4. If a user has already signed up, you can add a role for him or her by clicking on the user from the **User Manager** page, clicking on the **edit** link, and then simply selecting the checkbox for the role that you want to add.

Notification on sign up

Good Eatin' Goal: Set up a notification system so that web site administrators can be notified each time a new user registers on the web site. This can help you to quickly review new members and follow up with them to ensure that they have a positive experience on the site.

Additional modules needed: Trigger (Core).

In order to notify administrators when a user has signed up, we will need to do two things. First, we will need to build an action that creates and sends the email. The second thing we need to do is create a trigger that tells Drupal when the email should be sent. Let's begin by creating the action.

Creating the email action

1. Actions are created by using the **Actions Manager**, which is accessed by selecting **Site Configuration** and then **Actions**, from the **Administer** menu.

2. As you can see in the following image, there are several basic actions that can be used. Alternatively, you can create your own actions.

Actions

Actions are individual tasks that the system can do, such as unpublishing a piece of content or banning a user. Modules, such as the trigger module, can fire these actions when certain system events happen; for example, when a new post is added or when a user logs in. Modules may also provide additional actions.

There are two types of actions: simple and advanced. Simple actions do not require any additional configuration, and are listed here automatically. Advanced actions can do more than simple actions; for example, send an e-mail to a specified address, or check for certain words within a piece of content. These actions need to be created and configured first before they may be used. To create an advanced action, select the action from the drop-down below and click the Create button.

Actions available to Drupal:

Action type	Description
comment	Unpublish comment
node	Publish post
node	Unpublish post
node	Make post sticky
node	Make post unsticky
node	Promote post to front page
node	Remove post from front page
node	Save post
user	Block current user
user	Ban IP address of current user

Make a new advanced action available

Choose an advanced action ▾   [Create]

As there is no basic action for emailing the administrator, we will need to create a new action.

3. Begin by selecting **Send email** from the **Advanced Options** drop-down list and then click **Create**.

4. Drupal will then display a form where you can enter information about the email that is to be sent, as shown below:

Configure an advanced action

An advanced action offers additional configuration options which may be filled out below. Changing the Description field is recommended, in order to better identify the precise action taking place. This description will be displayed in modules such as the trigger module when assigning actions to system events, so it is best if it is as descriptive as possible (for example, "Send e-mail to Moderation Team" rather than simply "Send e-mail").

Description:

New User Email

A unique description for this advanced action. This description will be displayed in the interface of modules that integrate with actions, such as Trigger module.

Recipient:

admin@drupalbyexample.com

The email address to which the message should be sent OR enter *%author* if you would like to send an e-mail to the author of the original post.

Subject:

A New User Registered registered on %site_name

The subject of the message.

Message:

A new user registered on %site_name with the user name %username. To approve this user, please login to %site_name. And visit the User Manager.

The %site_name team.

The message that should be sent. You may include the following variables: %site_name, %username, %node_url, %node_type, %title, %teaser, %body. Not all variables will be available in all contexts.

Save

---

5. Click on **Save** and the action will be added to the **Action Manager**. You can modify the email at any point by clicking on the **configure** link, or you can delete the action by clicking **delete**.

Creating the new user trigger

We now need to create the **Trigger** that will determine when our new email is to be sent.

1. Begin by enabling the **Trigger module**, which is installed as part of the core Drupal installation.

2. Once the Trigger module has been installed, you can access the **Trigger manager** by selecting **Site building** and then **Triggers**, from the **Administer** menu. The **Trigger Manager** is divided into several sections, depending on its usage.

3. To access the manager for user-related Triggers, click on the **Users** tab in the **Trigger Manager**. Drupal will display a list of all possible Triggers, and you can assign actions to each as shown in following screenshot:

Triggers

Triggers are system events, such as when new content is added or when a user logs in. Trigger module combines these triggers with actions (functional tasks), such as unpublishing content or e-mailing an administrator. The Actions settings page contains a list of existing actions and provides the ability to create and configure additional actions.

Below you can assign actions to run when certain user-related triggers happen. For example, you could send an e-mail to an administrator when a user account is deleted.

[more help...]

Trigger: After a user account has been created

| New User Email ▾ | Assign |

Trigger: After a user's profile has been updated

| Choose an action ▾ | Assign |

Trigger: After a user has been deleted

| Choose an action ▾ | Assign |

Trigger: After a user has logged in

| Choose an action ▾ | Assign |

Trigger: After a user has logged out

No available actions for this trigger.

Trigger: When a user's profile is being viewed

| Choose an action ▾ | Assign |

4. Change the action for the **Trigger: After a user account has been created** to **New User Email** and then click **Assign**. Drupal will add the action and save the form. The administrator will then be automatically emailed each time a new user account is created. If you want to disable this action in the future, simply click the **unassign** link in the **Trigger Manager**.

Working with comments

In this group of tasks, we will explore Drupal's built-in functionality to allow users to comment on your content. We will cover setting permissions for to determine who can comment and also describe the approval process for comments, to help prevent unwanted messages from being posted your site.

Enable comments for a node

Good Eatin' Goal: Allow registered users to leave comments on a new guest book page. All comments must be approved before they are published, unless the customer is a VIP customer, in which case their comments will be automatically approved.

Additional modules needed: None.

The first step in enabling content for a single page is to create the page by clicking on **Create content** and then **Page**.

We will use the following information for our **Guest book** page.

Guest book

Title: *

Guest book

▸ **Menu settings**

[Split summary at cursor]

Body:

We love to hear from our customers! Please leave us feedback here on our guest book. We promise to read each and every comment. To post a comment, you much register on the site which you can do at <a href="http://goodeatin.drupalbyexample.com/user/register">our registration page</a>. Comments will be added to the website shortly after posting.

▸ **Input format**

▸ **Revision information**

▾ **Comment settings**

  ○ Disabled

  ○ Read only

  ◉ Read/Write

▸ **URL path settings**

▸ **Authoring information**

▸ **Publishing options**

[Save] [Preview] [Delete]

By setting the **Comment settings** to **Read/Write**, users will be able to enter new comments on the site .

If you are creating your own custom content type using CCK there are many more settings you can choose from. We discussed many of these options when we built our menu item type.

Adding new comments

Good Eatin' Goal: Demonstrate how visitors will add comments to the guest book.

Additional modules needed: None.

Basic steps

When a page has been created with comments enabled, you will find a link at the bottom of the page, which a visitor can click to create a comment, as shown:

Guest book

We love to hear from our customers! Please leave us feedback here on our guest book. We promise to read each and every comment. To post a comment, you much register on the site which you can do at **our registration page**. Comments will be added to the website shortly after posting.

» **Add new comment**

When the user clicks on the **Add new comment** link, Drupal displays a form that allows the user to enter the subject of the comment and its text.

Reply

Your name:
mnoble

Subject:
Excellent food and service

Comment: *

My wife and I recently visited the Good Eatin' restaurant, and were extremely pleased with our meal. The food was cooked perfectly and our server Laura was very attentive to our needs. We never had to wait for more bread or drinks. Chef Wanyama even came out to personally greet us and ask how our meals were. We will definitely be visiting Good Eatin' again soon!

▸ **Input format**

Preview

After the visitor has entered a comment, he or she can click **Preview** to review the comment and can also make the changes that he or she wants. Otherwise, he or she simply clicks on the **Save** button to save the changes.

If the user has permissions to post comments without approval, the comment will be automatically published. If the user does not have permission to post comments without approval, the comment will be placed in the moderation queue.

Manage comments

Good Eatin' Goal: Demonstrate how to manage comments, view unpublished comments, and either publish the comment or delete it.

Additional modules needed: None.

Basic steps

1. Comments can be viewed in the **Comment Manager**, which can be accessed by selecting **Content management** and then **Comments**, from the **Administer** menu.

2. The Comment Manager contains two tabbed pages—one for published comments and another for unpublished comments. The unpublished comments are shown in the **Approval queue**, which is shown in the following screenshot:

3. To approve a comment, simply select the checkbox to the left of the comment that you want to approve, make sure that the **Update options** drop-down list is set to **Publish the selected comments**, and then click **Update**.

4. If you want to delete a comment, select the comment that you want to delete, change the **Update options** to **Delete the selected comments** and then click **Update**.

Setup email notification when comments are posted

Good Eatin' Goal: Automatically notify the administrator when a new comment has been submitted to the web site.

Additional modules needed: Trigger (core).

Basic steps

To create automatic notifications for new comments, we will follow a procedure similar to the one we used when we added notifications for new user registrations:

1. First, we will build an action that handles emailing the administrator. Begin by selecting **Site configuration** and then **Actions**, from the **Administer** menu.

2. Choose **Send e-mail...** from the **Advanced actions** drop-down and click on the **Create** button.

3. Fill out the action as follows:

Configure an advanced action

An advanced action offers additional configuration options which may be filled out below. Changing the Description field is recommended, in order to better identify the precise action taking place. This description will be displayed in modules such as the trigger module when assigning actions to system events, so it is best if it is as descriptive as possible (for example, "Send e-mail to Moderation Team" rather than simply "Send e-mail").

Description:

New Comment Email

A unique description for this advanced action. This description will be displayed in the interface of modules that integrate with actions, such as Trigger module.

Recipient:

admin@drupalbyexample.com

The email address to which the message should be sent OR enter *%author* if you would like to send an e-mail to the author of the original post.

Subject:

New Comment Added

The subject of the message.

Message:

A new comment was added to the %site_name by %username. Check the moderation queue to approve or delete this comment.

The message that should be sent. You may include the following variables: %site_name, %username, %node_url, %node_type, %title, %teaser, %body. Not all variables will be available in all contexts.

Save

---

4. Click **Save** to add the new action to your site.

5. Next, we need to create the trigger that will tell Drupal when to send our email. Open the Trigger Manager by selecting **Site building** and then **Triggers**, from the **Administer** menu.

6. Go to the comments section within the Trigger Manager and then change the value for **Trigger: After saving a new comment** to **New Comment Email**, and click on the **Assign** button. Drupal will then send our new email automatically whenever a user enters a new comment.

Set up user ratings for content

Chef Wanyama wants feedback about the dishes he creates because he wants to know what should be kept on the menu and what could be rotated off. He would like to allow visitors to add some more information about the dish when they rate it, so we will enable ratings when the visitor adds comments.

As we need only a single rating, we will use the Fivestar ratings settings for the content type, rather than an individual CCK field.

Add Fivestar content ratings to a node

This task will explain how to implement user ratings. For the client site, this will demonstrate how to allow users to rate menu items.

Good Eatin' Goal: Allow customers to rate their favorite menu items so that Chef Wanyama can get feedback on his food, keep popular meals, and remove unpopular food.

Additional modules needed: Fivestar (`http://drupal.org/project/fivestar`).

Basic steps

1. First, select the Content Type that you want to add ratings to, by opening the **Content Type Manager** and then editing the **Content Type**.

2. Expand the **Fivestar ratings** section, as shown here:

▾ Fivestar ratings

To rate this content, enable Fivestar rating below. These settings will be used for both comments (if available) and direct rating.

☑ Enable Fivestar rating

Number of stars:

5 ▾

▸ Star Labels

Direct rating widget

These settings allow you to display a rating widget to your users while they are viewing content of this type. Rating will immediately register a vote for that piece of content.

Star display style:

Display average vote value ▾

Text display style:

Both user and average vote ▾

☑ Show widget title

☑ Allow users to undo their votes

☑ Enable feedback during vote saving and deletion

Teaser display:

<Hidden> ▾

Full node display:

Clickable widget below node body ▾

Direct rating widget preview:

Average:
◔ ★★★☆☆
Your rating: 4 Average: 2.5 (20 votes)

Comment widget

Enabling Fivestar for comments will display a rating widget when a user posts a comment. The rating of the comment will affect its parent content.

Fivestar comment settings:

○ Disabled

◉ Optional rating

○ Required rating

Comment widget preview:

◔ ★★★★☆

---

3. For Chef Wanyama's site, we have selected the **Enable Fivestar rating** option, and customized the display of the rating. We have also enabled **ratings** when the user comments on our menu item.

4. Save the **Content Type** and your changes will be automatically applied.

5. The final change you need to make to your site is to allow users to rate content on the web site. This is done by modifying the permissions for the user by selecting **User Management** and then **Permissions**, from the **Administer** menu. The available permissions are shown in the following screenshot:

fivestar module			
rate content	☐	☐	☐
use PHP for fivestar target	☐	☐	☐

We can turn on rating content for both anonymous users and authenticated users, which will automatically enable it for all users as all users will either be anonymous or authenticated.

View content by rating

Good Eatin' Goal: Allow both Chef Wanyama and the customers to view a list of the most popular menu items.

Additional modules needed: Fivestar (`http://drupal.org/project/fivestar`), Views (`http://drupal.org/project/views`).

Basic steps

To create a display of menu items sorted according to rating, we will need to create another view to hold this information. We will include a full display for Chef Wanyama and a top-five that which can be included on the home page of the site for the visitors.

1. Begin by opening the **Views Manager** and selecting **Site building** and then **Views**, from the **Administer** menu.

2. Add a new view by selecting the **Add** link in the **Views Manager**.

3. Fill out the basic view information, as shown in the following screenshot:

Views

View name: *

menu_items_by_popularity

This is the unique name of the view. It must contain only alphanumeric characters and underscores; it is used to identify the view internally and to generate unique theming template names for this view. If overriding a module provided view, the name must not be changed or instead a new view will be created.

View description:

king menu items based on how they have been rated by users.

This description will appear on the Views administrative UI to tell you what the view is about.

View tag:

Menu Items by Popularity   ○

Enter an optional tag for this view; it is used only to help sort views on the administrative page.

View type:

⊙ Node

Nodes are a Drupal site's primary content.

---

4. Click **Next** to save the view and start editing the details of the view.

5. We need to add a Filter, which we can do by clicking on the + symbol next to the **Filter label**. Select **Node: Type**, and then click **Add**.

Defaults: Add filters

Groups:

Node

☐ Node. Sticky
    Whether or not the node is sticky.

☐ Node: Teaser
    The stored teaser field. This may not be valid or useful data on all node types.

☐ Node: Title
    The title of the node.

☑ Node: Type
    The type of a node (for example, "blog entry", "forum post", "story", etc).

☐ Node: Updated date
    The date the node was last updated.

☐ Node: Updated/commented date
    The most recent of last comment posted or node updated time.

[Add] [Cancel]

---

6. Set the actual type to **Menu Item** and click **Update**.

7. Add a relationship by clicking the + symbol next to the **Relationships** label. We will want the relationship as **Node: Voting results** as shown in the following screenshot:

Defaults: Add relationships

Groups:
Node

☐ Node: Individual votes
    Votes cast by users on node content.
☑ Node: Voting results
    The aggregate results of votes cast on node content.

8. After you have added the relationship, you will be prompted for more details of the relationship. We will need to set up this relationship so that any menu item that has not been rated will not be eligible. The other settings will control how the values are returned, as shown here:

Defaults: Configure Relationship "Node: Voting results"

Label:
Voting results

The label for this relationship that will be displayed only administratively.

☑ Require this relationship
If required, items that do not contain this relationship will not appear.

Data filters

For each piece of content, many pieces of voting data may be saved. Use these options to specify exactly which types should be available via this relationship. **Warning!** Leaving any of these filters empty may result in multiple copies of each piece of content being displayed in listings.

Value type:
Points

Vote tag:
Default vote

Aggregation function:
Average

[Update] [Cancel] [Remove]

9. Next, add a couple of new fields to the View by clicking the + symbol next to the **Fields** label. Add the following fields:
   ◦ **Node: Title** with the label **Title** and a link to the node
   ◦ **Voting API results: Function** with the label **Average Rating**

10. Change the settings for the **Row style options**, and set the **Node: Title** and **Voting API results: Function** to be inline fields, as shown here:

⊕ Defaults: Row style options

Inline fields:

☑ Voting API results: Function
☑ Node: Title

Inline fields will be displayed next to each other rather than one after another.

Separator:

The separator may be placed between inline fields to keep them from squishing up next to each other. You can use HTML in this field.

[Update] [Cancel]

11. Add a new sort criteria by clicking the **+** symbol next to the **Sort criteria** label.

12. The new sort criteria should be on **Voting API results: Function**. The results should be sorted in **Descending** order, as shown in following screenshot:

Defaults: Configure sort criterion "Voting API results: Function"

Relationship:
Voting results ▼

Sort order:

○ Ascending
◉ Descending

[Update] [Cancel] [Remove]

13. Modify the **Style** to be a list. This option is located in the **Basic settings** section, on the leftmost side of the screen.

14. We now need to add a page view so that Chef Wanyama can view the results of the voting. From the drop-down list for the view type, select **Page** and then click **Add display**.

15. Change the **Path** to **menu-by-rating** and change the **Title** to **Menu Items by Rating**.

16. Create a second display by selecting a drop-down value of **Block** and clicking the **Add display** button.

17. Change the title for the block display to **Most Popular**, set the number of **Items** to be displayed to **5**, and then set the **Block Admin Settings** to **Popular menu items**. When updating the title, make sure that you click the **Override** button rather than the **Update default display** button, to avoid changing the title for the page.

18. Save the view and our new block, and the page will be available.

19. To add the block to the home page, open the **Blocks Manager** by selecting **Site building** and then **Blocks** from the Administer menu.

20. Find the **Popular menu items** block and change the region to **Right sidebar**. Then save the block.

21. To ensure that the block only shows up on the home page and on menu pages (if any), click on the **configure** option and then modify the **Page specific visibility settings**, as shown in the following screenshot:

```
▾ Page specific visibility settings

Show block on specific pages:

  ○  Show on every page except the listed pages.
  ◉  Show on only the listed pages.
  ○  Show if the following PHP code returns TRUE (PHP-mode, experts only).

Pages:
┌─────────────────────────────────────────────────────────────────────┐
│ home                                                                  │
│ menu/*                                                                │
│                                                                       │
│                                                                       │
│                                                                       │
│                                                                       │
└─────────────────────────────────────────────────────────────────────┘
Enter one page per line as Drupal paths. The '*' character is a wildcard. Example paths are blog for the blog page and blog/* for
every personal blog. <front> is the front page. If the PHP-mode is chosen, enter PHP code between <?php ?>. Note that executing
incorrect PHP-code can break your Drupal site.
```

Change the display of the ratings

Good Eatin' Goal: Customize the rating display to make the ratings more dramatic.

Additional modules needed: Fivestar (`http://drupal.org/project/fivestar`).

Basic steps

The Fivestar module provides you with a wide assortment of images that can be used when displaying or selecting a rating. These are accessed by selecting **Site Configuration** and then **Fivestar**, from the **Administer** menu.

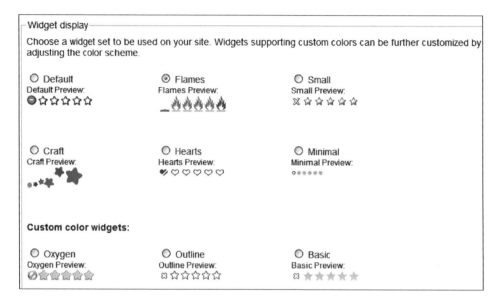

The top section contains a variety of different icons that are used for display. For our Good Eatin' site, we will use the **Flames** setting, because that works well with our restaurant theme.

If you select one of the widgets in the **Custom color widgets** section, you can customize the colors used in the display to suit the theme of your site, by using the options as shown in the following screenshot:

Working with polls

Polls are a great way to quickly get information from your users. Visitors like to answer short polls, especially if the results are immediately available and the questions are interesting. In Drupal, polls can contain only a single question, along with a set of predefined responses that the user can choose from.

Create a poll

Good Eatin' Goal: Create a poll to allow Chef Wanyama to get feedback from customers. The first poll will ask customers what their favorite meal is at Good Eatin'.

Additional modules needed: Poll (core).

Basic steps

1. We begin the process of building a poll by ensuring that the **Poll module** is active. The Poll module is included as a part of the Core Drupal installation.

2. Once you have confirmed that this module is available, select **Create content** and then **Poll** from the main Navigation menu. Drupal will open a new form, where you can enter information about the poll.

3. By default, you are given the space to specify two choices, but you can include additional choices by clicking **Add another choice**. For our Good Eatin' site, we are allowing visitors to select between Breakfast, Lunch, Dinner, and Desert.

4. The **Poll status** controls whether or not visitors can enter new votes into the system. If you want to manually manage the duration of the poll, you can simply close the poll by editing the poll and setting the **Poll status** to **Closed** when the poll is over.

5. The **Poll duration** can be used to automatically close a poll after a specified interval. The poll can be kept open for various intervals from 1 day to 1 year.

6. When you click **Save**, Drupal will add the poll to the web site, and allow you to vote in it, as shown in the following screenshot:

What is your favorite meal at Good Eatin'

Poll *What is your favorite meal at Good Eatin'* has been created.

Submitted by admin on Sun, 07/06/2008 - 10:53

○ Breakfast

○ Lunch

○ Dinner

○ Desert

[Vote]

7. The final step to setting up the poll is making sure that the users can submit answers to the poll. This is controlled via the **Permissions Manager**, which is accessed by selecting **User management** and then **Permission**, from the **Administer** menu.

8. There are several permissions available to control access to the polls, as shown in following screenshot:

Permission	anonymous user	authenticated user	VIP user
poll module			
cancel own vote	☑	☑	☑
create poll content	☐	☐	☐
delete any poll content	☐	☐	☐
delete own poll content	☐	☐	☐
edit any poll content	☐	☐	☐
edit own poll content	☐	☐	☐
inspect all votes	☐	☐	☐
vote on polls	☑	☑	☑

9. The only permissions we want to grant are the abilities to vote and cancel votes, for all users. Select these options, and then click **Save permissions**.

Adding the poll to the home page

Good Eatin' Goal: Add our new poll to the home page on the right-hand side, so that customers will see the poll.

Additional modules needed: Poll (core).

Basic steps

1. We can add the poll to the home page by creating a block. We do this by selecting **Site building** and then **Blocks**, from the **Administer** menu.

2. The **Most recent poll** block is already set up to do what we need, so we will change the location to **Right sidebar**, as shown in following screenshot:

3. We can now configure the display by clicking on the **configure** link. We will restrict the poll to only be displayed on the home page, as shown in the following screenshot. Because we have created an alias for our home page, called home, we can simply enter **home**. However, if you are using the automatically-generated home page, you will need to enter <front> instead.

▼ **Page specific visibility settings**

Show block on specific pages:

○ Show on every page except the listed pages.

◉ Show on only the listed pages.

○ Show if the following PHP code returns TRUE (PHP-mode, experts only).

Pages:

```
home
```

Enter one page per line as Drupal paths. The "*" character is a wildcard. Example paths are *blog* for the blog page and *blog/** for every personal blog. *<front>* is the front page. If the PHP-mode is chosen, enter PHP code between *<?php ?>*. Note that executing incorrect PHP-code can break your Drupal site.

4. The block on the home page appears as follows, before a vote is cast:

Submitting a poll

Good Eatin' Goal: Demonstrate how a customer will submit his or her answers to our poll.

Additional modules needed: Poll (core).

Basic steps

Visitors can easily submit an answer to the poll by selecting their preferred option and then clicking on **Vote**.

After voting, the display will be updated to show the results of the poll, as shown here:

Viewing poll results

Good Eatin' Goal: Demonstrate how Chef Wanyama can view the poll results, and show the results of the poll to customers who have already answered the poll.

Additional modules needed: Poll (core).

Basic steps

Users with the **Inspect all votes permission** can view a list of all of the votes that have been cast for a poll. This is done by viewing the poll and clicking on the **Votes** tab, to list all the votes, as shown in the following screenshot:

This view is useful for ensuring that all votes are legitimate, and for comparing votes submitted by registered users and anonymous users. For registered users their user name will be displayed; for unregistered users, the IP address of the machine from which they submitted their vote will be displayed.

Upgrading to Advanced Poll

Good Eatin' Goal: Explain some of the differences between Poll and Advanced Poll.

Additional modules needed: Advanced Poll (`http://drupal.org/project/advpoll`).

The **Advanced Poll** module provides several additional features that do not exist in the core Poll module, including: three new types of voting systems in addition to the basic poll, enhanced vote management, enhanced time management, write-in votes, and improved display.

The Advanced poll module has not been ported to Drupal 6 as of the time of writing.

Adding user surveys

User surveys allow more complex methods of querying visitors for information. Surveys support multiple questions that are asked at one time and questions that require more complex answers than a simple selection between a finite number of predefined choices. Chef Wanyama will use the user survey to get more comprehensive information about his customers' dining experience and what they expect from the restaurant in the future.

Creating a user survey

Good Eatin' Goal: Add a survey to the Good Eatin' web site that asks visitors for their opinion on the various aspects of the restaurant, including specifics about what new food items they are interested in, what their favorite visiting times are, how frequently they visit, and so on.

Additional modules needed: Webform module (`http://drupal.org/project/webform`).

Basic steps

1. Install the Webform module on your site, and activate it by using the Module Manager.

2. There are several settings provided for controlling the basic aspects of the Webform module. These can be accessed by clicking on **Site configuration** and then **Webform**. For the Good Eatin' site, all of the default values are acceptable.

3. To build a new Webform, select **Create Content** and then **Webform**, from the **Main menu**. Drupal will display a form that allows you to build your survey.

4. The first section of the form allows you to enter a title, description, and information to be displayed when the user finishes the survey. We will fill this form out as shown in the following screenshot:

▾ Webform Settings

Title: *
```
Customer Survey
```

Description:
```
Please fill out this customer survey to help us better serve you.  The survey should take no more than 5 to
10 minutes to complete. All information is kept confidential and is only used to help us improve our
services.
```
Text to be shown as teaser and before the form.

Confirmation message or redirect URL:
```
Thank you for taking our survey! We look forward to serving you again soon!
```

Message to be shown upon successful submission or a path to a redirect page. Redirect pages must start with *http://* for external
sites or *internal:* for an internal path. i.e. *http://www.example.com* or *internal:node/10*

— ▸ **Input format**

---

5. The next section of the form controls which users should be able to submit the form. The default allows anyone to fill out the survey, which is fine for our needs.

6. The next section allows you to control whether or not survey results are mailed to a user, and if they are mailed, who they should be sent to. We won't automatically email survey results, so this section can be left as it is.

7. We will also disable comments, and set the URL path to the survey.

8. Finally, we will add a menu item for this form, called **Customer Survey** which will appear in our main menu, using the settings shown in the following screenshot:

▾ Menu settings

Menu link title:
```
Customer Survey
```
The link text corresponding to this item that should appear in the menu. Leave blank if you do not wish to add this post to the
menu.

Parent item:
```
<Navigation>
```
The maximum depth for an item and all its children is fixed at 9. Some menu items may not be available as parents if selecting
them would exceed this limit.

Weight:
```
14
```
Optional. In the menu, the heavier items will sink and the lighter items will be positioned nearer the top.

---

9. Save the form by clicking the **Save** button.

10. Drupal will then display a form that allows us to add new questions to our survey, as shown in the following screenshot:

View	Edit	Results

Configuration | **Form components**

Customer Survey

This page displays all the components currently configured for this webform node. You may add any number of components to the form, even multiple of the same type. To add a new component, fill in a name and select a type from the fields at the bottom of the table. Submit the form to create the new component or update any changed form values.

Click on any existing component's name to edit its settings.

- The new webform *Customer Survey* has been created. Add new fields to your webform with the form below.
- This webform is currently unpublished. After finishing your changes to the webform, use the *Publish* button below.

Name	Type	Value	Mandatory	E-mail	Operations
	No Components, add a component below.				
⊹ New component name	textfield ▼		☐	☑	Add

| Submit | Publish |

11. To add a new question, enter the question in the **Name** field, and select the type of answer from the drop-down list for the **Type**.

Name	Type	Value	Mandatory	E-mail	Operations
	No Components, add a component below.				
⊹ What meals have you visited	select ▼		☐	☐	Add

For surveys, most questions will be of the type **textfield** (for questions with open ended answers) or **select** for yes/no or multiple choice questions. After you are satisfied with the information, click the **Add** button.

12. You can now customize the available answers for the question and choose various other options related to the display of the question. We will enter available answers of breakfast, lunch, and dinner, and allow multiple values to be selected. When you have finished modifying the options, click the **Submit** button to add the question.

13. Other questions can be entered in a similar manner. When you have finished entering all of your questions, click the **Publish** button to publish your survey to the site.

Protecting the survey with Captchas

Good Eatin' Goal: Add a Captcha to the survey to help prevent automated entry into the survey, to prevent spam.

Additional modules needed: Webform module (`http://drupal.org/project/webform`), Captcha module (`http://drupal.org/project/captcha`).

Basic steps

1. Begin by installing and activating the Captcha module via the Module Manager.

2. We will then need to modify the settings of the Captcha module. These are accessed by selecting **User management** and then **CAPTCHA**, from the **Administer** menu.

3. The key setting we need to enable is the **Add CAPTCHA administration links to forms** option, as shown in the following screenshot:

☑ Add CAPTCHA administration links to forms
This option is very helpful to enable/disable challenges on forms. When enabled, users with the "*administer CAPTCHA settings*" permission will see CAPTCHA administration links on all forms (except on administrative pages, which shouldn't be accessible to untrusted users in the first place). These links make it possible to enable a challenge of the desired type or disable it.

This will allow us to add the Captcha to our Survey.

4. You can also configure Captchas for several predefined forms, specify whether or not users have to answer Captchas for each form they submit, specify whether or not incorrect answers are logged, and what the various options for each type of Captcha are.

5. You can view examples of each type of Captcha by clicking on the **Examples** link. Several examples are shown in the following screenshot:

CAPTCHA

This page gives an overview of all available challenge types, generated with their current settings.

Challenge "*Math*" by module "*captcha*"

Math Question: *

11 + 0 = [   ]

Solve this simple math problem and enter the result. E.g. for 1+3, enter 4.

10 more examples of this challenge.

Challenge "*Image*" by module "*image_captcha*"

What code is in the image?: *

[   ]

Copy the characters (respecting upper/lower case) from the image.

10 more examples of this challenge.

Challenge "*Text*" by module "*text_captcha*"

What is the fifth word in the phrase "hutobi nohe ayawe iyiloki duki"?: *

[   ]

10 more examples of this challenge.

6. Now that the Captcha has been configured, you can edit or simply view the Customer Survey. There, you will find a new section titled **CAPTCHA**, which you can expand.

▾ CAPTCHA

Place a CAPTCHA here for untrusted users.

7. Click the **Place a CAPTCHA here for untrusted users** link to expand this section. You can now select the **Challenge type** that visitors will be presented with, as shown in the following screenshot:

CAPTCHA point adminstration

Form ID:

webform_client_form_10

The Drupal form_id of the form to add the CAPTCHA to.

Challenge type:

Math (captcha) ▾

The CAPTCHA type to use for this form

[Save]

8. Click the Save button to save your settings. An untrusted user will see a Captcha when he or she attempts to submit an answer.

Answering a survey

Good Eatin' Goal: Demonstrate how a visitor will fill out the survey to submit new answers.

Additional modules needed: Webform module (`http://drupal.org/project/webform`).

Basic steps

When the users click on the **Customer Survey** link from the menu, they will be presented with the survey form that is to be filled out.

After they have entered all of their responses, they will need to answer the Captcha question, if they are not registered users.

What days do you visit Good Eatin'?:

☐ Monday

☐ Tuesday

☐ Wednesday

☑ Thursday

☐ Friday

☑ Saturday

☐ Sunday

What is your favorite dish:

Alligator Tail

What dish would you like to see us add to the menu?:

Something with Ostrich

CAPTCHA

This question is for testing whether you are a human visitor and to prevent automated spam submissions.

Math Question: *

13 + 1 = 14

Solve this simple math problem and enter the result. E.g. for 1+3, enter 4.

Submit

The users then click **Submit** to send their responses to the site.

If any required information is missing, or if the Captcha is entered incorrectly, the user will be asked to correct this information, and then they can try to submit their responses again.

Once the information has been successfully submitted, the user will be taken to your completion page, which was set up when you created the survey.

Viewing survey results

Good Eatin' Goal: Demonstrate how Chef Wanyama will view the results of surveys.

Additional modules needed: Webform module (`http://drupal.org/project/webform`).

The Webform module offers different ways of reviewing the survey submissions. These are all accessed by opening the survey and then clicking on the **Results** link.

Submissions view

The **Submissions** page shows a list of all of the responses to the survey, as shown here. This view can be sorted, so you can easily identify duplicate submissions. You can view individual responses, and delete them if necessary.

Analysis view

The **Analysis** page groups responses so that you can view statistics of the survey and easily see how the answers for each question are broken down. A partial view is shown in the following screenshot:

Table view

The **Table** view displays all of the results of the survey in a single, easy to read format, as shown in the following screenshot:

#	Submitted	User	IP Address	How often do you visit Good Eatin'?	What meals have you visited us?	What days do you visit Good Eatin'?	What is your favorite dish	What dish would you like to see us add to the menu?
1	07/06/2008 - 21:43	Anonymous	24.9.170.138	Monthly	Breakfast Dinner	Thursday Saturday	Alligator Tail	Something with Ostrich
2	07/06/2008 - 21:46	Anonymous	24.9.170.138	Daily	Breakfast Lunch Dinner	Monday Tuesday Wednesday Thursday Friday Saturday Sunday	Everything is incredible	Octopus Tartare

(View | Edit | Results tabs; Submissions | Analysis | Table | Download | Clear. Customer Survey)

Download view

The **Download** view allows you to download all of the survey responses into a comma-delimited file, which can then be opened in a program such as Microsoft Excel, for further analysis.

Clear

Clicking on the **Clear** link will remove all of the survey responses from the site. This can be useful if you are testing the survey and want to restart, or if you want to restart the survey at the beginning of each month.

Summary

In this chapter, we explored various methods of soliciting feedback from visitors to your site, including comments, ratings, polls, and surveys. Using these techniques will help you to improve the products and services you provide to your customers.

In the next chapter, we will create a company blog to allow Chef Wanyama to promote his restaurant to interested readers. We will also load feeds from other web sites into the Good Eatin' site, to leverage content from other sources.

5
Creating a Company Blog

A blog is a series of typically short postings that are displayed in reverse chronological order. Blogs normally allow users to comment on each posting. With a regularly updated blog or blogs, you can ensure that your site always has fresh content, which ensures that both visitors and the search engines keep coming back.

In this chapter, we will create a blog where Chef Wanyama can discuss the Good Eatin' restaurant, cooking, the restaurant business, and more. He plans to use the blog to make the site more interactive and to draw search engine traffic.

Each employee will also be given the opportunity to have his or her own blog, where they can create blog entries if they so choose. Employee blogs will be monitored, and posts will be added to an approval queue before they are released to the public at large.

Finally, we will demonstrate how users can view the blogs using RSS feeds and add related blog posts to their own blogs.

Creating blogs

In this section, we will discuss how to set up the blog module so that a user can create blogs. We will demonstrate how Chef Wanyama creates blog posts, and will look at ways at ways to moderate blogs and use alternate editors to build the blog.

Setting up the blog system

Good Eatin' Goal: Set up the blog system, so that Chef Wanyama can begin posting to the blog.

Additional modules needed: Blog (core).

Basic steps

1. Activate the blog module within the **Module Manager**.

2. Drupal will allow any user with the `create blog entries` permission to create a blog. To make it easier to control who can create blogs, we will create a new role called blogger. To build a new role, click on **User management** and then **Roles**.

3. Enter **blogger** as the role name and then click **Add role**, as shown below:

Name	Operations	
anonymous user	locked	edit permissions
authenticated user	locked	edit permissions
VIP user	edit role	edit permissions
blogger	Add role	

4. Once the role has been created, click on the **edit permissions** links, so that we can define what this role can do. We will select the following settings as follows:

Permission	blogger
blog module	
create blog entries	☑
delete any blog entry	☐
delete own blog entries	☑
edit any blog entry	☐
edit own blog entries	☑

These settings will allow users to maintain their own blog, but not modify anyone else's blog.

Adding a new blog post

Good Eatin' Goal: Demonstrate how Chef Wanyama will add new posts to his blog.

Additional modules needed: Blog (core).

Basic steps

Creating a blog post is similar to building content pages.

1. We will start by clicking on the **Create content** link and then on the **Blog entry** link in the main Navigation menu.

2. Drupal will display a form you can enter the body of the post as well as a title for the post, as shown in the following screenshot:

> **Create Blog entry**
>
> **Title:** *
> Good Eatin' Website
>
> ▸ **Menu settings**
>
> [Split summary at cursor]
>
> **Body:**
> We've been working hard on our new website which has a new look and tons of new functionality. Please let us know what you think of the site by posting a comment here.

3. Once you are satisfied with the text of your post, simply click **Save** and your new post will be saved.

4. If you would prefer that visitors didn't comment on a specific post, you can disable comments by expanding the **Comment settings** section of the form and selecting the **Disabled** option.

> ▾ **Comment settings**
>
> ○ Disabled
> ○ Read only
> ◉ Read/Write

5. After you have saved the post, the final blog entry will appear as follows:

> **Home » Blogs » admin's blog**
>
> | View | Edit |
>
> **Good Eatin' Website**
>
> Blog entry *Good Eatin' Website* has been created.
>
> *Submitted by admin on Thu, 07/10/2008 - 23:24*
>
> We've been working hard on our new website which has a new look and tons of new functionality. Please let us know what you think of the site by posting a comment here.
>
> » admin's blog   Add new comment

Adding moderation for blog posts

Good Eatin' Goal: Configure the blogging systems so that posts must be moderated prior to publication, to ensure that the posts are appropriate. We will also add a moderator role that can edit posts or delete them, as necessary.

Additional modules needed: Blog (core).

Creating the moderator role

Before we can set up moderation for the blog posts, we will need to create a moderator role. We can create it by using the following steps:

1. Begin by opening the **Role Manager** and **User management** and then **Roles**, from the **Administer** menu.

2. Now, enter **moderator** as the name of the new role and click **Add role**, to build the role.

Roles

Roles allow you to fine tune the security and administration of Drupal. A role defines a group of users that have certain privileges as defined in user permissions. Examples of roles include: anonymous user, authenticated user, moderator, administrator and so on. In this area you will define the role names of the various roles. To delete a role choose "edit".

By default, Drupal comes with two user roles:

- *Anonymous user: this role is used for users that don't have a user account or that are not authenticated.*
- *Authenticated user: this role is automatically granted to all logged in users.*

[more help...]

Name	Operations	
anonymous user	locked	edit permissions
authenticated user	locked	edit permissions
blogger	edit role	edit permissions
Store Administrator	edit role	edit permissions
VIP user	edit role	edit permissions
moderator	Add role	

3. Next, click on the **edit permissions** link to set up the permissions for our moderator role. The only permission that is needed to publish the blog posts is **administer nodes**, as shown in the following screenshot:

Permission	moderator
node module	
access content	☐
administer content types	☐
administer nodes	☑

4. The **administer nodes** permission will also allow users assigned to this role to create, edit, or delete content, so you need to make sure that you assign this permission carefully. After you have selected the desired permissions, click the **Save permissions** button.

Setting up moderation for the blog posts

If you allow many users to post blog entries, it may be useful, when moderating the blog postings, to ensure that all posts conform to the standards you set. To do this, we will use Drupal's publishing functionality.

1. We will begin by editing the blog content type by selecting **Content management** and then **Content types**, from the Administer menu.

2. Then, select the **Blog entry** content type.

3. Expand the **Workflow settings** section, and deselect the **Published** checkbox, as shown in the following screenshot:

▾Workflow settings

Default options:

☐ Published
☑ Promoted to front page
☐ Sticky at top of lists
☐ Create new revision

Users with the *administer nodes* permission will be able to override these options.

4. Click the **Save content type** button to update the blog entry type.

5. With this setting turned off, all posts will need to be manually approved. You can view all of the posts that need to be approved in the **Content Manger**, which is accessed by selecting **Content management** and then **Content**, from the **Administer** menu.

6. To view only those posts that require moderation, change the **status** field to **not published** and click the **Filter** button.

Show only items where		
⦿ status	is	not published
○ type		Blog entry
○ category		Appetizer

Filter

7. Drupal will now show only those items that should be moderated, as shown in the following screenshot:

Content

[more help...]

Show only items where
status is **not published**
and where   ⦿ status   is   not published   [Refine] [Undo] [Reset]
              ○ type   Blog entry
              ○ category   Appetizer

Update options
Publish   [Update]

	Title	Type	Author	Status	Operations
☐	Good Eatin' Website	Blog entry	admin	not published	edit

8. To approve a post, you can select the checkbox next to its **Title**, set the **Update options** to **Publish**, and then click **Update**. Alternatively, you can edit the post and select the **Published** checkbox in **Workflow** settings for the post.

Automatically moderating content based on keywords

Good Eatin' Goal: Add the automatic moderation of posts, based on the content entered within a post.

Additional modules needed: Actions (core), Trigger (core).

Basic steps

An alternative to forcing all posts into moderation is to allow posts to be automatically published, but to force specific posts to be moderated if they do not meet your guidelines. This can help you cut down on your moderation time and allow most posts to be available immediately after they are written.

1. We will begin by creating a new action which will unpublish a post. Select **site configuration** and then **Actions**, from the Administer menu to open the **Actions manager**.

2. Select a new action of **Unpublish post containing keyword(s)** and click **Create**.

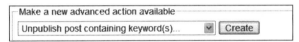

Drupal will now display a form on which you can enter the keywords that a post should contain if it is to be held for moderation. Enter the words separated by commas. If a term that you want to filter on includes a comma, you must enclose the entire term in quotes.

Configure an advanced action

An advanced action offers additional configuration options which may be filled out below. Changing the Description field is recommended, in order to better identify the precise action taking place. This description will be displayed in modules such as the trigger module when assigning actions to system events, so it is best if it is as descriptive as possible (for example, "Send e-mail to Moderation Team" rather than simply "Send e-mail").

Description:

Unpublish post containing keyword(s)

A unique description for this advanced action. This description will be displayed in the interface of modules that integrate with actions, such as Trigger module.

Keywords:

http, viagra, competitor, bad, horrible, loud, ugly, nasty, wrong, awful

The post will be unpublished if it contains any of the character sequences above. Use a comma-separated list of character sequences. Example: funny, bungee jumping, "Company, Inc.". Character sequences are case-sensitive.

Save

For a publicly-accessible blog, you will want to enter common terms used in spam such as http, viagra, and so on. For an internal company blog, you may want to moderate based on competitor names, or terms that may indicate derogatory posts. When you are satisfied with your list of terms, click **Save**.

3. We now need to trigger the new action when a new blog post is created. Select **Site building** and then **Triggers**, from the Administer menu.

4. In order to ensure that both new posts and edited posts are clean, we will set the trigger so that when a user either saves a new post or updates an existing post, our new Unpublish post containing keyword(s) action is carried out.

Triggers

Triggers are system events, such as when new content is added or when a user logs in. Trigger module combines these triggers with actions (functional tasks), such as unpublishing content or e-mailing an administrator. The Actions settings page contains a list of existing actions and provides the ability to create and configure additional actions.

Below you can assign actions to run when certain content-related triggers happen. For example, you could send an e-mail to an administrator when a post is created or updated.

[more help...]

Trigger: When either saving a new post or updating an existing post

Unpublish post containing keyword(s) ▾ | Assign

5. Click **Assign** to save your changes. All posts that meet our criteria (that is, they contain any of the specified keywords) will now automatically be unpublished and put in the moderation queue.

Enabling customers to read your blogs

In order to make the most of our blogs, we need to make sure that our customers can easily find and read them.

In this section, we will explore various ways of displaying the blogs to our customers.

Displaying a list of available blogs

Good Eatin' Goal: Modify the web site to display a list of available blogs, so that visitors can quickly find their favorite blog.

Additional modules needed: Blog (core).

Now that we can create new blog posts, we need to let our visitors know about them. We will add both a menu that links to our blog and a block showing the most recent posts in the blog.

Creating a blog menu

1. To enable the menu link for our blog, open the **Menu Manager** by clicking on selecting **Site building**, then **Menus**, and finally **Navigation**, from the **Administer** menu.

2. At the bottom of the list of menu items, you will find the **Blogs** menu item, as shown below:

Menu item	Enabled	Expanded	Operations
⊹ Blogs (disabled)	☐	☐	edit
⊹ My blog	☑	☐	edit

3. To activate the **Blogs** menu, simply select the **Enabled** checkbox and then click the **Save configuration** button at the bottom of the screen. The new **Blogs** item will now show up in the **Navigation** menu. If you want to change the name of the menu item, you can click on the **Edit link in the Operations column.**.

4. When a user clicks on the **Blogs** link, they will be taken to a page that contains the most recent posts for all blogs, as shown in the screenshot below:

Blogs

- Create new blog entry.

Trying new recipes

Submitted by Chef Wanyama on Fri, 07/11/2008 - 16:01

We received an order of alligator tail today and I got to spend part of the morning playing with different ways of preparing this delicacy.

I tried everything from light sautes to deep fried delights to stews. About the only thing we didn't try was carpaccios (something about raw alligator doesn't sit right with me).

The staff loved the new selections and we will be adding some new items to our seasonal menu. Come in and let us know what you think of these new dishes.

» Chef Wanyama's blog   Add new comment

Good Eatin' Website

Submitted by admin on Thu, 07/10/2008 - 23:24

We've been working hard on our new website which has a new look and tons of new functionality. Please let us know what you think of the site by posting a comment here.

» admin's blog   Add new comment

From this page, users can read recent posts, create a new blog entry (if they have permissions to post), comment on posts, or see all the posts that a given user has made by clicking on the link to the user's blog.

Creating a blog block

1. The blog block is enabled by selecting **Site building** and then **Blocks**, from the Administer menu, to open the **Block Manager**.

2. The **Recent blog posts** block will be in the **Disabled** section. Change the **Region** to the **Left sidebar** and then click **Save blocks**.

3. After saving the blocks, the **Recent blog posts** block will be displayed on the leftmost side of the screen. It will look similar to this:

Creating an RSS feed for newsreaders

Good Eatin' Goal: Publish blogs using RSS feeds, so customers can follow blogs in their favorite newsreader.

Additional modules needed: Blog (core).

Each blog automatically has an RSS feed created for it. RSS stands for Really Simple Syndication, and is a technology that allows readers to automatically retrieve posts from one or more sites, into a newsreader. The newsreader checks for new content at specified intervals and then automatically downloads new posts if they are available. This is a fantastic way for a user to get updates from his or her company on a regular basis.

To add an RSS feed from your site to their newsreader, a user clicks on the RSS link icon, which appears at the bottom of all the blogs, and looks like this: 🔲

The actual signup process will vary somewhat, depending on the web browser that the site visitor is using. In Firefox, the process is as follows (other browsers will also use a similar process):

After clicking on the **subscription** icon, the user will be asked what program they would like to use to follow the feed, as shown in the following screenshot.

The users can select from several common newsreaders, or they can select an application of their choice. To complete the subscription, they simply click the **Subscribe Now** button.

Adding subscription buttons

Good Eatin' Goal: Allow the user to easily add the news feed to their favorite reader by providing subscription buttons.

Additional modules needed: FeedButtons (`http://drupal.org/project/feedbuttons`).

Basic steps

You can make subscribing to your blog easier and more obvious to visitors by adding a set of buttons that will automatically add your blog to their newsreader.

1. Begin by installing and activating the FeedButtons module on your site.

2. The settings for the FeedButtons module are accessed by selecting **Site configuration** and then **Feed Buttons settings** from the **Administer** menu.

The buttons shown above are only a small sample of the buttons that you can add.

3. Select the buttons that you would like your visitors to be able to use and, then click **Save configuration**.

4. We now need to activate the block. Open the block manager by selecting **Site building** and then **Blocks**, from the **Administer** menu. Change the location of the **Subscribe Buttons** block to the **Right sidebar**, and then click the **Save blocks** button.

5. As the subscription buttons are somewhat distracting, and the blog is not a key feature of the Good Eatin' site, we will limit the display of this block to only on the blog pages. To do this, click the **configure** link for the block and then set the visibility settings as follows.

▼ Page specific visibility settings

Show block on specific pages:

○ Show on every page except the listed pages.

◉ Show on only the listed pages.

○ Show if the following PHP code returns TRUE (PHP-mode, experts only).

Pages:

```
blog
blog/*
```

Enter one page per line as Drupal paths. The '*' character is a wildcard. Example paths are *blog* for the blog page and *blog/** for every personal blog. *<front>* is the front page. If the PHP-mode is chosen, enter PHP code between *<?php ?>*. Note that executing incorrect PHP-code can break your Drupal site.

Including information from other blogs

In this section, we will add content from blogs on other sites that is relevant to the customers to our site. This can help customers recognize you as an authority in your area and make the site more useful to them.

Allowing your site to read content

Good Eatin' Goal: Set up the Aggregator module to collect posts from other blogs and display them on the Good Eatin' site.

Additional modules needed: Aggregator (core).

Basic steps

1. Activate the **Aggregator module** in the **Module Manager**.

2. The **Feed aggregator** can now be accessed by **clicking on Content management** and then **Feed aggregator**, from the **Administer** menu.

3. There are several settings available to the Feed aggregator; these can be found by clicking on the **Settings** tab. These settings are shown below:

```
   List      Add category      Add feed      Settings

Feed aggregator

Allowed HTML tags:
<a> <b> <br> <dd> <dl> <dt> <em> <i> <li> <ol> <p> <strong> <u> <ul>
A space-separated list of HTML tags allowed in the content of feed items. (Tags in this list are not removed by Drupal.)

Items shown in sources and categories pages:
3 items  [v]
Number of feed items displayed in feed and category summary pages.

Discard items older than:
16 weeks  [v]
The length of time to retain feed items before discarding. (Requires a correctly configured cron maintenance task.)

Category selection type:

( ) checkboxes

( ) multiple selector

The type of category selection widget displayed on categorization pages. (For a small number of categories, checkboxes are easier to
use, while a multiple selector work well with large numbers of categories.)

[ Save configuration ]  [ Reset to defaults ]
```

For the Good Eatin' site, the default values are all acceptable.

4. If you plan to import many feeds from different sources, it is a good idea to categorize them so that your visitors can easily find the information they want. The Good Eatin' site will have two categories: recipes and restaurant ownership.

5. To add a new category, click on the **Add category** tab. Drupal will display a form that allows you to enter a **Title** and **Description** for your category, as shown in the following screenshot:

| List | **Add category** | Add feed | Settings |

Feed aggregator

Categories allow feed items from different feeds to be grouped together. For example, several sport-related feeds may belong to a category named Sports. Feed items may be grouped automatically (by selecting a category when creating or editing a feed) or manually (via the Categorize page available from feed item listings). Each category provides its own feed page and block.

[more help...]

Title: *
Recipes

Description:
A collection of recipes from the internet. We add our favorites to our menu.

Save

6. After you have created your categories, you can edit them by clicking on the **List** tab.

| **List** | Add category | Add feed | Settings |

Feed aggregator

Thousands of sites (particularly news sites and blogs) publish their latest headlines and posts in feeds, using a number of standardized XML-based formats. Formats supported by the aggregator include RSS, RDF, and Atom.

Current feeds are listed below, and new feeds may be added. For each feed or feed category, the latest items block may be enabled at the blocks administration page.

[more help...]

Feed overview

Title	Items	Last update	Next update	Operations

Category overview

Title	Items	Operations
Recipes	0 items	edit
Restaurant ownership	0 items	edit

7. To add a new feed to the **Feed aggregator**, click on the **Add feed** tab. Drupal will display a form where you can enter the URL for the feed, as well as additional information for the feed, as shown below:

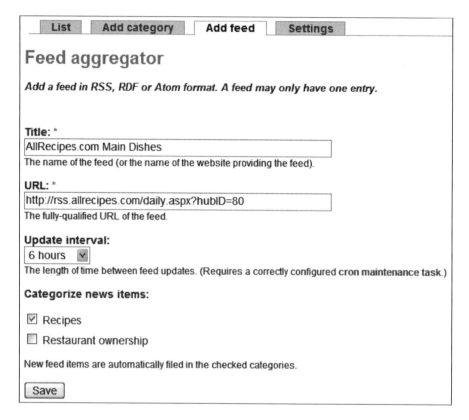

To reduce traffic on the site that you are receiving feeds from, you should try to set the **Update interval** in line with the frequency at which that site is updated. For example, there is no reason to poll a site every 15 minutes if the site states that the feed is only updated once a day, or once a week.

8. After you are satisfied with your selections, click the **Save** button.

9. After you create the feed, it will be displayed on the **List** page, as shown in the following screenshot:

Feed overview				
Title	Items	Last update	Next update	Operations
AllRecipes.com Main Dishes	0 items	never	never	edit remove items update items

10. As you can see, there are no **Items** available for this feed, and it has never been updated. To update the feed manually, click the **update items** link.

Viewing feeds

Good Eatin' Goal: Demonstrate how feeds will appear on the Good Eatin' site.

Additional modules needed: None.

Basic steps

1. In order for a feed to be visible to users, you must update the user role permissions. Select **User management** and then **Permissions**, from the **Administer** menu. Select the checkbox for **access news feeds** for each user role that you want to see the feeds, as shown in the following screenshot:

Permission	anonymous user	authenticated user	blogger	VIP user
aggregator module				
access news feeds	☑	☑	☐	☐
administer news feeds	☐	☐	☐	☐

2. If a user has permission to view news feeds, they will have a **Feed aggregator** menu item in the **Navigation** menu. This menu item can be either modified or disabled in the menu item, if you wish.

3. When a user clicks on the **Feed aggregator** link, a list of current posts will be displayed, as shown in the following screenshot:

Feed aggregator

Burgers: Grilled Spicy Lamb Burgers | Submitted By: Alan Hollister
AllRecipes.com Main Dishes - Fri, 07/11/2008 - 16:05

Something new for all the grill-daddies! An EASY burger to make, and guests rave over this one.

Categories: Recipes

Casserole Recipes: Green Bean and Canadian Bacon Casserole | Submitted By: Cathy H.
AllRecipes.com Main Dishes - Fri, 07/11/2008 - 16:05

Green beans, onion and Canadian bacon are baked in a creamy sauce and topped with bread crumbs for a delicious family supper.

Categories: Recipes

Pizza and Calzones: Deep Dish Alfredo Pizza | Submitted By: EMKING
AllRecipes.com Main Dishes - Fri, 07/11/2008 - 16:05

---

4. The visitor can also display news items by **Category** or by **Source**. The Category view is shown in the following screenshot:

Categories

Recipes

- **Main Dish Fish and Shellfish: Cod with Italian Crumb Topping | Submitted By: Verona** *7 hours 51 min old, AllRecipes.com Main Dishes*
- **Stuffed Peppers: Quick and Easy Stuffed Peppers | Submitted By: Jen** *7 hours 51 min old, AllRecipes.com Main Dishes*
- **Deep Fried: Oat Crusted Fish | Submitted By: Pierre** *7 hours 51 min old, AllRecipes.com Main Dishes*

More

The Sources view is as follows:

Sources

AllRecipes.com Main Dishes

- **Main Dish Fish and Shellfish: Cod with Italian Crumb Topping | Submitted By: Verona** *7 hours 53 min old*
- **Stuffed Peppers: Quick and Easy Stuffed Peppers | Submitted By: Jen** *7 hours 53 min old*
- **Deep Fried: Oat Crusted Fish | Submitted By: Pierre** *7 hours 53 min old*

More

---

5. We can also add a block for the Feeds, by using the block manager. There is a block for each category of news feed, in addition to a category for a specific feed. You can add these blocks to any section of the site you want to, by changing the location and then saving the blocks.

✛	AllRecipes.com Main Dishes feed latest items	\<none\>	configure
✛	Recipes category latest items	\<none\>	configure
✛	Restaurant ownership category latest items	\<none\>	configure

Automatically updating your feeds with cron jobs

Good Eatin' Goal: Set up a cron job to automatically read the news feeds at regular intervals and update the Good Eatin' site.

Additional modules needed: None.

Basic steps

We can manually update each feed by clicking the **update items** link in the **Feed Aggregator Manager**. However, it can be time consuming and error prone to have to do this for each feed, once a day, or more frequently. Drupal allows you to automate the process of updating the feeds by using cron jobs.

A cron job is an automated task that runs at specific intervals. The cron job is activated by navigating to `http://yoursite.com/cron.php`. Each module that has been activated can run tasks every time the cron job is started. Even if you are not using the Aggregator, you should set up cron because Drupal uses the cron job for maintenance tasks, and many other modules use cron to perform maintenance.

The method of setting up a cron job depends on the operating system that you are using. If you are running a control panel on your web server, such as cPanel or Plesk, you may be able to configure the cron job from within the control panel. In all cases, you will be instructing the operating system to automatically load the `http://yoursite.com/cron.php` page on your web site at specific intervals.

Setting up a cron job in Unix or Linux

To use a cron job in Unix or Linux, you will need either `lynx` or `wget` installed and available to the user under whom the cron job will run.

1. Login to your server using SSH or another suitable tool.

2. At the command line, type `crontab -e` to edit your `crontab` file.

3. Add a new line to the file using the following format.
   `mm hh dd MM ww command`

   where:
   `mm`: is the minute at which the command should be run (0-59)
   `hh`: is the hour to run the command should be run (0-23)
   `dd`: is the day of the month on which the command should be run (1-31)
   `MM`: The month of the year in which the command should be run (1-12)
   `ww`: The day of the month on which the command should be run (0-6), where 0 is Sunday

To specify every available interval for a field, use * for the field.

To specify multiple values for a field, separate them with commas.

To specify a range of values, separate the start and end values with a hyphen.

4.   Save the file.

For example, to run cron every 15 minutes, every day of the week using wget enter:

```
0,15,30,45 * * * * /usr/bin/wget -O - -q http://yoursite.com/
cron.php
```

To run cron twice a day at 10am and 7pm Monday to Friday using lynx, enter:

```
0 10,19 * * 1-5 /usr/bin/lynx -source http://yoursite.com/cron.php
```

Setting up a cron job in Windows

Windows uses **Scheduled Tasks** to run tasks at specific intervals.

1.   Open the Scheduled Tasks dialog by selecting **Start | All Programs | Accessories | System Tools | Scheduled Tasks**.

2.   Click **Add Scheduled Task**, to open the **Scheduled Task Wizard**.

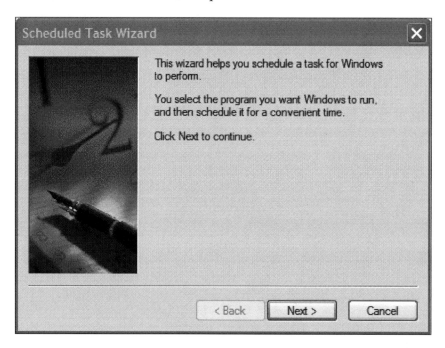

3. Click **Next**, and the Scheduled Task Wizard will allow you to select the program to be run.

You can use Internet Explorer, Firefox, or any other browser of you choice to load the page.

4. Click **Next** and you can change the interval at which the job should be run.

5. Click **Next**, and you can select the time at which you want to load the page.

6. If you want to run the task as a specific user, you can enter a user name and password in the next step. In the **Advanced** options, you need to modify the task to load your cron page, as shown below:

7. You can also modify the task to run more than once a day, via the **Schedule** tab.

Additional ways of setting up cron

The Drupal site has a wealth of information about setting up cron on various other systems, at `http://drupal.org/cron`.

Using poormanscron as an alternative way of updating feeds

Good Eatin' Goal: Set up a 'cron' job for a web site that has no other method of creating a cron job.

Additional modules needed: Poormanscron (`http://drupal.org/project/poormanscron`).

Poormanscron checks each time a page is loaded to determine if cron needs to be run. This allows you to run cron on a site where you are having trouble configuring a traditional cron job. This convenience comes at a performance cost, because Drupal will check to see if cron needs to be loaded every time a page is loaded by a visitor, which can have a significant impact, especially on sites with lots of traffic.

1. Install and activate the Poormanscron module.
2. The settings for Poormanscron are available by selecting **Site configuration** and then **Poormanscron**, from the **Administer** menu. The settings are shown in the following screenshot:

3. You should set the **cron interval** to be small enough to ensure that the site stays up-to-date, but not so frequently that cron is running all of the time, even if there are no changes.

4. If you elect to log successful cron runs or the progress of runs, you can view the logs by selecting **Reports** and then **Recent log entries**, from the Administer menu. The report will look similar to the following screenshot:

Recent log entries

The dblog module monitors your website, capturing system events in a log to be reviewed by an authorized individual at a later time. The dblog log is simply a list of recorded events containing usage data, performance data, errors, warnings and operational information. It is vital to check the dblog report on a regular basis as it is often the only way to tell what is going on.

[more help...]

‣ Filter log messages

Type	Date ▼	Message	User	Operations
cron	07/14/2008 - 22:06	Cron run completed (via poormanscron).	admin	
aggregator	07/14/2008 - 22:06	There is new syndicated content from ...	admin	
cron	07/13/2008 - 23:21	Cron run completed (via poormanscron).	admin	
update	07/13/2008 - 23:21	Fetched information about all available new releases ...	admin	view
aggregator	07/13/2008 - 23:21	There is new syndicated content from ...	admin	

Summary

In this chapter, we have explored how to create a blog for your company, and how to incorporate news feeds from other web sites into your site. Using blogs and other web sites will help to keep your web site content fresh, and will keep visitors and search engines alike interested in your site so that they visit frequently.

In the next chapter, we will work with several very useful modules to allow Chef Wanyama to create newsletters and a calendar of events to publicize current events at the Good Eatin' restaurant.

6
Newsletters and Calendars

In this chapter, we will add new features which will allow Chef Wanyama to keep his customers informed of current events at Good Eatin'.

We will provide two new means of communication. The first feature is a quarterly newsletter that customers can subscribe to. The newsletter will contain valuable information from Chef Wanyama including coupons, news, recipes, and more.

The second feature is a calendar that will help customers learn about upcoming events at the Good Eatin' restaurant.

Creating newsletters

A newsletter is a great way of keeping customers up-to-date without them needing to visit your web site. Customers appreciate well-designed newsletters because they allow the customer to keep tabs on their favorite places without needing to check every web site on a regular basis.

Creating a newsletter

Good Eatin' Goal: Create a new newsletter on the Good Eatin' site, which will be contain relevant news about the restaurant, and will be delivered quarterly to subscribers.

Additional modules needed: Simplenews (`http://drupal.org/project/simplenews`).

Basic steps

Newsletters are containers for individual issues. For example, you could have a newsletter called Seasonal Dining Guide, which would have four issues per year (Summer, Fall, Winter, and Spring). A customer subscribes to the newsletter and each issue is sent to them as it becomes available.

1. Begin by installing and activating the **Simplenews** module, as shown below:

Enabled	Name	Version	Description
☑	Simplenews	6.x-1.0-beta3	Send newsletters to subscribed e-mail addresses. Depends on: Taxonomy (enabled) Required by: Simplenews action (disabled)
☐	Simplenews action	6.x-1.0-beta3	Provide actions for Simplenews. Depends on: Simplenews (disabled), Taxonomy (enabled)

At this point, we only need to enable the **Simplenews** module, and the **Simplenews action** module can be left disabled.

2. Next, select **Content management** and then **Newsletters**, from the **Administer** menu. Drupal will display an administration area divided into the following sections:

   a) Sent issues

   b) Drafts

   c) Newsletters

   d) Subscriptions

3. Click on the **Newsletters** tab and Drupal will display a page similar to the following:

Sent issues	Drafts	Newsletters	Subscriptions

List newsletters | Add newsletter

Newsletters

Newsletter name	Operations
GoodEatin' newsletter	edit newsletter

As you can see, a default newsletter with the name of our site has been automatically created for us. We can either edit this default newsletter or click on the **Add newsletter** link to create a new newsletter.

4. Let's click the **Add newsletter** option to create our seasonal newsletter. Drupal will display a standard form where we can enter the name, description, and relative importance (relative importance weight) of the newsletter.

| Sent issues | Drafts | Newsletters | Subscriptions |

List newsletters   **Add newsletter**

Newsletters

You can create different newsletters (or subjects) to categorize your news (e.g. Cats news, Dogs news, ...).

Newsletter name: *

Seasonal Dining Guide

This name is used to identify the newsletter.

Description:

A guide to picking meals from our menu which use the freshest seasonal ingredients as well as recipes you can try from the comfort of your own home which feature the same ingredients used in the restaurant. New issues are released at the beginning of the Summer, Fall, Winter, and Spring each year.

The description can be used to provide more information.

Weight:

0

In listings, the heavier (with a higher weight value) terms will sink and the lighter terms will be positioned nearer the top.

Save

5. Click **Save** to save the newsletter. It will now appear in the list of available newsletters.

6. If you want to modify the **Sender information** for the newsletter to use an alternate name or email address to your site's default ones, you can either expand the **Sender information** section when adding the newsletter, or you click **Edit newsletter** and modify the **Sender information**, as shown in the following screenshot:

— ▼ Sender information —

From name:

Good Eatin' Newsletters

From e-mail address: *

newsletters@drupalbyexample.com

Allowing users to sign-up for the newsletter

Good Eatin' Goal: Demonstrate how registered and unregistered users can sign-up for a newsletter, and configure the registration process.

Additional modules needed: Simplenews (`http://drupal.org/project/simplenews`).

Basic steps

1. To allow customers to sign-up for the newsletter, we will begin by adding a block to the page.

2. Open the **Block Manager** by selecting **Site building** and then **Blocks**, from the **Administer** menu. Add the block for the newsletter that you want to allow customers to subscribe to, as shown in the following screenshot:

    ┼ Newsletter: Seasonal Dining Guide   Left sidebar ☑ configure

3. We will now need to give users permission to subscribe to newsletters by selecting **User management** and then **Permissions**, from the **Administer** menu. We will give all users permissions to subscribe to newsletters and to view **newsletter** links, as shown below:

Permission	anonymous user	authenticated user	blogger	VIP user
simplenews module				
administer newsletters	☐	☐	☐	☐
create newsletter	☐	☐	☐	☐
delete any newsletter	☐	☐	☐	☐
delete own newsletter	☐	☐	☐	☐
edit any newsletter	☐	☐	☐	☐
edit own newsletter	☐	☐	☐	☐
send newsletter	☐	☐	☐	☐
subscribe to newsletters	☑	☑	☑	☑
view links in block	☑	☑	☑	☑

4. If the customer does not have permission to subscribe to newsletters then the block will appear as shown in the following screenshot:

However, if the customer has permissions to subscribe to newsletters, and is logged in to the site, the block will appear as shown in the following screenshot:

If the customer has permission to subscribe, but is not logged in, the block will appear as follows.

5. To subscribe to the newsletter, the customer will simply click on the **Subscribe** button. Once they he subscribed, the **Subscribe** button will change to **Unsubscribe** so that the user can easily opt out of the newsletter. If the user does not have an active account with the site, they will need to confirm that they want to subscribe to the site.

Managing sign-ups

Good Eatin' Goal: Generate a list of all of the users who have signed up for a newsletter, and demonstrate how to remove suspicious users.

Additional modules needed: Simplenews (`http://drupal.org/project/simplenews`).

Basic steps

After customers have begun to sign up for your newsletter, you can view a list of all existing subscriptions by selecting **Content management** and then **Newsletters** from the **Administer** menu, and finally on **Subscriptions**. Drupal will display a page similar to the following image:

Home » Administer » Content management » Newsletters

| Sent issues | Drafts | Newsletters | Subscriptions |

List subscriptions   Import subscriptions   Export subscriptions

Newsletters

Subscription filters

Subscribed to: All newsletters

E-mail address:

[Filter]

Update options

Activate [Update]

☐	E-mail ▲	Username	Status	Operations
☐	mnoble@drupalbyexample.com	mnoble	☑	edit

You can filter the display to list only specific newsletters, or to list only those newsletters that a specific customer has subscribed to. To edit individual subscriptions, click on the **edit** link. This will display a page similar to the following:

You can also activate, deactivate, or delete subscriptions by selecting the subscription you want to modify, selecting the appropriate action in the **Update options** drop-down list and then clicking the **Update** button. This allows you to remove malicious users who have subscribed to your newsletters. If you receive a significant number of invalid sign-ups, you may want to add a Captcha to the sign-up form.

Importing subscriptions from an existing list

Good Eatin' Goal: Import subscriptions from another list management system that was in use prior to you starting to manage your newsletter by using Simplenews.

Additional modules needed: Simplenews (`http://drupal.org/project/simplenews`).

Basic steps

If you already have a large list of subscribers to your newsletter, you probably wouldn't want to throw this list away because a good contact list takes time to build and can be very lucrative for you.

You can import a comma-delimited list of email addresses by clicking on the **Mass subscribe** link from the **Newsletter** administration page. This will display a page similar to the following:

Home » Administer » Content management » Newsletters

| Sent issues | Drafts | Newsletters | Subscriptions |

| List | **Mass subscribe** | Mass unsubscribe | Export |

Newsletters

[more help...]

Email addresses:

test1@test.com,test2@sample.com

Supply a comma separated list of email addresses to be subscribed.

Subscribe to: *

☑ GoodEatin' newsletter
☑ Seasonal Dining Guide

Subscribe

Simply copy and paste the list of email addresses from your current management system and then click **update**. Drupal will display a list of addresses that were added.

Creating a new issue of the newsletter

Good Eatin' Goal: Build a new issue of the seasonal specials newsletter in preparation for it to be sent to newsletter subscribers.

Additional modules needed: Simplenews (`http://drupal.org/project/simplenews`).

Basic steps

1. Creating a new newsletter issue is similar to creating any other page within Drupal. We will begin by clicking on **Create content** and then on **Newsletter issue**.

2. This will display a form where you can select the newsletter for which you want to create an issue, and can enter information about the issue, as shown in the following screenshot:

Create Newsletter issue

Add this newsletter issue to a newsletter by selecting a newsletter from the select list.

Send a newsletter or a test newsletter by selecting the appropriate radio button and submitting the node.

Install Mime Mail module to send HTML emails. Mime Mail is also used to send emails with attachments, both plain text and HTML emails.

Title: *
> Fall 2008 - Seasonal Dining Guide

Newsletter:
> Seasonal Dining Guide ☑

— ▸ **Menu settings**

[Split summary at cursor]

Body:
> Welcome to the Fall 2008 edition of the Good Eatin' Seasonal Dining Guide. In this issue, we will highlight some wonderful farm raised grass fed Bison which we are featuring on our menu this fall.

This will be the body of your newsletter. Available variables are: !site (the name of your website), !uri (a link to your homepage), !uri_brief (homepage link without the http://), !date (today's date), !login_uri (link to login page).

---

3. You can also modify the sending options to indicate whether newsletter should be sent to all subscribers, to just a test address, or should simply be saved as a draft.

▾ **Newsletter sending options**

Priority:
> none ☑

☐ Request receipt

Sending:

○ Don't send now

◉ Send one test newsletter to the test address

○ Send newsletter

It is highly recommended that you send a test newsletter before you send it to the entire subscription list to prevent errors in the final newsletter. The test address defaults to the administration email address for your site. You can change the test address on the **Simplenews Settings** page, which is accessed by selecting **Site configuration** and then **Simplenews**, from the **Administer** menu. The available settings are shown in the following screenshot:

Test addresses

Supply a comma-separated list of email addresses to be used as test addresses. The override function allows to override these addresses in the newsletter editing form.

Email address:

admin@drupalbyexample.com

☐ Allow test address override

---

4. When you are satisfied with your issue, click the **Save** button.

5. After you have sent a test email and checked that it was delivered correctly, you can send the newsletter to the full list of subscribers by editing your draft and then changing the **Newsletter sending options** to **Send newsletter**.

6. Once the newsletter has been scheduled to be sent, it will be sent to a portion of the subscriber list each time that cron is run. This is done to avoid flooding the network. You can configure the number of emails that are sent each time that cron is called by editing the **Mail backend settings** for the Newsletter, which is accessed by selecting **Site Configuration** and then **Simplenews** from the **Administer** menu. The available settings are shown in the following screenshot:

▾ **Mail backend options**

☑ Use cron to send newsletters
When checked cron will be used to send newsletters (recommended). Test newsletters and confirmation emails will be send immediately. Leave unchecked for testing purposes.

Cron throttle:
20
Sets the numbers of newsletters sent per cron run. Failure to send will also be counted.

Mail spool expiration:
Immediate
Newsletter mails are spooled. How long must messages be retained in the spool after successfull sending. Keeping the message in the spool allows mail statistics (which is not yet implemented). If cron is not used, immediate expiration is advised.

☐ Log emails
When checked all outgoing simplenews emails are logged in the system log. A logged email does not guarantee that it is send or will be delivered. It only indicates that a message is send to the PHP mail() function. No status information is available of delivery by the PHP mail() function.

By default, only 20 emails are sent each time that cron is run. This is fine, if you are running cron frequently, but if you are running it less frequently, you may want to increase the number of emails that are sent each time. Some web hosting companies only allow a specific number of emails to be sent every hour, to help prevent spammers from utilizing their servers. Before sending newsletters to large mailing lists, you should check with your host to ensure that you comply with their policies.

Adding a calendar

A calendar is a fantastic way of keeping customers coming back to your site and your business at regular intervals so that they can take advantage of specials, sales, and other time-limited events.

We will create a basic event calendar, which displays information about musical concerts, special events, and more, for the Good Eatin' restaurant.

Adding new events to the calendar

Good Eatin' Goal: Create an event that will be displayed on the calendar.

Additional modules needed: Event (`http://drupal.org/project/event`).

Basic steps

1. In order to add an event, you must first install and activate the **Event module** in the **Module manager** as shown in the following screenshot:

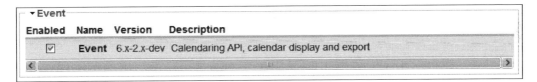

Activating the **Event** module will a create a new Event content type. There are also several settings that control how events are displayed and how time zones are handled.

2. To modify the time zone settings, select **Site configuration**, then **Events**, and finally **Timezone handling**, from the **Administer** menu.

3. Drupal will display a page similar to the following:

Timezone handling

Event time zone input: *

◉ Use the sitewide time zone

○ Use the time zone of the user editing or creating the event

○ Allow users to set event time zones

Events are saved with a time zone value. This setting allows you to determine how the time zone is determined when creating or editing an event.

Event time zone display: *

◉ Use the event's time zone

○ Use the user's time zone

○ Use the sitewide time zone

Events are saved with a time zone value. This setting allows you to determine if the event's time zone, the sitewide time zone, or the user's personal time zone setting is used to display the time for an event.

Time notation preference: *

◉ 24h

○ 12h

The time notation system used for entering event times.

[Save configuration] [Reset to defaults]

---

4. You will want to customize these settings according to where the majority of your users live, and the types of events that you are holding. For example, if most of your users are in the U.S., 12 hour notation is probably appropriate, but if most of you users are in Europe, 24 hour notation is better. If the events are held online with a mix of users in different time zones, it would make sense to have the events displayed in the user's time zone. However, if the event is being held at a single site, it would make sense to use the local time of the event. For the Good Eatin' site, we will use the site's time zone for events, display the events in the event time zone, and use the 12 hour time notification.

5. Before we can create an event, we must set the default time zone for the site. This is done by selecting **Site configuration** and then **Date and time**, from the **Administer** menu.

Date and time

Locale settings

Default time zone:

US/Mountain

Select the default site time zone.

User-configurable time zones:

○ Disabled

◉ Enabled

When enabled, users can set their own time zone and dates will be displayed accordingly.

First day of week:

Sunday

The first day of the week for calendar views.

Formatting

Short date format:

07/30/2008 - 22:58

The short format of date display.

Medium date format:

Wed, 07/30/2008 - 22:58

The medium sized date display.

Long date format:

Wednesday, July 30, 2008 - 22:58

Longer date format used for detailed display.

The Good Eatin' restaurant is located in Colorado, so we will set the time zone to **US/Mountain**.

6. Click **Save configuration** to save your changes.

7. To add an event, select **Create content** and then **Event**, from the main **Navigation** menu.

8. Enter a title and a description for the event, as shown in the following screenshot, and then set the start time and optionally the end time for the event.

Create Event

Title: *

Winter 2008 Menu party

▸ **Menu settings**

Split summary at cursor

Body:

Join us for the unveiling of our Winter 2008 seasonal menu. You can sample all dishes from the new menu and enjoy complimentary beverages designed to enhance the flavors of the menu.

▸ **Input format**

▸ **CAPTCHA**

☑ Event has time
Is time important for this event? Uncheck if event takes all day.

Start date:

September | 01 | 2008 | 18 | 00

☑ Event has end date
Check if you want to specify an end date for this event, then choose end date below.

End date:

September | 01 | 2008 | 22 | 00

9. Click **Save** when you are happy with the event settings.

Displaying events

Good Eatin' Goal: Display events on the site in various formats including a block of upcoming events, a table of events, and a calendar of events.

Additional modules needed: Event (`http://drupal.org/project/event`).

Basic steps

The **Event** module provides several methods for allowing customers to view events. We will explore each of these in turn.

1. The easiest way to allow visitors to browse events is by using the event page, which is accessed by at `http://yoursite.com/event`. The page appears as follows:

Home » Events

Events

(all) ⌄
Select event terms to filter by

— ▸ CAPTCHA

(all) ⌄
Select event type to filter by

— ▸ CAPTCHA

Week   Day   Table   List

September 2008 »

Sun	Mon	Tue	Wed	Thu	Fri	Sat
	Winter 2008 Menu party Start: 09/01/2008 - 18:00 End: 09/01/2008 - 22:00 `1`	`2`	`3`	`4`	`5`	`6`
`7`	`8`	`9`	`10`	`11`	`12`	`13`

2. If you want the user to be able to access this page without knowing the URL in advance, you can create a menu item for the page. Open the **Menu Manager** by selecting on **Site building** and then **menus**, from the **Administer** menu.

3. Select the menu that you want to add to the menu item and then click the **Add item** tab.

4. Enter the information about the new menu item, as shown in the following screenshot, and then click **Save** when you are satisfied.

| List items | **Add item** | Edit menu |

Navigation

Menu settings

Path: *

    event

The path this menu item links to. This can be an internal Drupal path such as *node/add* or an external URL such as *http://drupal.org*. Enter *<front>* to link to the front page.

Menu link title: *

    Upcoming Events

The link text corresponding to this item that should appear in the menu.

Description:

    Browse all upcoming events for the Good Eatin' restaurant.

The description displayed when hovering over a menu item.

---

5. The second method of presenting events to users is by using the upcoming events block. To add this, open the **Blocks Manager** by selecting **Site building** and then **Blocks**, from the **Administer** menu.

6. Set the region for the **List of upcoming events** to **Right sidebar**.

| ✛ | List of upcoming events. | | Right sidebar ▾ | configure |

---

7. The new block will appear as follows:

8. The final method of displaying calendar entries is a block showing upcoming events in a calendar view. To add this block, open the **Block Manager** by selecting **Site building** and then **Blocks**, from the **Administer** menu. Set the region for **Calendar to browse events** to **Right sidebar**.

| ✛ | Calendar to browse events. | Right sidebar ⌄ | configure |

9. The display for the calendar will appear as follows:

Events

August 2008»

Sun	Mon	Tue	Wed	Thu	Fri	Sat
					1	2
3	4	5	6	7	8	9
10	11	12	13	14	15	16
17	18	19	20	21	22	23
24	25	26	27	28	29	30
31						

You can decide which of these methods to use for your own site, based on how the user will work with your site.

Adding other content types to the event calendar

Good Eatin' Goal: Discuss how to add custom content types to the event calendar.

Additional modules needed: Event (`http://drupal.org/project/event`).

An easy way of adding additional content types to your existing event calendar is by modifying the content type and then setting the **Event calendar** options.

1. Open the **Content Manager** by selecting **Content management** and then **Content types**, from the **Administer** menu.

2. Edit the type that you want to add to the event calendar.

3. Open the **Event calendar** section and modify the options, as shown here:

> ▼ Event calendar
>
> **Show in event calendar:**
>
> ⊙ All views
>
> ○ Only in views for this type
>
> ○ Never
>
> All views: This content type will be available for display on all calendar views, including with other events.
> Only in views for this type: This content type will only appear in calendar views specific to this type and never with other events.
> Never: This content type will not be associated with the events calendar.

> If you prefer to have a calendar just for the type, you can use the **Only in views for this type** option.

4. Save the changes to your content type, and the event calendar will be automatically updated.

Creating events using CCK

Good Eatin' Goal: Build events using the CCK module and the Date module, rather than the Event module, thereby giving additional control over the events.

Additional modules needed: CCK (`http://drupal.org/project/cck`), Date (`http://drupal.org/project/date`).

Basic steps

Depending on your site, it may be more convenient to use CCK and the Date API to build dates. This strategy also gives you additional control over what information is included in the event and in the display. In addition, all required modules should be updated more quickly after each new Drupal release. However, you will need to carry out more initial setup for events and displays if you use this strategy.

1. Install and activate the **CCK** and **Date modules** if you have not done so already.

2. Open the **Content Type Manager** by selecting **Content management** and then **Content types**, from the Administer menu.

3. Click **Add content type** to begin creating your new event type. We will call this type **Event CCK** to avoid conflicts with the **Event module**, as shown below:

Content types

To create a new content type, enter the human-readable name, the machine-readable name, and all other relevant fields that are on this page. Once created, users of your site will be able to create posts that are instances of this content type.

Identification

Name: *

    Event CCK

The human-readable name of this content type. This text will be displayed as part of the list on the *create content* page. It is recommended that this name begin with a capital letter and contain only letters, numbers, and **spaces**. This name must be unique.

Type: *

    event_cck

The machine-readable name of this content type. This text will be used for constructing the URL of the *create content* page for this content type. This name must contain only lowercase letters, numbers, and underscores. Underscores will be converted into hyphens when constructing the URL of the *create content* page. This name must be unique.

Description:

    An alternative way of entering events without needing to use the event
    module.

A brief description of this content type. This text will be displayed as part of the list on the *create content* page.

4. After you are satisfied with the information for the new content type, click **Save Content Type** to create the new event type.

5. We now need to add fields to store the date and the time of the event. Click on the **Add field** link to begin the process.

6. We will call the field **event_time_cck** and make the type a **Datetime** field so that we can enter both the day on which the event occurs and the time of day at which it starts, as shown in the following screenshot:

Create new field

Field name: *

field_ | event_time_cck

The machine-readable name of the field. This name cannot be changed later! The name will be prefixed with 'field_' and can include lowercase unaccented letters, numbers, and underscores. The length of the name, including the prefix, is limited to no more than 32 characters.

Label: *

Event Time

A human-readable name to be used as the label for this field in the *Event CCK* content type.

Field type: *

Datetime ▾

The type of data you would like to store in the database with this field.

---

7. Click **Continue** to save the new field. You will now need to select the display widget for the field. **Text field with jQuery pop-up calendar** is appropriate. Click **Continue** to complete the field definition. You can optionally modify various settings related to how the field is displayed. You should make the time **Required**. If you want to define end dates or times for the event, you should modify the **To Date** to **Optional** or **Required**.

8. You can now create CCK-based events using the same techniques that we used to create other content—just select **Create content** and then **Event CCK**, from the main **Navigation** menu.

9. Enter the information for the event, as shown in the following screenshot:

Create Event CCK

Title: *

```
Swingin' at Good Eatin'
```

▸ **Menu settings**

[Split summary at cursor]

Body:
```
Good Eatin' is proud to welcome Herbert Henry and his big band to the Good
Eatin' stage on Saturday August 30th.  Join us for a fun filled night of dinin'
and dancin'.
```

▸ **Input format**

▸ **CAPTCHA**

Event Time

From date: *
```
30/08/2008          18:00
```
Format: 02/08/2008 13:49 Format: 02/08/2008 13:49
To date:
```
30/08/2008          23:00
```
Empty 'To date' values will use the 'From date' values. Format: 02/08/2008 13:49

10. When you are satisfied with the event, click **Save** to add the new event to the site's calendar.

Displaying a calendar using views and CCK

Good Eatin' Goal: Display a calendar that gives more details than a block view on a page.

Additional modules needed: Calendar (`http://drupal.org/project/calendar`), Views(`http://drupal.org/project/views`), Date API (`http://drupal.org/project/date`).

Basic steps

Now that we can create events using CCK, we need to display them on the site. We will begin by creating a page where visitors can browse all of the upcoming events using a convenient calendar.

1. Begin by installing and activating the **Views** and **Calendar** modules if you have not done so already. Note that, some versions of Calendar released prior to June 28, 2008 require you to activate both **Calendar** and **iCal** at the same time. If you experience an error when installing the **Calendar** module, either upgrade to the latest development module or install both modules at the same time.

2. The easiest way to build new views using the calendar is to clone the default calendar view and customize it to meet your needs.

3. Go to the **Views Manager** by selecting **Site building** and then **Views**, from the **Administer** menu.

4. Drupal will display a list of all of the views that have currently been established on the site. If you scroll the list, you will see the **Default Node view**: **calendar** as shown in the following screenshot:

```
◉ Default Node view: calendar (Calendar)                           Enable
Path: calendar                        A multi-dimensional calendar view
Calendar block, Calendar block view,  with back/next navigation.
Calendar page, Calendar page day,
Calendar page month, Calendar page
week, Calendar page year
```

5. Temporarily enable the default view by clicking on the **Enable** link.

6. After the view has been activated, a new set of links will appear, labeled: **Edit, Export, Clone,** and **Disable**.

7. Click on the **Clone** link to make a copy of the calendar. Drupal will allow you to change the name and description of the view. Change the name to **event_calendar** and then click **next** to edit the view.

8. The default settings for the view are shown in the following screenshot. We will edit several settings for our purposes.

Edit view "*event_calendar*"

| View | Export | Clone | View "Calendar page" | *New view* |

event_calendar, displaying items of type Node.

Defaults ▶

Calendar page

Year view

Month view

Day view

Week view

Calendar block

Block view

Page ⌄

Add display

Analyze

❷ **Defaults** *Default settings for this view.*

View settings

Tag: Calendar

Basic settings

Name: Defaults
Title: None
Style:
Calendar
navigation
Use AJAX: No
Use pager: No
Items to display:
Unlimited
More link: No
Distinct: No
Access:
Unrestricted
Header: None
Footer: None
Empty text:
None
Theme:
Information

❷ Relationships + ↑↓
None defined

❷ Arguments + ↑↓
Date: Date
(node.changed)

❷ Fields + ↑↓
Node: Title Title
Node: Updated
date Updated
date
Node: Body
Body

❷ Sort + ↑↓
criteria
None defined

❷ Filters + ↑↓
None defined

Click on an item to edit that item's details.

Save   Cancel

9. The first change we need to make is to create a new Filter by clicking on the **+** symbol next to the **Filters** label. Select the **Node: Type** filter, as shown in the following screenshot:

Defaults: Add filters

Groups:

Node ⌄

The stored teaser field. This may not be valid or useful
data on all node types.
☐ Node: Title
The title of the node.
☑ Node: Type
The type of a node (for example, "blog entry", "forum post",
"story", etc).
☐ Node: Updated date
The date the node was last updated.
☐ Node: Updated/commented date
The most recent of last comment posted or node updated
time.

Add   Cancel

In most cases, you should also select the **Node: published** or **admin** filter to prevent unauthorized access to private information.

10. Click the **Add** button and set the allowable types to **Event CCK**.

11. The next change we will need to make is to modify the fields by selecting **Node: Updated date**.

12. Click **Remove** to remove this field from the view.

13. Click the **+** next to the **Fields** label to add a new field.

14. Select **Content: Event Time** for the new field to be added, as shown in the following screenshot:

Defaults: Add fields

Groups:

Content

Content Taxonomy Fields - Appears in: Menu Item
☐ Content: Content Taxonomy Fields: Served For (field_served_for)
Content Taxonomy Fields - Appears in: Menu Item
☐ Content: Datetime: Event Time (field_event_time)
Datetime - Appears in: Event
☐ Content: Decimal: Price (field_price)
Decimal - Appears in: Menu Item
☑ Content: Event Time (field_event_time_cck value)
Datetime - Appears in: Event CCK
☑ Content: Event Time (field_event_time_cck value2)
Datetime - Appears in: Event CCK

[Add] [Cancel]

15. Click **Add** to save the changes. You will now need to configure the display of the field.

Defaults: Configure field "Content: Event Time (field_event_time_cck value)"

Format: *

Default

☐ Exclude from display
Check this box to not display this field, but still load it in the view. Use this option to not show a grouping field in each record, or when doing advanced theming.

☐ Link this field to its node

Label:

○ None
◉ Widget label (Event Time)
○ Custom

[Update] [Cancel] [Remove]

In most cases, including this one, the defaults are acceptable. So we will just click **Update** to continue. You will also need to update the settings for the end time (value 2), as described above.

16. The final change we need to make to the view is in the **Arguments**. Select the **Date:Date** link in the **Arguments** section.

17. Drupal will display a list of parameters that you can use to customize the arguments.

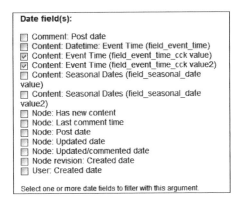

We will need to change this to use our Content Event time fields, and then click **Update** to save the changes.

18. Now that all of the required changes have been made, click **Save** to finish building the **View**.

19. We can now return to the list of all views by clicking on the **List** link, and disable the default calendar view by selecting the **Disable** link for the default calendar view.

20 Now that our view has been completely set up, we can use it to browse our events. The calendar view, which we used as a starting point, provides several methods of displaying the content as shown below:

You may use any of these views, or you can add more views according to your site's needs. If you do not want to use a display type, you can delete it. If you click on the **Calendar Page** display type and review the **Page settings**, you will see that a Page is provided, which can be accessed using the path `http://yoursite.com/calendar`. No menu is provided. You can either add a menu link here, or use the **Menu Manager** if desired. If you open the calendar page, the display appears as follows:

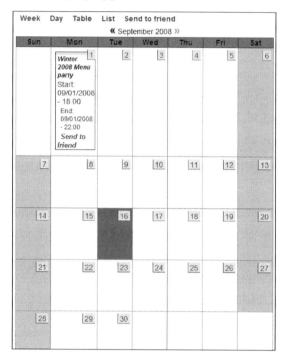

21. The calendar view also provides several block displays that can be activated and added to your site via the **Block Manager**. These blocks include a **Calendar** block that is similar to the display provided by the event block, and a **Legend** block that can be used to allow visitors to understand the information in the calendar more easily.

Summary

Congratulations! You have now added newsletters and events to your sites. These will provide valuable ways of communicating with your customers to ensure that they keep coming back to your web site and, more importantly, to your business.

In the next chapter, we will leverage sites such as YouTube, Flickr, and Google to provide advanced functionality to Chef Wanyama's Good Eatin' web site.

7
Buzzword Compliance: Whisking in Some Web 2.0

Now that we are comfortable with building content, we will begin to add more content that is developed and maintained on other web sites. Some of this content will be built by you, while some may be created by other people in your community, or even across the world.

You may wonder why you would want to store content on another site that you don't have control over, especially when we have shown that it is so easy to build content with Drupal. Although you do give up some control, there are several great reasons to use some of these resources:

1. Bandwidth can be expensive. If your site is popular and makes heavy use of large pictures, or videos, you can easily exceed your monthly bandwidth limits. By storing the pictures and video on someone else's server (possibly for free), you avoid overage charges.

2. Their servers are better than yours. The servers that are used to store and serve the pictures and videos are typically best-in-class servers. Because they are used to store data from many different people, the actual cost is spread out, so you don't have to pay the full cost.

3. You can leverage the work of other community members to help you build and maintain the content. This is especially important if you have a lot of content that regularly changes, or you want to collect content that other people have created. For example, if you want to offer pictures of your town, you can use Flickr to store the pictures, and also link to pictures that other people have taken and posted on Flickr. Please make sure that you have permission to use the images before linking to them, though!

4. By allowing the third-party site to maintain the content separately, you can also leverage any enhancements that they make to the technology of their site. The sites we describe linking to are all very large and actively maintained. They also tend to have new functionality released frequently, which could be difficult and expensive to do on your own.

Online cooking class

In this section, we will add video content from YouTube that demonstrates various cooking techniques used at the restaurant.

Embedding a YouTube video with a filter

Good Eatin' Goal: Add videos that are stored on YouTube to an existing page.

Additional modules needed: Video Filter (`http://drupal.org/project/video_filter`).

Basic steps

YouTube (`www.youtube.com`) is a popular video sharing site where you can view videos that have been created and submitted by people across the globe. YouTube allows you to link to videos stored on their site so that you can share them with your own visitors, without incurring bandwidth charges. In fact, you can even earn revenue from the videos if you have a Google AdSense account.

To insert a video into a page, we will use the following process:

1. Install and activate the **Video Filter** module.
2. We now need to build a new input format that will process the filter. To do this, select **Site configuration** and then **Input formats**, from the **Administer** menu.
3. Click on the **Add input format** link.
4. We will name the input format **YouTube** and allow only administrators to use this format. Depending on your site's needs, you will need to decide who should be able to use the input format. Just make sure that anyone with access to this format will comply with your site's terms and not link to videos that you wouldn't want on your site.

5. Finally, enable the **Video Filter** filter and **Save** the configuration.

> ☑ Video Filter
> Substitutes [video:URL] with embedded HTML.
>
> Save configuration

6. We can now use the new input format in a new page. We will create the page by clicking on **Create content** and then on **Page**.

7. We will title the new page **Cooking Classes**, and enter a description as follows:

> **Home » Create content**
>
> ## Create Page
>
> **Title:** *
>
> Cooking Classes
>
> ▸ **Menu settings**
>
> Split summary at cursor
>
> **Body:**
>
> Chinese dumplings are a popular appetizer on the Good Eatin' menu. We make ours with a variety of rare meats including ostrich, emu, and crocodile rather than more traditional chicken and pork. [video:http://www.youtube.com/watch?v=JjXcjdOPBHY]
>
> ▾ **Input format**
>
> ○ Filtered HTML
> - Web page addresses and e-mail addresses turn into links automatically.
> - Allowed HTML tags: <a> <em> <strong> <cite> <code> <ul> <ol> <li> <dl> <dt> <dd>
> - Lines and paragraphs break automatically.
>
> ○ Full HTML
> - Web page addresses and e-mail addresses turn into links automatically.
> - Lines and paragraphs break automatically.
>
> ○ Image Format
> - Allowed HTML tags: <img> <a> <em> <strong> <cite> <code> <ul> <ol> <li> <dl> <dt> <dd>
> - Lines and paragraphs break automatically.
> - Slideshows can be added to this post.
>
> ⦿ YouTube
> - You may insert videos with [video:URL]
>
> **More information about formatting options**

After you save the page, the final result will appear as follows:

You can also use the Video Filter module to display videos from Google Video, GodTube, DailyMotion, Eyespot, Jumpcut, Revver, and Vimeo by using the same techniques. To use these alternative sources, simply enter the full URL to the page to embed in the filter.

Before adding a YouTube video to your site, please make sure that you comply with the terms of use for YouTube, and check that the material is not copyrighted. See http://www.youtube.com/t/terms for more details.

Creating a YouTube playlist and display a random video

Good Eatin' Goal: Enhance the YouTube filter to play from a list of videos, and explore other features of the Video Filter module.

Additional modules needed: Video Filter (`http://drupal.org/project/video_filter`).

Basic steps

Now that you can add a single video to your page, you may want to add more videos that are displayed in random order, automatically start the video when the page loads, or control the size of the video. All of this is possible by using the Video Filter.

To add multiple videos to a filter, you just need to add multiple videos separated by commas. For example, you could enter:

```
video:http://www.youtube.com/watch?v=0Q2aPi9ZEgs,
http://www.youtube.com/watch?v=dTDVKDzVOcg,http://www.youtube.com/
watch?v=eV__oOckAPM
```

If you want a video to start automatically, you need to add `autoplay:1` to your filter separated by a space from the remainder of the filter. For example:

```
video:http://www.youtube.com/watch?v=DqoqFymiGkk autoplay:1
```

To resize your video, you will need to enter the width and height of the video, again separated from the remainder of the filter by a space. The filter will ensure that the aspect ratio of the video is correct, and that the actual width and height are no greater than the sizes you specify. An example appears below:

```
video:http://www.youtube.com/watch?v=BYhrHdvI6m8 width:240
height:160
```

The final formatting option is to control the alignment of the video on the page. Note that you can currently only specify the alignment as being either left or right. This is controlled with the align option, as shown below:

```
video:http://www.youtube.com/watch?v=wPhBiu6Sx_w align:right
```

Enhancing content with the Embedded Media Field

Good Eatin' Goal: Integrate a YouTube video into an existing content type instead of using a filter.

Additional modules needed: Embedded Media Field (`http://drupal.org/project/emfield`).

Basic steps

In the last two topics, we explored inserting YouTube videos into existing content. But what if you want to add video fields to all instances of a specific content type? For example, if you have a content type for a cooking class, you could include fields for:

- Class Name
- Class Description
- Class Dates
- Video giving a preview of the class

In this case, it would be much better to have a specific field for the video rather than embedding it into text with a filter.

Let's build the example above using the Embedded Media module to add the video field.

1. Begin by installing and enabling the **Embedded Media Field** and **Embedded Video Field** modules in the Module Manager.

2. We can now create our new content type by selecting **Content Management** and then **Content types**, from the **Administer** menu. Finally, click on **Add content** type.

3. We will fill out the basic information for the content type as follows:

---Identification---

Name: *

Cooking Class

The human-readable name of this content type. This text will be displayed as part of the list on the *create content* page. It is recommended that this name begin with a capital letter and contain only letters, numbers, and **spaces**. This name must be unique.

Type: *

cooking_class

The machine-readable name of this content type. This text will be used for constructing the URL of the *create content* page for this content type. This name must contain only lowercase letters, numbers, and underscores. Underscores will be converted into hyphens when constructing the URL of the *create content* page. This name must be unique.

Description:

A class offered at Good Eatin' where customers can come to learn cooking techniques from the basics to the advanced.

A brief description of this content type. This text will be displayed as part of the list on the *create content* page.

Click **Save content type** to save the type.

4. We can now add fields to the new type. We will use the title for the **Class Name** and description for the **Class Description** so we just need to add a date field and a video field. We have already created several date fields, so we will just describe how to add the video field in detail.

5. Click **Add field** to begin building the new video field.

6. Enter the basic information including the **name**, **label**, and **type** as shown below:

Create new field

Field name: *

field_ | video |

The machine-readable name of the field. This name cannot be changed later! The name will be prefixed with 'field_' and can include lowercase unaccented letters, numbers, and underscores. The length of the name, including the prefix, is limited to no more than 32 characters.

Label: *

| Video Preview |

A human-readable name to be used as the label for this field in the *Cooking Class* content type.

Field type: *

| Embedded Video ▾ |

The type of data you would like to store in the database with this field.

[Continue]

Click **Continue** to finish creating the basic information.

7. You will now need to set the **Widget type** for the field. The only possible value is **3rd Party Video**, so you can simply click **Continue**.

8. You can now modify various options for the field including valid providers, video display settings, video preview settings, thumbnail settings, and global settings.

9. The complete list of possible providers is shown below. We will only select **YouTube** for our field.

```
┌─ ▼ Providers Supported ────────────────────────────┐
│  Select which third party providers you wish to allow for this content type
│  from the list below. If no checkboxes are checked, then all providers will be
│  supported. When a user submits new content, the URL they enter will be
│  matched to the provider, assuming that provider is allowed here.
│
│  Providers:
│
│  ☐ Blip.tv
│  ☐ Brightcove
│  ☐ Dailymotion
│  ☐ Google
│  ☐ GUBA
│  ☐ IMEEM
│  ☐ JumpCut
│  ☐ Last.fm
│  ☐ Live Video
│  ☐ MetaCafe
│  ☐ MySpace
│  ☐ Revver
│  ☐ Sevenload
│  ☐ Spike TV
│  ☐ Tudou
│  ☐ Veoh
│  ☐ Vimeo
│  ☐ YouTube
│  ☐ Custom URL
└──────────────────────────────────────────────────┘
```

10. The next sets of settings are the **Display** and **Preview** settings , each of which contains the same set of options as shown in the following screenshot:

```
┌─ ▼ Video Display Settings ──────────────────────────┐
│  These settings control how this video is displayed in its full size, which
│  defaults to 425x350.
│
│  Video display width: *
│  ┌──────────────────────────────────────────────┐
│  │ 425                                            │
│  └──────────────────────────────────────────────┘
│  The width of the video. It defaults to 425.
│
│  Video display height: *
│  ┌──────────────────────────────────────────────┐
│  │ 350                                            │
│  └──────────────────────────────────────────────┘
│  The height of the video. It defaults to 350.
│
│  ☐ Autoplay
│  If supported by the provider, checking this box will cause the video to automatically
│  begin after the video loads when in its full size.
└──────────────────────────────────────────────────┘
```

You can use the **Preview** settings to display a smaller video under certain circumstances. We will leave all other settings with their default values.

11. The next set of settings control the preview image, as shown in the following screenshot:

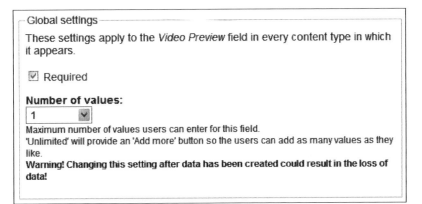

12. Finally, the **Global settings** can be set as shown below. We will mark the field as **Required**.

13. Click the **Save field settings** button to complete adding the field.

Now that the content type has been fully defined, we can use the new content type to build content.

1. Start by clicking on **Create Content** and then on **Cooking Class**.

2. Enter the information for your class as shown below, and click **Save** to finish adding the new class.

Create Cooking Class

Title: *

Dumpling Class

‣ **Menu settings**

Split summary at cursor

Body:

Learn to make delicious Chinese dumplings to serve at your next dinner party. We will explore all aspects of dumplings including creating several different fillings, making wrappers from scratch, and properly steaming and pan frying dumplings.

‣ **Input format**

Video Preview: *

http://www.youtube.com/watch?v=JjXcjdOPBHY

Enter the URL or Embed Code here. The embedded third party content will be parsed and displayed appropriately from this.
The following services are provided: YouTube

Class Dates

Empty 'To date' values will use the 'From date' values.

From date:

08/19/2008

Format: 08/19/2008

To date:

08/20/2008

Format: 08/19/2008

3. The final page will appear as follows:

Flickr integration: Another alternative for images and slideshows

Flickr is an extremely popular web site that allows you to post and share pictures with people around the world. You can either upload your own pictures to Flickr and use it for storage, or embed images that other people have taken into your own site. Of course, you need to check the license for all of the images that you want to embed before using them on your site.

Embedding media from Flickr

Good Eatin' Goal: Add a preview image for our Cooking Class content type using Flickr.

Additional modules needed: Embedded Media Field (http://drupal.org/project/emfield).

Basic steps

We have previously used the **Embedded Media Field** module to display YouTube movies on our site. In this step, we will also use it to display images from Flickr.

1. If you have not already installed and activated the **Embedded Media Field** module, do so now. We also need to activate the **Embedded Image Field** module, which will allow Flickr integration.

2. Before we can add content from Flickr, we will need to apply for a Flickr API Key. You can request an API key at `http://www.flickr.com/services/api/keys`. If you do not already have a Yahoo account, you will be prompted to create one.

3. After you sign into your Yahoo and Flickr accounts, you can apply for an API key by accepting the terms of service. You will need to specify whether the key is for commercial or non-commercial use, and enter your name and email account. When the sign-up is complete, you will receive a long key for use with Flickr. You should store this key in a safe place.

4. We can enter the Flickr key for the Embedded Media field by selecting **Content Management** and then **Embedded Media Field configuration**. Expand the **Embedded Image Field** section, which appears as follows, and enter your key.

```
▼ Embedded Image Field
The following settings configure content with any fields controlled by
Embedded Image Field.
  ▼ Providers
  The following settings determine what providers are allowed, and what
  provider-specific options, if any, are set.
    ▼ Flickr configuration
    These settings specifically affect images displayed from Flickr.

    ☑ Allow content from Flickr
    If checked, then content types may be created that allow content to be provided by
    Flickr.

      ▼ Flickr API
      You will first need to apply for an API Developer Key from the Flickr
      Developer Profile page.

      Flickr API Key:
      [                                              ]
      Please enter your Flickr Developer Key here.

      Flickr API Secret:
      [                                              ]
      If you have a secret for the Flickr API, enter it here.


      ▶ Supported features


  ▶ ImageShack configuration

  ▶ Photobucket configuration

  ▶ Picasa configuration
```

5. Open the **Content Type Manager** by selecting **Content management** and then **Content types**, from the **Administer** menu.

6. Click on the **add field** link next to the Cooking Class content type.

7. Enter the name and label for the new field as shown in the following screenshot, and make sure that you set the **Field type** to **Embedded Image**.

```
┌─ Create new field ──────────────────────────────────────────────┐
│                                                                  │
│  Field name: *                                                   │
│  field_ │example                                      │          │
│  The machine-readable name of the field. This name cannot be     │
│  changed later! The name will be prefixed with 'field_' and can  │
│  include lowercase unaccented letters, numbers, and              │
│  underscores. The length of the name, including the prefix, is   │
│  limited to no more than 32 characters.                          │
│                                                                  │
│  Label: *                                                        │
│  │An example of what you will make                    │          │
│  A human-readable name to be used as the label for this field    │
│  in the Cooking Class content type.                              │
│                                                                  │
│  Field type: *                                                   │
│  │ Embedded Image            ▼ │                                 │
│  The type of data you would like to store in the database with   │
│  this field.                                                     │
│                                                                  │
└──────────────────────────────────────────────────────────────────┘

[ Continue ]
```

8. Click **Continue** to select the Widget type. The only available type is **3rd Party Image**, so we will leave that set, and click **Continue** again.

9. We can now set several options for the field, including the allowable providers and the size to display images when they are displayed full size, preview size, or thumbnail size.

10. We will first set the providers to allow images only from Flickr. Depending on your site, you may want to add other providers as well.

Cooking Class settings

These settings apply only to the *An example of what you will make* field as it appears in the *Cooking Class* content type.

▾ Providers Supported

Select which third party providers you wish to allow for this content type from the list below. If no checkboxes are checked, then all providers will be supported. When a user submits new content, the URL they enter will be matched to the provider, assuming that provider is allowed here.

Providers:

☑ Flickr

☐ ImageShack

☐ Photobucket

☐ Picasa

---

11. The image resizing options contain the following possibilities:

▾ Full size display settings

These settings control how this image is displayed in its full size, which defaults to 500x800. Note that if one of the dimensions is 0, then the image will be resized to be no larger than the other dimension.

Full size display width: *

```
500
```

The width of the image. It defaults to 500. Set it to 0 if you want to leave the image at its original aspect ratio.

Full size display height: *

```
800
```

The height of the image. It defaults to 800. Set it to 0 if you want to leave the image at its original aspect ratio.

Full size link:

`Link to provider ▾`

Where the image will link when displayed in its full size. 'Content' links to the content page, 'provider' links to the provider's image page, and 'none' displays the image with no link.

In our case, the defaults are acceptable, so we will leave them alone.

12. Click **Save field settings** to complete the new field definition.

13. We can now either create a new cooking class, or edit one that we created previously, to add information to our new field.

In either case, the edit field will appear as follows:

An example of what you will make:

http://www.flickr.com/photos/kendiala/40170940/

Enter the URL or Embed Code here. The embedded third party content will be parsed and displayed appropriately from this.

The following services are provided: Flickr

14. Simply enter the information and click **Save** to add the image.

Using the Flickr module to insert photos using a filter

Good Eatin' Goal: Add images to an existing block of text using a filter.

Additional modules needed: Flickr module (`http://drupal.org/project/flickr`).

Basic steps

Although the **Embedded Media Field** is very convenient for adding pictures as a field, there may be times when you want to display an image within a block of text. To do this, we will use the **Flickr** module.

1. Begin by installing and activating the **Flickr** module. There are several available modules included, but we only need the **Flickr** and the **Flickr Filter** modules.

Enabled	Name	Version	Description
☑	Flickr	6.x-1.0-alpha1	Flickr and Drupal integration. Required by: Flickr Block (disabled), Flickr Filter (disabled), Flickr Sets (disabled), Flickr Tags (disabled), Flickrfield (disabled)
☐	Flickr Block	6.x-1.0-alpha1	Flickr Block for inserting photos into content. Depends on: Flickr (disabled)
☑	Flickr Filter	6.x-1.0-alpha1	Flickr Filter for inserting photos into content. Depends on: Flickr (disabled)
☐	Flickr Sets	6.x-1.0-alpha1	Add photoset capability to Flickr module. Depends on: Flickr (disabled)
☐	Flickr Tags	6.x-1.0-alpha1	Adds tags capability to Flickr module. Depends on: Flickr (disabled)

If you only plan on using images from Flickr, you could use the **Flickr Field** rather than the **Embedded Media Field** to add images to a content type as a field.

2. We need to configure the Flickr module to enter our API key. We can do this by selecting **Site configuration** and then **Flickr** from the **Administer** menu.

3. Drupal will display a page similar to the following where you can enter the API key and a shared secret.

Flickr

You will need a Flickr API key to use this module. You can apply for one at http://www.flickr.com/services/api/keys/apply/

[more help...]

API Key: *

[   ]

API Key from Flickr

API Shared Secret: *

[   ]

API key's secret from Flickr.

Default Flickr User Id:

[   ]

An, optional, default Flickr username or user id. This will be used when no user is specified. Disabled until a valid API Key is set.

Update interval:

[1 hour   ▾]

The refresh interval indicating how often you want to check cached Flickr API calls are up to date.

[Save configuration]   [Reset to defaults]

---

4. After you have entered this information, click on **Save configuration**.

5. We can now build an input format that allows us to embed Flickr images into content, by clicking on **Site configuration** and then **Input format**, from the **Administer** menu.

6. Next, click **Add Input format** to begin building the new format.

7. We will call the Input format **Flickr**, and enable only the **Flickr linker** filter.

☑ Flickr linker
Insert photos or photosets from Flickr without tags: [flickr-photo:id=230452326]

8. Click **Save configuration** to finish building the input format.

9. We can now use the new input format in a new page or in an existing page. We will modify the **About page** to include an image from Flickr. Navigate to the **About page** and then select the **Edit** link.

10. We will modify the description to include a Flickr image, and change the **Input format** to **Flickr**, as shown in the following screenshot:.

Body:

[flickr-photo:id=1414283257,size=m]
<em>Good Eatin' Bistro</em> is a full service restaurant serving breakfast, lunch, and dinner daily. Good Eatin' Bistro was founded in 2008 by <cite>Mark Noble</cite> to serve as an example website for the <strong>Drupal Sitebuilder Cookbook</strong>.

▼ Input format

○ Filtered HTML
  • Web page addresses and e-mail addresses turn into links automatically.
  • Allowed HTML tags: <a> <em> <strong> <cite> <code> <ul> <ol> <li> <dl> <dt> <dd>
  • Lines and paragraphs break automatically.

○ Full HTML
  • Web page addresses and e-mail addresses turn into links automatically.
  • Lines and paragraphs break automatically.

○ Image Format
  • Allowed HTML tags: <img> <a> <em> <strong> <cite> <code> <ul> <ol> <li> <dl> <dt> <dd>
  • Lines and paragraphs break automatically.
  • Slideshows can be added to this post.

○ YouTube
  • You may insert videos with [video:URL]

◉ Flickr
  • Insert Flickr images: [flickr-photo:id=230452326,size=s] or [flickr-photoset:id=72157594262419167,size=m].

More information about formatting options

11. On saving, the resulting page appears as follows:

12. In addition to embedding pictures, you can also embed photosets, which is an easy way to add multiple images to your site at once. To use a photoset, first create the photoset on Flickr, and then embed it using a filter in the form [flickr-photoset:id=72157594262419167,size=m].

Adding Google maps

Maps are invaluable for directing customers to your store, or for helping them learn more about an area, community, or town. Google offers a very powerful mapping solution, which you can embed into your web site free of charge.

Getting a Google maps API key

Good Eatin' Goal: Obtain a Google Maps API key, which will allow us to embed maps into our web site.

Additional modules needed: None.

Basic steps

Google requires you to obtain a key from them if you want to use one or more of their maps on your web site. This is a very simple process.

1. The full process is described on Google's web site at:
   `http://code.google.com/apis/maps/signup.html`.

2. If you do not already have a Google account, you will need to sign-up for a new account.

3. After you have signed up for an account, you will need to read and accept the terms of service, enter the URL of your web site, and then click on **Generate API Key**, as shown in the following screenshot:

```
Google Maps API Terms of Use

Thank you for using the Google Maps API! By using the Google Maps API
(the "Service"), you ("You") accept and agree to be bound by the
Google Terms of Service, the Terms of Service for Google Maps as well
as these additional terms and conditions (the "Terms of Service"). It
is important for You to read each of these three documents, as they
form a legal agreement between You and Google regarding your use of
the Service.

  1. Service.

     1.1 Description of Service. The API allows You to display
certain content, including map images and driving directions on your
website, subject to the limitations and conditions described below.
The informationaccessible through the Service, not limited to map
```

☑ I have read and agree with the terms and conditions (printable version)

My web site URL: `http://goodeatin.drupalb`

[Generate API Key]

4. After you click on **Generate API Key**, Google will issue you a long string that you will need to use as your key. Make sure that you save this key in a safe place so that you can use it later.

Insert a simple map with GMapEZ

Good Eatin' Goal: Add a basic map in a new page to the web site. We will control where it is centered as well as the zoom level.

Additional modules needed: GmapEZ (`http://drupal.org/project/gmapez`).

Basic steps

1. Begin by installing and activating the **GmapEZ** module.

2. We now need to enter our API Key by clicking on **Site configuration** and then on **GmapEZ**. The configuration options are shown in the following screenshot:

    Simply enter your map key and then click on **Save configuration**. You can now begin adding maps to pages.

3. We will create a new page which will contain a map called **Our Locations**. Select **Create content** and then **Page**, from the **Navigation** menu.

4. To insert a map into a page, you will need to enter a block similar to the following one, on your page. You will also need to modify your input format to a format that includes `divs`. You may even want to create a format specifically for maps.

    ```
    <div class="GMapEZ GSmallMapControl" style="width: 600px;
                                        height: 480px;">
    <a href="http://maps.google.com/maps?q=111%20Main%20Street,
                                %20Parker,%20CO"></a>
    </div>
    ```

5. With the above information , the page will appear as follows:

Our Locations

Page *Our Locations* has been updated.

Good Eatin' has several locations offering our fine cuisine. Just click on a location to get information.

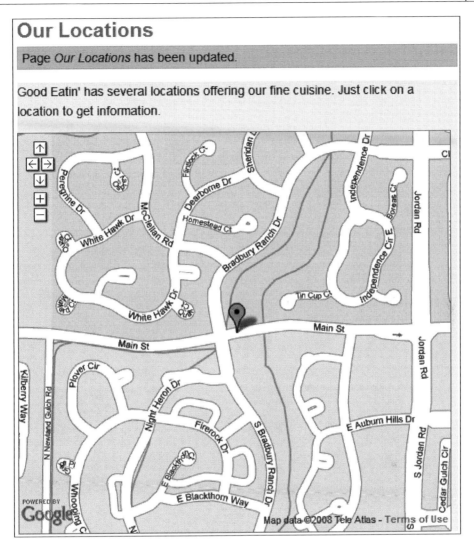

6. You can specify the center of the map by modifying the portion of the URL after the q. This can be an actual street address, the name of a well-known building or monument, or a specific latitude and longitude. You can verify whether or not Google will be able to find the address by checking on `maps.google.com`.

An example of a URL based on an address or place name is:

`q=Washington+Monument`

An example of a URL based on a specific latitude and longitude is:

`ll=39.521985,-104.784765`

You can retrieve the latitude and longitude either from a GPS or from a Google map.

When you build your own URLs, make sure that you substitute either a **+** symbol or **%20** for all of the spaces, as spaces are not allowed within URLs.

7. You can also build URLs by finding the location that you want on Google maps and then copying and pasting it into the `<a>` tag.

8. To change the size of the map on the page, simply modify the width and height that are specified in the `div` tag.

9. If your map does not appear, make sure that your input filter allows `div` tags to be included in content. You may need to change the active **Input filter** for your page if the default does not allow `div`s.

10. If you want to specify multiple locations on the map, you can simply add multiple links in the form of `<a>` tags to the div. When using multiple markers, you must include the latitude and longitude in all of the links. If you don't, only the first marker will be displayed.

11. An example of a map with multiple markers is shown in the following screenshot:

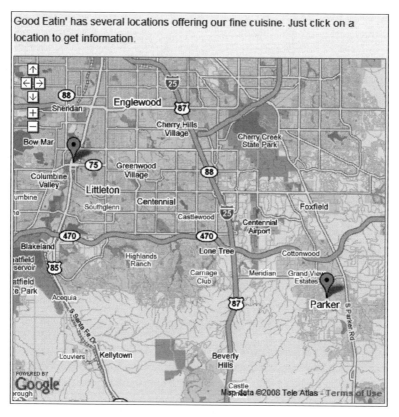

Displaying content in pop-ups

Good Eatin' Goal: Enhance our map location by displaying a pop-up balloon when a visitor clicks on our pin.

Additional modules needed: GmapEZ (`http://drupal.org/project/gmapez`).

Basic steps

If you have played with your map, you may have noticed that there is no information available when you click on the pin. Google allows you to display information in the pins. To do this, we will use the following steps:

1. Adding pop-up info windows to a location is very easy. You simply need to add a `div` tag containing the contents of the info window.

2. Edit the page with your map so that you can change the contents.

3. We will now edit the **Parker** location to add an info window using the following information:

```
<a href="http://maps.google.com/maps?q=111+Main+Street,
+Parker,+CO&ie=UTF8&ll=39.521985,-
104.784765&spn=0.030853,0.077248&z=14&iwloc=cent">
    </a>
    <div>
    Our original Parker location sets the bar.
    At 111 Main Street
Call 555-111-2222 for reservations
</div>
```

4. The resulting info window will appear as follows when a user clicks on it:

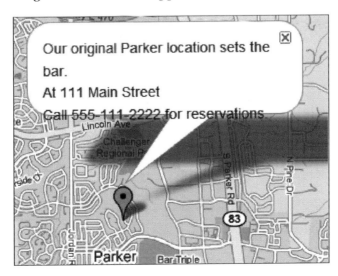

5. You can also add images to the info windows, in addition to text.

6. If you add more than one div to a link, the info window will be displayed in several tabs, one for each div.

Using links to change the map

Good Eatin' Goal: Add links to each restaurant location and have the map automatically zoom in to the location.

Additional modules needed: GmapEZ (`http://drupal.org/project/gmapez`).

Basic steps

If you want to allow customers to be able to jump easily from location to location, you can add links within the text surrounding the map, which will cause GmapEZ to automatically re-center the map to the location that you linked it to.

1. You will first need to add IDs to each anchor (`<a>`) tag.

2. For example, we will modify our links as follows.

   ```
   <a id="original" href="http://maps.google.com/maps?q=111+Main+
   Street,+Parker,+CO&ie=UTF8&ll=39.521985,-104.784765&spn=0.030853,
   0.077248&z=14&iwloc=cent">
   </a>
   ```

3. We can now link to the location from the text by creating another anchor tag as follows:

   ```
   <a href="#original" class="ZOOM">Original Location</a>
   ```

4. The `#original` indicates that the browser should link to the anchor tag on the same that has an ID of **original**.

Content sharing, bookmarking, and twittering—oh my!

After you have built high quality content for your web site, you need to make sure that everyone knows about it. One of the best ways to do this is by letting your customers add your content to social bookmarking sites such as Digg, del.ico.us, technorati and more.

Diggin' Digg It with DiggThis

Good Eatin' Goal: Give our customers the opportunity to vote on our content at Digg, to help draw traffic to the site.

Additional modules needed: DiggThis (`http://drupal.org/project/diggthis`).

Basic steps

Digg is a popular place for people to discover content on the Internet. It works by allowing community members to submit content to the site and then allowing anyone to vote either for the content by selecting **Digg It**, or against the content by selecting **Bury It**. Visitors can also comment on content to give more information about their votes. Content with the most number of votes is listed first on the home page and in each section of the site.

1. Begin by installing and activating the **DiggThis** module.

2. You can configure the **DiggThis** module by selecting **Content management** and then **DiggThis**, from the **Administer** menu.

3. The first configuration option controls the display of the link as well as the content types that should have the **Digg** button added to them.

---

digthis settings

Button skin:

standard ▼

The Button skin option controls the look at the button. If set to *standard* the button defaults to a standard digg button (much like the one you see on Digg itself). If specified as *compact*, then a smaller horizontal visual design is used that will fit better into a list of links.

Button background color:

#ffffff

Enter a hexadecimal color value here, e.g. #ff9900. Include the leading # and enter 6 numbers/digits

Weight:

10 ▼

Specifies the position of the Digthis button. A low weight, e.g. -20 will display the button above the content and a high weight, e.g. 20 below the content.

Node Types:

☐ Blog entry

☑ Cooking Class

☑ Event

---

4. We can also control some additional **API settings** for Digg. These settings control how frequently Digg is updated, and the domain that should be used in the display.

---

diggthis API settings

Digg Stories Domain:

drupalbyexample.com

Enter the domain, e.g. *mydomain.com*, that will be used to show top Digg stories for.

Minimum cache lifetime:

12 hours ▾

The time the response from the Digg API is cached before being requested again.

---

5. After configuring the module, a link will be displayed on your site allowing users to easily vote for your content on Digg. You can also add a link to the site that contains the top-ranked content from your site.

Tagging content for del.ico.us!

Good Eatin' Goal: Allows you to consume content from `del.icio.us` based on specified tags.

Additional modules needed: Delicious (`http://drupal.org/project/delicious`).

Basic steps

del.icio.us or **delicious.com**, allows you to organize your bookmarks with one or more tags. You can also share your bookmark list with other users and search the bookmarks by popularity, or by tag.

1. To begin using **del.icio.us**, install and activate the **del.icio.us** module.

2. To configure the **del.icio.us** module, select **Site configuration** and then **delicious**, from the **Administer** menu. Please note that this module may appear at the bottom of the page because the first letter of "delicious" is not capitalized.

3. The **del.icio.us** module offers several settings that control whether or not it tries to automatically generate tags, and which pages should have the **del.icio.us** tags generated.

delicious settings

☐ Enable del.icio.us related crosslink
Enable a link to a del.icio.us tag corresponding to the node's first term.

☑ Enable del.icio.us "smart tagging"
Words in node bodies matching del.icio.us tags will be linked to del.icio.us.

Node Types:

☐ webform

☑ blog

☐ poll

☐ image

☐ simplenews

☑ cooking_class

☑ event

☐ event_cck

☑ menu_item

☑ page

☑ story

SELECT all node types that allow crosslinking and/or smarttagging.

[Save configuration] [Reset to defaults]

We added the **cooking_class** and **event** types to the defaults provided by the module.

4. There are several permissions that you will need to set in order to properly access the tags.

delicious module				
administer delicious	☐	☐	☐	☐
create delicious links	☐	☐	☑	☑
view delicious links	☑	☑	☑	☑

5. Permissions can be set by selecting **User management** and then **Permissions**, from the **Administer** menu.

Twitter when you post

Good Eatin' Goal: Provide Twitter notifications each time content is updated on our site to ensure that customers always stay up-to-date.

Additional modules needed: Twitter (`http://drupal.org/project/twitter`).

Basic steps

Twitter allows users to post very brief messages at frequent intervals, so that other people can remain updated on what they are doing. You can subscribe to a person to follow everything they do, or search for specific posts.

Once you have installed and activated the **Twitter module**, a message is sent via Twitter each time a user with the required permissions adds a new post. You can control what types of nodes to send messages to Twitter for, as well how the post should be formatted, in the **Twitter settings**. The **Twitter settings** can be accessed by selecting **Site configuration** and then **Twitter setup** from the **Administer** menu.

Social bookmarking with service links

Good Eatin' Goal: Allow customers to easily add our content to several different social bookmarking sites.

Additional modules needed: Service Links (`http://drupal.org/project/service_links`).

Basic steps

If you would like to display links to several social bookmarking links at the same time, you can do so with the **Service Links** module. This can be useful if you need many links and don't need specific controls over each individual site.

1. Begin by installing and activating the **Service Links** module.

2. The **Service Links** options can be configured by selecting **Site configuration** and then **Service Links** from the **Administer** menu.

3. The first configuration that needs to be done is to set the types of nodes that you want to display links for, as shown below:

Where to show the service links

Set the node types and categories you want to display links for.

Node types:

- ☐ Blog entry
- ☑ Cooking Class
- ☑ Event
- ☐ Event CCK
- ☐ Image
- ☐ Menu Item
- ☑ Newsletter issue
- ☐ Page
- ☐ Poll
- ☐ Story
- ☐ Webform

We will allow links from our **Cooking Class**, **Event**, and **Newsletter issue** as these change frequently and are important to draw attention to.

4. The next configuration is the categories that you want to display the links for. The categories are not relevant for the content types we wish to display links for, so we will leave all of these settings with their default values.

5. We can now update which sites we want to link to, as shown here:

What bookmark links to show

- ☑ Show del.icio.us link
- ☑ Show Digg link
- ☐ Show StumbleUpon link
- ☐ Show Propeller link
- ☑ Show Reddit link
- ☐ Show ma.gnolia.com link
- ☐ Show Newsvine link
- ☐ Show Furl link
- ☐ Show Facebook link
- ☑ Show Google link
- ☑ Show Yahoo link

We can also choose to include search links, as shown in the following screenshot:.

```
┌─What search links to show──────────────────────────────┐
│                                                        │
│   ☑ Show Technorati link                               │
│                                                        │
│   ☐ Show IceRocket link                                │
│                                                        │
└────────────────────────────────────────────────────────┘
```

6. The final configuration step is to tell the **Service Links** module where the links should be displayed, and whether they should be displayed as image links, as text links, or both.

```
┌─When and how to show the links──────────────────────────┐
│                                                         │
│   Service links in links:                               │
│   ┌──────────────────────────┐                          │
│   │ Disabled              ▼ │                          │
│   └──────────────────────────┘                          │
│   When to display the services in the links section.    │
│                                                         │
│   Service links in nodes:                               │
│   ┌──────────────────────────┐                          │
│   │ Full-page view        ▼ │                          │
│   └──────────────────────────┘                          │
│   When to display the services after the node text.     │
│                                                         │
│   Service links style:                                  │
│   ┌──────────────────────────┐                          │
│   │ Image and text links  ▼ │                          │
│   └──────────────────────────┘                          │
│                                                         │
└─────────────────────────────────────────────────────────┘
```

7. With these settings, the final display will appear as follows:

```
┌─────────────────────────────────────────────────────────┐
│ Bookmark/Search this post with:                          │
│  ■ Delicious   🎲 Digg   ⓢ Reddit   G Google   Y Yahoo  ☻│
│ Technorati                                               │
└─────────────────────────────────────────────────────────┘
```

Summary

In this chapter, we have explored a number of ways to integrate your web site with sites created by other developers and other companies around the world, either by including information from their sites into your site or by publishing information from your site to them.

Including content from other web sites is an extremely powerful way of building new content for your web site without having to dedicate hundreds and thousands of hours and precious resources on the development of functionalities that have already been created by other developers. This allows you to focus on your core business and on the development of functionalities that are critical to the success of your site.

In the next chapter, we will discuss various ways of providing free content to your visitors, as well as ways of transferring information to them via the download of menus, pictures, brochures, or other content.

8
Freebies and Downloads

In this chapter, we will explore various ways of adding downloads to your web site to provide free content, or to deliver paid content to users. We will also discuss the automatic conversion of pages to PDF files, which your users can download to read or print.

Free content is a fantastic way of building customer loyalty. Depending on the content that you provide, you can also keep your brand in front of people. For example, a simple tastefully-done screen saver or desktop background can be used to always keep your logo on your customers' desktop. Of course, you need to make sure that the free content is of the highest possible quality to ensure that the customers will actually use the content.

Many visitors want to print content or save it to their computers for later use when they are not online or are not working on their computers. We will build PDF files automatically, to give your visitors this convenience.

If you allow visitors to download content from your site, you need to be careful that your site security is solid, so that an unscrupulous user cannot download content that you don't want them to have access to. We will discuss how to protect your content in this chapter.

Adding downloads and PDFs to the web site

In this section, we will discuss how to add downloads and PDFs to the web site.

Controlling how files are downloaded

Good Eatin' Goal: Ensure that Drupal has full control over any files that are uploaded, so that we can specify who can download the files.

Additional modules needed: None.

Basic steps

Drupal allows you to set downloads to either **Public** or **Private**. The public setting does not have any additional download security. The private setting allows Drupal to secure and manage the downloaded files.

You can control this functionality using the **File system** settings, which are available by selecting **Site configuration** and then **File system**, from the **Administer** menu, as shown in the following screenshot:

```
File system

File system path:
sites/default/files
A file system path where the files will be stored. This directory must exist and be writable by
Drupal. If the download method is set to public, this directory must be relative to the Drupal
installation directory and be accessible over the web. If the download method is set to private,
this directory should not be accessible over the web. Changing this location will modify all
download paths and may cause unexpected problems on an existing site.

Temporary directory:
/tmp
A file system path where uploaded files will be stored during previews.

Download method:

   ○  Public - files are available using HTTP directly.

   ◉  Private - files are transferred by Drupal.

Choose the Public download method unless you wish to enforce fine-grained access
controls over file downloads. Changing the download method will modify all download paths
and may cause unexpected problems on an existing site.

[ Save configuration ]   [ Reset to defaults ]
```

Because we want Drupal to provide additional security for the downloaded files, we will select the **Private** setting and then save the configuration.

You can also control where the files are stored on the web site, and also specify a temporary location to be used while files are being transferred. In most cases, the defaults are acceptable. However, you may need to customize the directories depending on how your server and site are configured. If you are using the private download method, the **File system path** should not be accessible via a web browser. To ensure that a directory is not available via a web browser, you should choose a folder that is not located within the Drupal installation. It should also not be located within your root web folder. On most systems, the root web folder is named htdocs. If you are unsure what your root web folder is, ask your webhost. Some hosting companies do not allow you to create folders outside the root web folder. If this is the case, you can contact your host to see if they can make an exception, or you will have to use the public download method.

Allowing files to be uploaded to the web site

Good Eatin' Goal: Allow authorized users to upload a file to the web site.

Additional modules needed: Upload (`core`).

Basic steps

In order to allow a user to download a file, you must first upload files to the web site. We will create a downloads page that stores all of the files that have been uploaded.

1. Begin by activating the **Upload** module, which is a part of the core Drupal distribution.

2. We can now customize the permissions for the **Upload** module by clicking on **User management** and then on **Permission**. The available permissions are shown in the following screenshot:

Permission	anonymous user	authenticated user	blogger	VIP user
upload module				
upload files	☐	☐	☐	☐
view uploaded files	☐	☑	☐	☐

It is a good idea to give only authenticated users the ability to view and download files. This will provide an additional incentive for visitors to register on your web site.

3. We can now build a new page for our uploaded files by clicking on **Create content** and then on **Page**.

4. The basic information for the page is shown below:

Create Page

Title: *

Free downloads

▸ **Menu settings**

[Split summary at cursor]

Body:

Registered members can download a variety of free pictures and screen savers here.

5. To add a file to the page, expand the **File attachments** section. The section appears as follows:

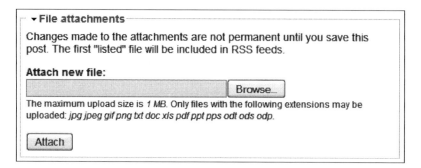

6. You can now **Browse** for the file to be uploaded, and then once you have selected it, click **Attach**.

7. After a file has been attached, it will be listed on the form as shown below:

Changes made to the attachments are not permanent until you save this post. The first "listed" file will be included in RSS feeds.

	Delete	List	Description	Size
✛	☐	☑	File System settings.png http://localhost/goodeatin/system/files/File%20System%20settings.png	27.04 KB

8. After you save the new page, users with the appropriate permissions will be able to download the file by clicking on the link. You can also add links within the text of a page.

Sending the correct file types to a user

Good Eatin' Goal: Ensure that the correct file type is sent to the browser so that the visitor's computer can accurately determine how to handle it.

Additional modules needed: File MIME (`http://drupal.org/project/filemime`).

Basic steps

As you add files to your site for download, it is important to make sure that a visitor's browser knows how to display the file. With web sites, this is done by setting the MIME type for the file. Some common MIME types are:

*   text/`html`: A standard web page
*   text/`csv`: A comma-delimited file

- text/`plain`: Plain text with no formatting
- audio/`mpeg`: Audio mpeg1 and mpeg2 files
- audio/`mp4`: Audio mp4 files
- image/`jpeg`: JPEG encoded image files
- image/`gif`: GIF encoded images
- application/`pdf`: A PDF document
- application/`javascript`: A script file written in Javascript

A full list of how Drupal handles each file type can be found at: `http://api.drupal.org/api/function/file_get_mimetype`.

The **File MIME** module automatically detects the type of file based on the file extension, and sets the appropriate MIME type, which is returned to the browser.

To use the File MIME module, carry out the following steps:

1. Download, install, and activate the **File MIME** module.

2. Configure the module by selecting **Site configuration** and then **File MIME**, from the **Administer** menu. The module allows you to specify the location of the `mime.types` file, which is installed along with your web server. The Apache web server installs this file in the same directory as where your `httpd.conf` file is installed.

File MIME

Local mime.types file path:

/xampp/apache/conf/mime.types

If a mime.types file exists and is readable, it will be parsed to extract MIME extension mappings. Example: */usr/local/etc/apache22/mime.types*

Additional MIME extension mappings:

application/vnd.ms-excel csv xls

Additional types provided here will be merged with the mime.types file. Specify the mappings using the mime.types file format. Example:
audio/mpeg mp3 m4a
audio/ogg ogg

[Save configuration] [Reset to defaults]

3. You can also add additional mappings for specific file types. For example, you may want `.csv` files to be treated as Microsoft Excel files if you know that a significant number of your users are running Windows-based machines and want to download `.csv` files into Excel. You can do this by adding the following line to the settings, as shown in the preceding screenshot:

```
application/vnd.ms-excel csv xls.
```

4. After the module has been properly configured, the module will automatically set the correct MIME types each time that a file is downloaded.

Forcing a file to be downloaded

Good Eatin' Goal: Force a file to be downloaded even if it could be displayed within the browser.

Additional modules needed: File Force (`http://drupal.org/project/file_force`).

Basic steps

In the previous section, we discussed setting the MIME type automatically so that the browser can handle the file correctly. However in some cases, you may want the file to always be saved to the user's computer, even if it is a common file type that can be read by the browser. For example, you may want to have PDF files or pictures to be downloaded to the customer's computer even though all modern browsers can display these types of files in the browser.

To use the **File Force** module, download, install, and activate it.

The File Force module does not require any configuration, so you can begin using it immediately. To use the File Force module, you simply need to prefix any link to downloadable content with the text `download`. So, if you have a link called: `/sites/default/files/song.mp3` that you want users to always download, you would replace the link with `/download/sites/default/files/song.mp3`. File Force will then modify the information returned to the browser to indicate that the file should be downloaded rather than be displayed or played.

If you do not add the `download` prefix to the link, the File Force module will not change the behavior of downloads, so you can offer files either as downloads or as play-now links.

Tracking download counts

Good Eatin' Goal: Track how many downloads have been completed, so that we can gauge the effectiveness of our promotions.

Additional modules needed: Download Count (`http://drupal.org/project/download_count`).

Basic steps

If you want to be able to determine the effectiveness of your downloads, you should track how many times each file has been downloaded. The **Download Count** module is specifically designed to help you with this.

1. To begin with, download and install the **Download Count** module.

2. The Download counter can be configured by selecting **Site configuration** and then **Download counter**, from the **Administer** menu.

3. The most important configuration is defining which file extensions should be included in the download counter, and which should be ignored.

▾ Ignoring certain file extensions

Excluded file extensions:

jpg jpeg gif png

This module only considers files that have been uploaded with the upload module and that become file attachments. However, if you are using a contributed module to upload images and display them in the body of nodes, these files may get flagged as downloaded whenever a visitor or robot views the node page, because strictly speaking they are file attachments. This will happen with the module img_assist. Note that this won't happen with the module imce, because imce treats inline images as nodes. If you do not want to set a download counter for image files, list their extension here. Separate extensions with a space and do not include the leading dot. For example, you could list these extensions : jpg jpeg gif png. If you do not want to exclude any file, leave that field blank.

Depending on how your site is configured, you may want to either add or remove extensions from the list of extensions to be excluded from the statistics.

4. You can also configure whether or not download counters are displayed to the administrator, and you can also add more information to the statistics page, which is available at `yoursite.com/download_counter`. These options are shown in the following screenshot:

5. You can also configure the download count permissions by selecting **User management** and then **Permissions** from the **Administer** menu. The available permissions are shown in the following screenshot:

6. The download count for a single page appears as follows:

Attachment	Size	Hits	Last download
File System settings.png	27.04 KB	2	4 sec ago
6403_03_1stDraft.odt	865.5 KB	1	24 sec ago
6403_02_1stDraft_WIP.odt	2.77 MB	0	Not yet downloaded

As you can see, this page shows the number of times each file has been downloaded, and when it was last downloaded.

7. You can also view statistics for all downloadable files by navigating to `yoursite.com/download_counter`. The resulting page is formatted as follows:

Download counter

filename	hits▼	last download	action
File System settings.png	2	2 min 29 sec ago	view Page
6403_03_1stDraft.odt	1	2 min 49 sec ago	view Page

This page shows all of the files that have been downloaded, regardless of the page they are on, and you can also sort the files depending on your needs.

Allow users to browse files

Good Eatin' Goal: Give users an intuitive interface to see which files are available for download, with additional information for each file.

Additional modules needed: Filebrowser (`http://drupal.org/project/filebrowser`).

Basic steps

The **filebrowser** module allows visitors to easily browse downloadable files on your site.

1. Begin by downloading and installing the **filebrowser** module.

2. In order to display a list of files in a directory, we need to create a **Directory Listing** page. To do this, first select **Create content** and then **Directory listing** from the **Navigation** menu.

3. Enter a title for the page, and specify the directory you wish to browse, as shown in the following screenshot:

Create Directory listing

Title: *

Browse Downloads

The system file path to the directory: *

sites/default/files

This can be an absolute path or should be relative to the Drupal root directory.

☑ Allow subdirectory listings.

☐ Enable private downloads
Some files won't download unless this private downloads are enabled (PHP files for instance).

A blacklist of all files that shouldn't be accessible by users:

.*, descript.ion, file.bbs, CVS

List files separated by commas. Use .* to signify all files starting with a period.

4. After you are happy with the settings, save the page. When you view the page, you will see a listing of the files in the directory as well as summary information for the directory, as shown in the following screenshot:

Browse Downloads

Submitted by admin on Wed, 09/03/2008 - 22:04

Displaying *sites/default/files*.

Contains 7 files totaling 3.95 MB in size.

Name▲	Size
images	
pictures	
6403_02_1stDraft_WIP.odt	2.77 MB
6403_03_1stDraft.odt	865.5 KB
File System settings.png	27.04 KB

5. Clicking on a filename will open the file in the browser, and clicking on a directory will open that directory.

6. The **filebrowser** module offers a variety of permissions that give you control over who can create directory listings, and who can edit and delete directory listings.

Permission	anonymous user	authenticated user	blogger	VIP user
filebrowser module				
create directory listings	☐	☐	☐	☐
delete any directory listings	☐	☐	☐	☐
delete own directory listings	☐	☐	☐	☐
edit any directory listings	☐	☐	☐	☐
edit own directory listings	☐	☐	☐	☐
view directory listings	☐	☑	☐	☐

You may want to only allow authenticated users to view directory listings, in order to provide an additional incentive for registration.

Automatically generating PDF files for a page

Good Eatin' Goal: Generate PDF files of our pages so that the users can automatically download the pages for printing, or for offline usage.

Additional modules needed: Printer, email, and PDF (http://drupal.org/project/print).

Basic steps

As you continue to work on your web site, you will find that many users want access to your content, even if they aren't online. With the **Printer**, **email**, and **PDF** module, you can easily and automatically provide content in various formats for offline usage.

1. To begin with, download and install the **Printer**, **email**, and **PDF** module.

Enabled	Name	Version	Description
☑	**PDF version**	6.x-1.0-rc9	Adds the capability to export pages as PDF. Depends on: Printer-friendly pages (core) (disabled)
☑	**Printer-friendly pages (core)**	6.x-1.0-rc9	Adds a printer-friendly version link to content and administrative pages. Required by: Send by e-mail (disabled), PDF version (disabled)
☑	**Send by e-mail**	6.x-1.0-rc9	Provides the capability to send the web page by e-mail. Depends on: Printer-friendly pages (core) (disabled)

▾ Printer-friendly pages

2. You can now configure the basic options for the module by selecting **Site configuration** and then **Printer-friendly pages** from the **Administer** menu.

3. The general settings are accessed by clicking on the **Settings** tab. These settings are shown below, and include options to style the printable pages, and to determine whether or not URLs and comments are displayed on the page. You can also control how the page is opened, and also which logos are displayed on it.

Printer-friendly pages

Common Settings

Stylesheet URL:

The URL to your custom print cascading stylesheet, if any. When none is specified, the default module CSS file is used.
Macros: %b (base path: "/goodeatin/"), %t (path to theme: "sites/all/themes/foliage")

☑ Printer-friendly URLs list
If set, a list of the destination URLs for the page links will be displayed at the bottom of the page.

☐ Include comments in printer-friendly version
When this option is active, user comments are also included in the printer-friendly version. Requires the comment module.

New window method:

○ Use HTML target (does not validate as XHTML Strict)
◉ Use Javascript (requires browser support)

Choose the method used to open pages in a new window/tab.

▸ Logo options

▸ Source URL

By expanding the **Source URL** section, you can cause the URL of the page to be included on the printed output. You can also optionally add the date and time when the page was generated to the printed output.

4. The printable page (web page) configuration options include a variety of options to control how the links to the printable versions are displayed, as well as how the printable pages are displayed.

Printer-friendly pages

Web page options

Printer-friendly page link:

☐ Links area

☑ Content corner

Choose the location of the link(s) to the printer-friendly page. The Links area is usually below the node content, whereas the Content corner is placed in the upper-right corner of the node content. Unselect all options to disable the link. Even if the link is disabled, you can still view the print version of a node by going to print/nid where nid is the numeric id of the node.

▸ **Advanced link options**

☑ Take control of the book module printer-friendly link
Activate this to have the printer-friendly link in book nodes handled by this module. Requires the (core) book module.

☐ Open the printer-friendly version in a new window
Setting this option will make the printer-friendly version open in a new window/tab.

☐ Send to printer
Automatically calls the browser's print function when the printer-friendly version is displayed.

▸ **Robots META tags**

---

5. We have modified the **Printer-friendly page link** to be in the **Content corner** rather than in the **Links area**. You can also optionally display the printable page in a new window and automatically call the print function, as needed.

6. Opening the **Advanced link options** gives you additional options for how the link is displayed, and what pages it should be displayed on, as shown in the following screenshot:

```
┌──────────────────────────────────────────────────────────────┐
│ ▼ Advanced link options                                        │
│                                                                │
│ Link style:                                                    │
│                                                                │
│   ○ Text only                                                  │
│   ◉ Icon only                                                  │
│   ○ Icon and Text                                              │
│                                                                │
│ Select the visual style of the link.                           │
│                                                                │
│ Link visibility:                                               │
│                                                                │
│   ◉ Show on every page except the listed pages.                │
│   ○ Show on only the listed pages.                             │
│                                                                │
│   ┌──────────────────────────────────────────────────────┐    │
│   │                                                        │    │
│   │                                                        │    │
│   └──────────────────────────────────────────────────────┘    │
│ Enter one page per line as Drupal paths. The '*' character is  │
│ a wildcard. Example paths are *blog* for the blog page and     │
│ *blog/** for every personal blog. *<front>* is the front page. │
│                                                                │
│ Link class:                                                    │
│   ┌──────────────────────────────────────────────────────┐    │
│   │ print-page                                             │    │
│   └──────────────────────────────────────────────────────┘    │
│ This can be used by themers to change the link style or by     │
│ jQuery modules to open in a new window (e.g. greybox or        │
│ thickbox). Multiple classes can be specified, separated        │
│ by spaces.                                                     │
│                                                                │
│ Show link in system (non-content) pages:                       │
│                                                                │
│   ○ Show on every page except the listed pages.                │
│   ◉ Show on only the listed pages.                             │
└──────────────────────────────────────────────────────────────┘
```

7. The **Robots META tags** section allows you to prevent search engines from indexing your printable version, which will help to ensure that visitors are directed only to your online content. This can also help prevent duplicate content penalties being imposed by search engines.

8. To create PDFs, we need to install a third-party tool to handle the conversion. You can choose from either TCPDF or dompdf, which are available at the following locations:

   - TCPDF: http://tcpdf.org
   - dompdf: http://www.digitaljunkies.ca/dompdf/faq.php

You can install and use either of these. You can also install both of them and switch between the two, while you evaluate which one will meet the needs of your site best.

9. After you have installed `TCPDF` and/or `dompdf`, you can access the **PDF** tabbed page in the **Printer-friendly pages** configuration.

10. The PDF generation options are similar to the printable web page options, but with a few additions. To begin with, you need to select which generation tool is to be used, as shown in the following screenshot:

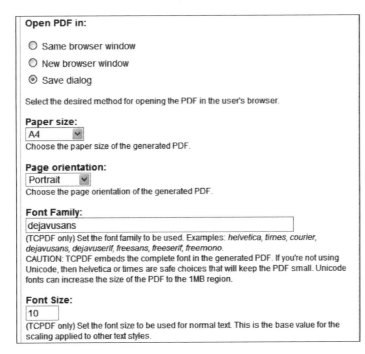

11. You can also control the paper size and orientation to be used in the PDF, as well as font sizes, and whether the PDF should be displayed after it is created, as shown in the following screenshot:

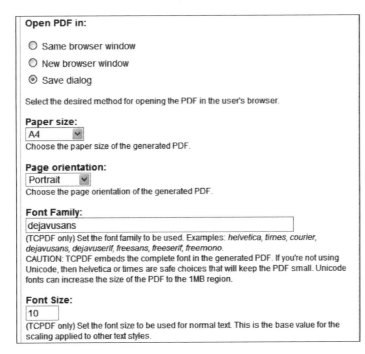

12. After all of the options have been updated, you will see a set of links for printing the page or exporting it to a PDF file, as shown below:

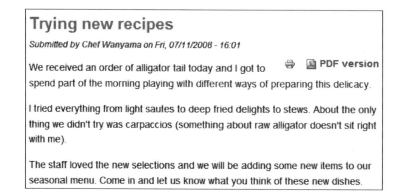

13. Clicking on the **printer icon** will remove most of the styling, as shown in the following screenshot, so that the user can print the page from within the browser.

14. If the user clicks on the **PDF icon**, a PDF will be generated, and either displayed to the user or saved to the user's hard drive, as shown in the following screenshot:

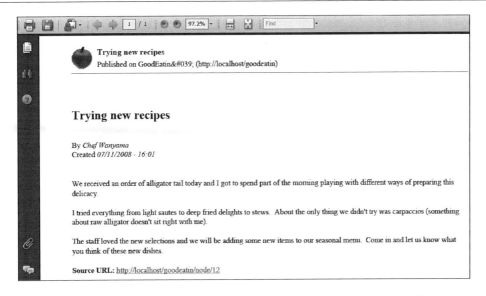

15. Giving visitors the ability to send pages to other users via email is configured in a similar way to configuring PDF generation. In the **Printer-friendly pages** configuration page, you simply click on the **e-mail** tab to edit the settings, as shown in the following screenshot:

16. It is a good idea to set a low **Hourly threshold** for the number of emails that can be sent, to prevent users from abusing this feature. Leaving the **Send only the teaser** option enabled is a great way of ensuring that email recipients are directed to your site to read the rest of the content.

17. When a customer wants to send content via email, they simply click on the **Send to a friend link** that appears on the page. Drupal will then present a form similar to the following screenshot:

Send page by e-mail

Your e-mail:

admin@drupalbyexample.com

Your name:

admin

Send to:

myfriend@drupalbyexample.com

Enter multiple addresses separated by commas and/or different lines.

Subject:

admin has sent you a message from GoodEatin'

Your message:

Checkout this cool information about Good Eatin'

☑ Send only the teaser

— ▸ CAPTCHA

[Send e-mail] [Clear form] [Cancel]

18. After the customer clicks **Send e-mail**, the site will generate the email for the customer, and send it to the specified recipient.

Summary

In this chapter, we reviewed some methods of making the most out of the downloadable content. As long as you provide high quality downloadable content, your customers will appreciate getting something useful from you. In return, you receive the opportunity to market to your customers.

The amount of downloadable content for a site will vary depending on the goal of the web site, as well as the requirements of the visitors to the site.

We have also discussed automatic creation of PDF files for offline use as well as for printing. This is a great way of allowing your users to make use of the site even when they are not actively browsing the site, online.

In the next chapter, we will create a take-out menu that our customers can order from and then pay for their orders online.

9
Online Orders and Payments

A common goal for many business web sites is to integrate their web site with their store, take reservations, and accept payments.

For example, a retail store may allow customers to browse their store inventory and then purchase items either for delivery or for pick-up at the store. A salon may allow patrons to view appointment times that are available, select a time for their appointment, and optionally pre-pay for their appointment online.

For the Good Eatin' site, we will allow customers to view a take out menu, select items that they want to purchase, and then pay for the order online. After an order has been submitted, the order will be sent via an email to the kitchen staff so that they can begin preparation of the order. The order will also be available for viewing online.

Take-out ordering

To expand its services, Good Eatin' is adding a take out menu that will allow patrons to select from a special menu which is available for pick-up. After the patron places the order, they can either pay for it online or in the store. The order is sent to the kitchen where the food is prepared. When the patron arrives at Good Eatin', their hot meal is ready and waiting for them to take home to their family.

Setting up the shopping system

Good Eatin' Goal: Set up the system that will allow visitors to purchase take-out from the web site.

Additional modules needed: Ubercart (`http://drupal.org/project/ubercart`).

Basic configuration

In order to utilize an e-commerce solution within a web site, you must either build a solution from scratch or use a ready-made solution. Because building a professional e-commerce solution from scratch would take an entire book and weeks or months to build, we are fortunate to have **Ubercart**, which is a professional quality e-commerce solution tailor-made for Drupal.

To begin using Ubercart, download and install the module. To use Ubercart, you will also need to install the **Token** module, which can be downloaded from http://drupal.org/project/token. We will begin by installing the Cart, Order, Product, Store, and Conditional actions modules. There are a variety of other modules that can be optionally enabled. We will explore some of these in future topics.

Ubercart installs a new menu within the **Administer** menu called **Store administration**, which includes the options shown in the following screenshot:

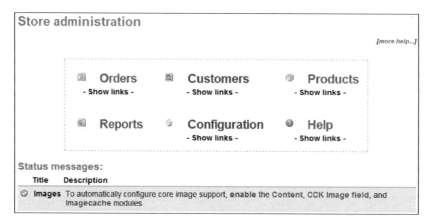

To begin using Ubercart, we will need to edit the **Configuration** settings, which are shown in the following screenshot:

Clicking on the **Store settings** link allows you to configure several options that control how information on the site is displayed, as well as specify some basic contact information for the site.

Name and contact information:

- Store name is *not set.*
- Store owner is *not set.*
- Store e-mail is *not set.*
- Store phone number is not set.
- Store fax number is not set.
- Store address is:

Display settings:

- Store admin page display type: Dashboard with collapsed submenu links
- Customer billing address used in lists.
- Footer using random message.

Format settings:

- Default currency: USD
- Currency format: $1,234.56
- Weight format: 36 lb.
- Date format: 08/18/2007

Reporting settings:

- Version information is being reported to Ubercart.org.

To edit the settings for a section, click on the title of the section. On the **Store settings** page, we simply need to update the **Name and contact information** for the store.

If your store is not located in the United States, you will also need to modify the **Format Settings**. The **Country settings** will also need to be changed if you are not in the United States or Canada.

Permissions

You should also create a role for store administration, by clicking on **User management** and then **Roles**. We will call our role **Store Administrator**.

Name	Operations	
anonymous user	locked	edit permissions
authenticated user	locked	edit permissions
blogger	edit role	edit permissions
VIP user	edit role	edit permissions
Store Administrator	Add role	

Click **Add role** to finish building the role. After the role has been added, click the **edit permissions** link for the role to define the permissions for the new role.

Ubercart includes several sections of permissions, all of which start with uc_, including:

- Store permissions

Permission	Store Administrator
uc_store module	
administer store	☑
view customers	☑
view store reports	☑

- Product permissions

Permission	Store Administrator
uc_product module	
administer product classes	☑
administer product features	☑
administer products	☑
create products	☑
create takeout_item products	☑
delete all products	☑
delete all takeout_item products	☑
delete own products	☑
delete own takeout_item products	☑
edit all products	☑
edit all takeout_item products	☑
edit own products	☑
edit own takeout_item products	☑

- Order Permissions

Permission	Store Administrator
uc_order module	
administer order workflow	☑
create orders	☑
delete any order	☑
delete orders	☑
edit orders	☑
view all orders	☑

If your site has employees, you may also want to create a separate role (or several roles) that do not give full control over the store for your employees. For example, you may not want an employee to be able to create or delete products, but you would like them to be able to take new orders.

Blocks

To make it easier for visitors to your site to see what they have ordered and to check out, you can enable the **Shopping Cart** block using the **Block manager**, which can be accessed by selecting **Site building** and then **Blocks**, from the Administer menu.

Block	Region	Operations
✛ Shopping cart*	Left sidebar ⌄	configure

These are the basic configuration options which need to be done after you install the module.

Building the take-out menu

Good Eatin' Goal: Create the take-out menu that visitors can order from.

Additional modules needed: Ubercart (`http://drupal.org/project/ubercart`).

Basic steps

Now that we have completed the basic configuration of the store, we can begin to add products to the store.

1. Products are added to Ubercart from the **Product manager**, which is accessed by selecting **Store administration** and then **Products** from the **Administer** menu.

2. We can now select **Manage classes**, which will allow us to define the content types that are used to build products. We will enter a new class, with the settings shown in the following screenshot:

Manage classes

[more help...]

Class ID	Name	Description	Operations

No product classes have been defined yet.

Add a class

Class ID: *

takeout_item

The machine-readable name of this content type. This text will be used for constructing the URL of the *create content* page for this content type. This name may consist only of lowercase letters, numbers, and underscores. Dashes are not allowed. Underscores will be converted into dashes when constructing the URL of the *create content* page. This name must be unique to this content type.

Class name: *

Take out Item

Description:

An item which is available for takeout or delivery.

This text describes the content type created for this product class to administrators.

Submit

3. Click **Submit** to save the new class.

4. We can now create a new **Take out Item** by clicking on **Create content** and then **Take out Item**.

5. We start by entering basic information for the take out item, including the **Name**, **SKU**, **prices**, and **shipping information**. If you will be shipping the product via a delivery service, you should enter the weight and dimensions so that Ubercart can correctly calculate shipping charges.

Create Take out Item

Name: *

Pork Dumplings

Name of the product.

▸ **Menu settings**

▾ **Product information**

SKU: *

01-01-001

Product SKU/model.

List price:	**Cost:**	**Sell price:** *
$	$	$
	1.57	4.49
The listed MSRP.	Your store's cost.	Customer purchase price.

☐ Product and its derivatives are shippable.

The SKU (stock-keeping unit) number is a number that uniquely identifies the product in your catalogue. If you have an existing catalogue, you should use that number here. If you do not already have a catalogue, you can create your own system here. Although you only need to enter the **selling price** for an item, entering the **List price** and **Cost** can help you to calculate your profit on each item.

6. You also need to enter a description off the item, as well as quantity information, as shown in the following screenshot:

In the example above, we are specifying that each order of dumplings contains six individual dumplings.

7. When you are happy with the product definition, click the **Save** button.

8. The resulting product will appear similarly to the product shown in the following screenshot:

Pork Dumplings

Take out Item *Pork Dumplings* has been created.

Submitted by admin on Sat, 09/13/2008 - 10:14

01-01-001

Delicious Pork dumplings with a fabulous soy ginger dipping sauce. 6 per order.

Price: $4.49

— ▸ CAPTCHA

[Add to cart]

» **Add new comment**   **Send to friend**

▨ **PDF version**

🖶 **$4.49**

9. To display a full catalogue of products, we will need to activate the **Catalog** module.

10. Once the catalog module has been activated, you can access the full product catalog at `yoursite.com/catalog`. If you open the catalog now, you will notice that the catalog is blank and our dumplings do not appear. This is because the catalog display depends on the **Catalog Taxonomy** being applied to the content. To allow the taxonomy to be applied to our 'take out' item type, we need to select **Content Management** and then **Taxonomy** to open the **Taxonomy manager**. Then, edit the **Catalog Taxonomy** and enable the **Take out item**, as shown in the following screenshot:

▾ Content types

Content types:

☐ Blog entry
☐ Cooking Class
☐ Directory listing
☐ Event
☐ Event CCK
☐ Image
☐ Menu Item
☐ Newsletter issue
☐ Page
☐ Poll
☑ Product
☐ Story
☑ Take out Item
☐ Webform

Select content types to categorize using this vocabulary.

---

11. Once the catalog taxonomy has been added to the **Take out item** type, we need to add new terms to the taxonomy so that the catalog can be generated. We will build terms for breakfast, lunch, dinner, and dessert. using the same techniques that we used when we built taxonomy for our menu items. The form for adding a new Breakfast term is shown in the following screenshot:

Add term to *Catalog*

[more help...]

Image:

Browse...

▾ **Identification**

Term name: *

Breakfast

The name of this term.

Description:

Items served available for breakfast at the Good Eatin' restaurant. Breakfast is served from 7:00am to 11:am daily.

A description of the term. To be displayed on taxonomy/term pages and RSS feeds.

▸ **Advanced options**

Save

You can optionally add images to each term. The images will be displayed on the catalog page, which can make for a nicer-looking catalog.

12. We can now edit our **Pork Dumpling** take-out item to add the correct taxonomy items, as shown below.

Pork Dumplings

Name: *

Pork Dumplings

Name of the product.

Catalog:

- None -
Breakfast
Desert
Dinner
Lunch

Hold Ctrl while clicking to select multiple categories.

13. The catalog can be accessed at `www.yoursite.com/catalog`. The catalog appears as follows:

```
Catalog
              Dinner                              Lunch
```

14. When a customer clicks on a category within the catalog they will see a list of all items available in that section, as shown in the following example for the Dinner category:

```
Home » Catalog

Dinner
Name ▲                                  Price   Add to cart
Pork Dumplings                          $4.49   [ Add to cart ]
```

15. To make it easier for customers to find your catalog, you should create a menu item that links to the catalog. This is done by using the **Menu manager**, and uses the same process as we used in Chapter 2. You can also activate the **Catalog block** in the **Block manager**. We will add the catalog block to the **Right sidebar**, as shown in the following example:

```
+   Catalog          [ Right sidebar ▼ ]  configure
```

The catalog block now appears as follows:

```
Catalog
  o  Dinner (1)
  o  Lunch (1)
```

Setting up a payment processor

Good Eatin' Goal: Add a payment processor to the site who will take credit card payments from your customers and transfer the payments to you.

Additional modules needed: Ubercart (`http://drupal.org/project/ubercart`).

Basic steps

Before we can allow visitors to order our products, we need to set up a payment processor so that we can accept money from our visitors over the Internet.

1. We will begin by adding the modules related to payments. Because this is only a demonstration site, we will only enable the **Test Gateway**, which allows you to test your site functionality without using actual money. We also need to enable the **Payment** module, which will allow us to accept payments. These modules are shown in the following screenshot:

2. After these modules have been enabled, we need to configure our payment settings by clicking on selecting **Store administration**, then **Configuration**, and finally **Payment settings**, from the **Administer** menu. The following settings are available:

Payment settings

☑ **Payment settings:**

- Payment tracking is enabled.
- Payments may be deleted by approved users.
- Payments are tracked in the order logs.
- Default payment details message:
  Continue with checkout to complete payment.

☑ **Payment methods:**

- Credit card is enabled for checkout.

☑ **Payment gateways:**

- Test Gateway is enabled.

Because we are only configuring a test payment gateway, we only need to be concerned with the **Payment methods** section.

3. On the **Payment methods** page you can prioritize the order in which you want to display the payment methods, if you accept more than one method. You can also configure several settings that control how the credit card information is handled and stored on your web site.

4. The first and most important section is the **Credit card data security** section. This section controls how credit card details are encrypted on your web site.

▾ **Credit card settings**

┌ Credit card data security

You are responsible for the security of your website, including the protection of credit card numbers. Please be aware that choosing some settings in this section may decrease the security of credit card data on your website and increase your liability for damages in the case of fraud.

Card number encryption key filepath:

/secure_keys

You must enable encryption by following the encryption instructions in order to accept credit card payments. In short, you must specify a path outside of your document root where the encryption key may be stored. Relative paths will be resolved relative to the Drupal installation directory. Once this is set, you should not change it.

☐ Operate in credit card debug mode.
In debug mode, credit card details may be stored in violation of PCI security standards. Debug mode is only recommended for testing transactions with fake credit card details.

You will need to specify the folder in which to store security keys. This folder should be accessible to as few users as possible. For testing purposes, you may want to select the **Operate in credit card debug mode** option, but you should remember to disable it before you begin accepting real payments.

5. The **Checkout workflow** section allows you to control whether or not credit card numbers should be validated before they are submitted to the processor, and whether or not cards should be processed when the order is submitted. Both settings should be left on unless you are testing your site.

Checkout workflow

These settings alter the way credit card data is collected and used during checkout.

☑ Validate credit card numbers at checkout.
Invalid card numbers will show an error message to the user so they can correct it.
This feature is recommended unless you are in debug mode.

☑ Attempt to process credit card payments at checkout.
Failed attempts will prevent checkout completion and display the error message from above.
This box must be checked to process customer credit cards if you are not in debug mode.

---

6. Next, you can specify the fields that must be entered when the visitor checks out.

Credit card fields

Specify what information to collect from customers in addition to the card number.

☑ Enable CVV text field on checkout form.
The CVV is an added security measure on credit cards. On Visa, Mastercard, and Discover cards it is a three digit number, and on AmEx cards it is a four digit number. If your credit card processor or payment gateway requires this information, you should enable this feature here.

☐ Enable card owner text field on checkout form.

☐ Enable card start date on checkout form.

☐ Enable card issue number text field on checkout form.

☐ Enable issuing bank text field on checkout form.

☐ Enable card type selection on checkout form.
If enabled, specify in the textarea below which card options to populate the select box with.

Card type select box options:

Visa
Mastercard
Discover
American Express

Enter one card type per line. These fields will populate the card type select box if it is enabled.

In most cases, the default settings are acceptable, unless your store experiences a large number of fraudulent transactions. If this is the case, requiring more information may reduce fraud. However, requiring too much information can make it more difficult for legitimate visitors to order from your web site.

7. Next, you can specify the types of cards that you want to accept. If your merchant account does not allow you to process specific types of cards, you will need to disable them here.

Accepted card types (for validation)

Use the checkboxes to specify which card types you accept for payment. Selected card types will show their icons in the payment method selection list and be used for card number validation.

☑ Visa

☑ Mastercard

☑ Discover

☑ American Express

---

8. Finally, you can set the messages that are to be displayed to let customers know what information they need to provide when ordering, and you can also define a failure message that is displayed if the credit card processor declines the purchase.

Customer messages

Here you can alter messages displayed to customers using credit cards.

Credit card payment policy:

Your billing information must match the billing address for the credit card entered below or we will be unable to process your payment.

Instructions for customers on the checkout page above the credit card fields.

Card processing failure message:

We were unable to process your credit card payment. Please verify your card details and try again. If the problem persists, contact us to complete your order.

Error message displayed to customers when an attempted payment fails at checkout.

---

9. When you are ready to set up your site to accept payments through a merchant account, PayPal, or another type of payment gateway, you should refer to the Ubercart documentation and your merchant account documentation for additional information.

Setting up notifications when orders are complete

Good Eatin' Goal: Ensure that the kitchen is notified when orders are submitted from customers, so that they can prepare the meal for the customer.

Additional modules needed: Ubercart (`http://drupal.org/project/ubercart`).

Basic steps

1. In order to be notified each time an order is placed, we will use **Conditional actions**. These are configured by selecting **Site configuration** and then **Conditional actions**, from the **Administer** menu.

2. As you can see from the following screenshot, there are several actions that are automatically added when you install Ubercart.

Conditional actions

[more help...]

Trigger: Customer completes checkout

Title	Class	Status	Weight	Operations
Email customer on checkout	order	Enabled	0	**edit**

Trigger: A payment gets entered for an order

Title	Class	Status	Weight	Operations
Ask for more money.	payment	Disabled	0	**edit**
Update order status on full payment	payment	Enabled	0	**edit**
Update order status on completed checkout of non-shippable items	payment	Enabled	1	**edit**

Trigger: Order status gets updated

Title	Class	Status	Weight	Operations
Email order update	order	Enabled	0	**edit**

Add a predicate

3. To add a new action, click on the **Add a predicate** link. This will open a form as shown below, which allows you to define the trigger for the action as well as a name for the action.

Conditional actions

[more help...]

Title: *
Send order to kitchen
Enter a title used for display on the overview tables.

Trigger: *
Customer completes checkout
Select the trigger for this predicate.
Cannot be modified if the predicate has conditions or actions.

Description:
Sends a copy of the order to the kitchen so they can begin preparing the order for pickup.
Enter a description that summarizes the use and intent of the predicate.

Class:
custom:
Classes let you categorize your predicates based on the type of functionality they provide.
Cannot be modified if defined by a module.

Status:

⦿ Enabled

○ Disabled

Disabled predicates will not be processed when their trigger is pulled.

Weight:
0
Predicates will be sorted by weight and processed sequentially.

Save predicate   Cancel

Enter the required information for your action, and click **Save predicate**.

4. You can now add additional conditions to the predicate, to refine the criteria for triggering the action. In our case, no additional refinement is necessary.

5. We can now generate the actions that we want to occur, by clicking on the **Actions** tab. This will display a list of possible actions that can be executed. In our case, the **Send an order email** action is what we want.

6. After you have selected the **Send an order email** action, click **Add action** and you will be prompted to configure the action. The action allows you to customize who the email should be sent to. In our case, we want the email to be sent to our kitchen staff. We will also customize the text of the email to give them additional information about the order. The information in brackets [ ] will be replaced with information from the actual order before the email is sent. You can view a full list of the possible replacement patterns by expanding the **Replacement patterns** section.

Send order to kitchen

Action added.

Actions

These actions will be performed in order when this predicate passes the conditions evaluation.

▾ **Action: Send an order email**

Title:

Send an order email

▸ **Arguments**

Sender: *

admin@drupalbyexample.com

The "From" address.

Recipients: *

kitchen@goodeatin.drupalbyexample.com

Enter the email addresses to receive the notifications, one on each line. You may use order tokens for dynamic email addresses.

Subject: *

New online order placed

Message:

A new order has been placed on the website. By [order-first-name] [order-last-name]. Full details of the order are available at: [order-url].

▸ **Input format**

▸ **Replacement patterns**

[Remove this action]

Available actions:

Display a message to the user ▾

[Add action]

[Save changes]

7. Click **Save changes** when you are satisfied with your email message. Drupal will now automatically send a notification email to the kitchen whenever a new order is placed.

Example order

Good Eatin' Goal: Walk through the purchase process from the perspective of a customer.

Additional modules needed: Ubercart (`http://drupal.org/project/ubercart`).

Basic steps

1. You can either provide a link to the **Catalog** page or you can provide a custom view or menu links to the product pages for the visitor to select from.

2. When the visitor finds a product that they want to order, they can add the item to the cart by clicking on the **Add to cart** button.

3. The selected items will then appear in the **Shopping cart**, where the customer can either increase the quantity that they they want to purchase of an item, or remove the item from the cart.

4. Once the customer is happy with their order, they will click **Checkout** to proceed with the purchase.

5. A summary of the order will be displayed and the customer can enter their billing information.

The customer will also need to enter their credit card information for the order.

6. When the customer is happy with the information they have provided, they will click the **Review order** button. At this point, Ubercart will validate the credit card details and display the order to the customer, for review.

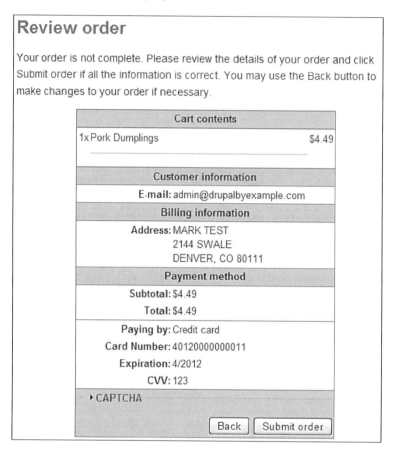

7. If the user is sure that the information is correct, they will click the **Submit order** button to finish processing the order.

8. After the order is complete, the user will be notified and the order will appear in the list of orders.

9. You can check for any pending orders by selecting **Store administration** and then **Orders**, from the **Administer** menu. All active orders will also be displayed for your review.

10. You can view the order by clicking on the **View** icon which is the leftmost icon under **Actions**, as shown above. This will display the order as shown in the following screenshot:

11. There are also several other views that you can use. If you accept partial payments for an order, you can use the **Payments** tab to enter each instalment.

Summary

In this chapter, we have truly integrated the web site into our business by allowing users to order from our menu and place orders from the site. You can apply many of the same techniques to your own site to make the most of your web site.

For more information about running an online store with Drupal, check out *Drupal e-Commerce* by Michael Peacock, also published by Packt: `http://www.packtpub.com/drupal-ecommerce/book`.

In the next chapter, we will discuss essential tasks for administering your web site and ensuring that your site stays up-to-date. We will cover backups, installing updates to Drupal, and third party modules, along with moderating content.

10
Keeping a Clean Kitchen

Now that we have built our site and integrated it into our business, we need to ensure that our site stays clean and up-to-date. In this chapter, we will explore various maintenance tasks to keep our site operating at peak performance.

We will begin by discussing how to back up our web site and then restore it again, to protect it against hardware failures or malicious users. Next, we will discuss performance tuning to ensure that your site can meet any level of traffic demand. Finally, we will review managing and moderating content.

At the end of this chapter, you will be prepared to publish your web site to the world, knowing that you are prepared for anything.

Web site backups

A strong backup plan is critical for any successful web site. A good backup plan will protect against hardware failure, allow you to transfer your web site to another host, and allow you to recover from malicious hacking into your web site.

When you create a backup plan, you should also test the restoration from this backup to make sure that the backup works correctly.

In this section, we will explore ways of performing backups regardless of the host that you are using. Your hosting provider may also offer a solution that will back up files and databases either one time, or on a recurring basis. If your host does provide backup capabilities, you should review them to see if they suit your needs completely, or if you want to augment them or replace them with the techniques in this section.

Manually backing up a site

Good Eatin' Goal: Back up the web site without using a custom backup module.

Additional modules needed: None.

Basic steps

If you do not want to use a dedicated module to perform your backups, you can manually download the files and the database information that make up the site. However, this can be more time-intensive and error-prone than using a custom backup module.

A manual backup has two steps, in which you must first back up the files that make up the site and then back up the database information.

To back up the files for the web site, use the following procedure:

1. Begin by opening the utility that you use to transfer files to the web site. This could be an FTP client, or an online file manager. My favorite FTP client is **FileZilla**, which is a freely-available open source client. The FileZilla client can be downloaded from `http://filezilla-project.org/`.

2. Select the backup location on your local computer to which you want to copy the files, and select the root directory of your web server as the remote directory. You may want to date the backup folder so that you can maintain a history of the site.

3. Next, download the files to your local directory. If you want, you can compress the files into a ZIP file or a compressed archive.

4. To reduce the amount of data that you need to download, you should be able to download just the `sites` directory, because that folder contains all of the custom files, pictures, themes, and modules that you have added to the site, assuming that you have followed all of the guidelines in this book.

To back up the database information, you can use your web site provider's database management utility. Many hosts provide **phpMyAdmin** for this purpose. If you are unsure whether or not your host gives you access to phpMyAdmin, you can contact their customer support group to check.

1. Begin by opening **phpMyAdmin** and selecting the database that has your site information within it. The screen should be similar to the following:

2. If you have multiple databases available on the host, you may need to select the database that you want to work with in the drop-down list at the upper left corner of the screen.

3. Next, select the **Export** tab at the top of the screen. phpMyAdmin will prompt you to select the tables that you want to download and the format that you want to download in, as shown in the following screenshot:

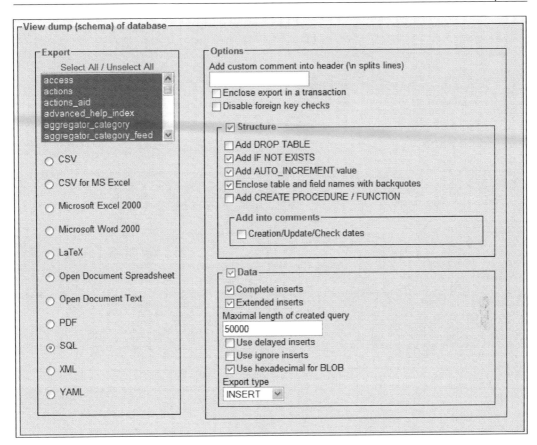

4. If you want to be able to rebuild the database at a later time, you should export all the tables in SQL format.

5. Next, you will need to specify the name of the file to download to. You can use ___DB___ as the database name.

You may want to zip the file to reduce storage space.

6. Then click **Go** to begin the download process. You will be prompted for the location to which you want to save the exported data.

When you are ready to restore the web site from backup, you simply reverse the process.

1. You should always import into a blank database, to avoid conflicts with existing data. You can either drop or delete all of the titles in the existing database, or you can create a new database to import the data into.

2. After you have cleaned out your database, select the **Import** tab in phpMyAdmin.

3. Now navigate to the file that you exported earlier, and click **Go** to begin the import. You may need to delete all of the tables in the database before you import the data, depending on the options you chose when you exported the data.

4. To reload the files, simply open your FTP client, select the same directories that you used when creating the backup and then upload the files, rather than downloading them.

Automatic site backups

Good Eatin' Goal: Back up a web site so that it can be stored for easy recovery.

Additional modules needed: Backup and Migrate (`http://drupal.org/project/backup_migrate`).

Basic steps

Although you can manually back up your files and database, this process can be time-consuming and error prone. Luckily, the **Backup and Migrate** module makes this process easier, and optimizes the backups to exclude unnecessary data.

1. Begin by downloading and installing the **Back up** and **Migrate** module.

2. You can now back up your data by selecting **Content management** and then **Backup and migrate**, from the **Administer** menu.

3. The **Backup and Migrate** module allows you to fully customize the backup files that are created. You can control which tables are included in the backup, and whether or not the data in the table is backed up. By default, the **Backup and Migrate** module does not back up cache information, session information, or watchdog information, because data in these tables is temporary and can easily be re-created.

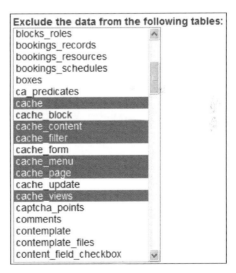

4. There are a variety of other options that you can choose from, which control how the resulting file is named, how it is compressed, and where it is compressed to.

Backup file name:

[site-name][site-date]

‣ Replacement patterns

Compression:

⦿ None
○ GZip
○ Zip

Destination:

⦿ Download
○ Save to Files Directory

☑ Append a timestamp.

Timestamp format:

Y-m-d\TH-i-s

Should be a PHP date() format string.

☑ Save these settings.

Backup Database

5. Once you have set the options as desired, click **Backup Database** to begin the backup process. If you have selected the **Download** option, the file will be sent to your computer so that you can store it. If you select the **Save to Files Directory** option, the backup file will be saved onto the server so that you can download it later, either directly from the server or using the **Saved Backups** tab.

| Backup/Export DB | Restore/Import DB | Saved Backups | Backup Schedule |

Manual Backups   Scheduled Backups

Backup and Migrate

[more help...]

GoodEatinThu09252008-2300.sql.zip 09/25/2008 11:00 pm 153.8 KB download restore delete

6. If you would like the **Backup and Migrate** module to back up your database automatically on a regular basis, you can schedule the back up to occur at specified intervals by clicking on the **Backup Schedule** tab, as shown here:

Backup/Export DB	Restore/Import DB	Saved Backups	**Backup Schedule**

Backup and Migrate

[more help...]

Backup every:

```
12
```
Hour(s)

Use 0 for no scheduled backup. Cron must be configured to run for backups to work.

Number of Backup files to keep:

```
6
```

The number of backup files to keep before deleting old ones. Use 0 to never delete backups

[Save configuration] [Reset to defaults]

Please note that the backups created by the **Backup and Migrate** module do not include the files from the site, so you will still need to back up these files independently. You can minimize the backup file size by only backing up the files that the users can upload. These files are typically stored in the `files` directory. The process for backing up files is identical to the process used in the section on manual backups.

Restoring a site from a backup

Good Eatin' Goal: Restore information from a backup file created by the Backup and Migrate module.

Additional modules needed: Backup and Migrate (`http://drupal.org/project/ backup_migrate`).

Basic steps

Restoring a backup created by the **Backup and Migrate** module is a simple process.

1. Navigate to the **Backup and Migrate manager** by selecting **Content management** and then **Backup and Migrate**, from the **Administer** menu.

2. Next, click on the **Restore/Import DB** tab.

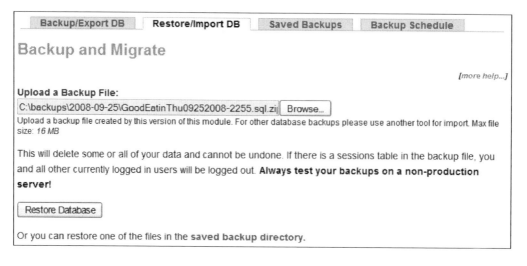

3. Navigate to the location of your backup file.

4. After you have selected the backup file, click on **Restore Database** to begin the restore process. Please read all displayed warnings carefully, and make sure that you test the import on a test installation for your site before running it on your production site. If you are sure that you want to proceed with the import, agree to the confirmation and click **restore**.

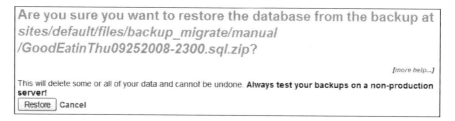

5. You may also need to import any saved files, if the server file system is not fully up-to-date. We discussed this previously in the section on manual backups.

Web site optimization

If your web site has a moderate to large number of visitors, you should tune your web site for maximum performance. This will ensure that all your visitors have a positive experience, and are not frustrated by delays in loading pages or accessing the web site.

We will discuss ways to optimize both the back end database, and the front end of the web site that displays the information to the visitor.

Optimizing the database tables

Good Eatin' Goal: Optimize the database where your site content is stored, to ensure the best possible performance.

Additional modules needed: DB Maintenance (`http://drupal.org/project/db_maintenance`).

Basic steps

When a database is used as frequently as the Drupal database is, it can become less optimized over time, because having a large number of records inserted and deleted from each table can result in the database having wasted space. All databases will allow you to run an optimization process that removes unused space and rebuilds the indexes to make the search for information faster.

The **DB Maintenance** module can automatically perform the optimization process for you when cron is run.

1. Begin by downloading and installing the **DB Maintenance** module.

2. You can edit the settings for the **DB Maintenance** module by selecting **Site configuration** and then **DB maintenance**, from the **Administer** menu.

3. The settings allow you to control several options, including:

    a) Whether or not to write to the log when each optimization is performed.

DB maintenance

Executes an optimization query on database tables during cron runs.

[more help...]

[more help...]

☐ Log OPTIMIZE queries
If enabled, a watchdog entry will be made each time tables are optimized, containing information which tables were involved.

---

b) How often the tables are optimized, with options from hourly to bi-monthly, or at each cron run.

c) Finally, you can control which tables are optimized. This allows you to not optimize tables that do not change frequently, which will allow the maintenance task to complete faster.

Once you have configured the settings properly, you simply save the settings, and the **DB maintenance** module will automatically perform the optimization at the specified intervals.

Using caching to improve performance

Good Eatin' Goal: Use caching to improve the performance of content display.

Additional modules needed: None.

Basic steps

Because dynamically-generated pages, such as those created with Drupal, can be time-consuming and resource-intensive to generate. Drupal uses a sophisticated caching mechanism to pre-load sections of content for display to users.

To set up the Drupal cache, carry out the following steps:

1. Access the settings for the Drupal cache by selecting **Site configuration** and then **Performance**, from the **Administer** menu.

2. The first section of settings relate to the **Page cache**, which is used to cache entire pages of data. The **Page cache** system will only cache pages for anonymous users, to prevent personal data for one user being made visible to other users, and also because it is simpler to ensure that the pages are successfully cached only if anonymous users are served cached content.

Page cache

Enabling the page cache will offer a significant performance boost. Drupal can store and send compressed cached pages requested by *anonymous* users. By caching a web page, Drupal does not have to construct the page each time it is viewed.

Caching mode:

○ Disabled

◉ Normal (recommended for production sites, no side effects)

○ Aggressive (experts only, possible side effects)

The normal cache mode is suitable for most sites and does not cause any side effects. The aggressive cache mode causes Drupal to skip the loading (boot) and unloading (exit) of enabled modules when serving a cached page. This results in an additional performance boost but can cause unwanted side effects.

The following enabled modules are incompatible with aggressive mode caching and will not function properly: *poormanscron, uc_cart, uc_store*.

Most sites should enable **Normal** caching as this can significantly improve load times for your visitors without any possibility of adverse side effects.

3. If you choose to use **Aggressive** site caching, you need to be aware of any modules that may have problems. Drupal will identify these modules for you and highlight them in red. You should only enable the **Aggressive** cache if there are no potential incompatibilities, or if the module maintainer of a potentially incompatible module states that the module is acceptable for use with Aggressive caching. Some modules are not compatible with Aggressive mode due to the initialization or cleanup code that is run when a page is loaded normally, but not when it has been aggressively cached.

4. If your site is exceptionally busy, you may want to enforce a minimum cache lifetime, which is the minimum amount of time that Drupal will wait for, before rebuilding cached pages. If your site receives infrequent updates, you may see a performance benefit by increasing this number to match your update schedule.

Minimum cache lifetime:

5 min

On high-traffic sites, it may be necessary to enforce a minimum cache lifetime. The minimum cache lifetime is the minimum amount of time that will elapse before the cache is emptied and recreated, and is applied to both page and block caches. A larger minimum cache lifetime offers better performance, but users will not see new content for a longer period of time.

5. The **Page compression** controls whether or not the cached pages are compressed. This can be left as **Enabled** unless your web server automatically caches all web pages.

Page compression:

○ Disabled

◉ Enabled

By default, Drupal compresses the pages it caches in order to save bandwidth and improve download times. This option should be disabled when using a webserver that performs compression.

---

6. Drupal also provides a **Block cache**, which caches just the content of the blocks rather than the entire page. Unlike the page cache, the block cache works for both anonymous users as well as users who have logged into the site.

Block cache

Enabling the block cache can offer a performance increase for all users by preventing blocks from being reconstructed on each page load. If the page cache is also enabled, performance increases from enabling the block cache will mainly benefit authenticated users.

Block cache:

○ Disabled

◉ Enabled (recommended)

Note that block caching is inactive when modules defining content access restrictions are enabled.

---

7. The final type of optimization provided by Drupal relates to minimizing the amount of content that is sent to the user, by combining the CSS files and JavaScript files created by each module into a single CSS file and a single JavaScript file, which can be downloaded once by the user. These options are disabled if you are using the private filesystem. If you want to make use of these options, you will need to use the public filesystem on your site.

Bandwidth optimizations

Drupal can automatically optimize external resources like CSS and JavaScript, which can reduce both the size and number of requests made to your website. CSS files can be aggregated and compressed into a single file, while JavaScript files are aggregated (but not compressed). These optional optimizations may reduce server load, bandwidth requirements, and page loading times.

These options are disabled if you have not set up your files directory, or if your download method is set to private.

Optimize CSS files:

◉ Disabled

○ Enabled

This option can interfere with theme development and should only be enabled in a production environment.

Optimize JavaScript files:

◉ Disabled

○ Enabled

This option can interfere with module development and should only be enabled in a production environment.

8. Although Drupal caching makes your site faster and gives users a better experience, it can interfere with your development of the web site because the cache may prevent you from seeing the most recent changes to your site. If this is the case, you can clear the cached data by clicking on the **Clear cached data** button.

Clear cached data

Caching data improves performance, but may cause problems while troubleshooting new modules, themes, or translations, if outdated information has been cached. To refresh all cached data on your site, click the button below. *Warning: high-traffic sites will experience performance slowdowns while cached data is rebuilt.*

[Clear cached data]

Maintaining content

As you continue to add content to your web site, you will need to ensure that your content is properly moderated, that old content is removed, and that changes to web site content are tracked.

Creating content revisions

Good Eatin' Goal: Create revisions of content to ensure that you have a complete record of changes to your web site's content.

Additional modules needed: None.

Basic steps

Throughout this book, we have simply updated our pages as necessary to add new functionality and content. However, if you have many editors, content that changes frequently, a need to view the history of a page, or need the ability to easily return to an old version of a page, you will want to store multiple revisions of your pages.

To do this, carry out the following steps:

1. Edit the content for which you want to create a new revision.

2. Make the changes as needed and, before saving, expand the **Revision information** section.

▼ Revision information

☑ Create new revision

Log message:

Modified to add information about new redecoration.

An explanation of the additions or updates being made to help other authors understand your motivations.

---

3. Select the **Create new revision** option and enter a message describing the changes that you have made to the node.

4. When you save the content, you will see a new tab called **Revisions**. Clicking on this tab will show you a list of all of the revisions that have been created for the page.

5. If you would like to return to an older version of the page, you can click the **revert** link. Or, if you want to remove an older revision, you can click the **delete** link to get rid of it permanently.

6. You can control which users have access to the revision system by using the **Permissions Manager**. Drupal allows you to control which users can: view revisions, revert revisions, and delete revisions.

7. If you want to force users to always create new revisions when editing content, edit the content type and then expand the **Workflow settings**.

8. Change the default options to select the **Create new revision** option. When editors change content, the **Create new revision** option will be selected by default, and they will not be able to change the option unless they have the administer nodes permission.

9. If you want to approve all revisions before publication, you can deselect the **Published** checkbox.

Comparing content revisions

Good Eatin' Goal: Compare the text of two different revisions of a page.

Additional modules needed: Diff (`http://drupal.org/project/diff`).

Basic steps

Although the built-in functionality for creating revisions in Drupal works perfectly well, it can be difficult to review the changes that were made in each revision. The **Diff** module makes comparing revisions very easy.

1. Begin by installing and activating the **Diff** module.

2. To use the **Diff** module, simply view the revisions for any page. You will notice that the **Revisions** list has changed to allow you to select the revisions to be compared.

3. Select the revisions to compare and then click on the **Show diff** button. Drupal will then display information about the text that has been changed, added, or deleted.

Moderate content

Good Eatin' Goal: Find questionable or offensive content, and remove it from your site, easily.

Additional modules needed: Modr8 (`http://drupal.org/project/modr8`).

Basic steps

An unfortunate side effect of having a web site on the Internet is that, at some point, a malicious user will attempt to post inappropriate content on your site. If your site is extremely busy, you may find yourself with a large amount of content to review and approve.

The **Modr8** module can help you manage the workload and can send emails to users letting them know when their content has been approved or rejected.

1. Begin by installing and activating the **Modr8** module.

2. The settings for the **Modr8** module can be accessed by selecting **Site configuration** and then **Modr8**, from the **Administer** menu.

3. The basic settings control how often logs are removed. Alternatively, you can choose to keep the logs forever. You can also change the number of items in the moderation queue to be displayed at a time, as well as the default action for the content that requires moderation.

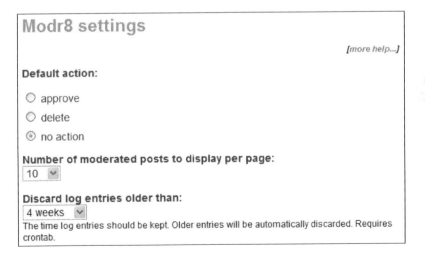

4. You can also configure the email settings for the moderation queue, including the text of the emails, and whether or not emails should be sent to the user who posted the content when their content is approved and/or when their content is rejected. You can also choose to send an email if the moderator does not take action for the item and wants to send a note to the author.

```
┌─ E-mail ──────────────────────────────────────────────────────────┐
│                                                                    │
│  Moderator email adress:                                           │
│  ┌──────────────────────────────────────────────────────────────┐ │
│  │moderater@drupalbyexample.com                                   │ │
│  └──────────────────────────────────────────────────────────────┘ │
│  E-mail notices sent by modr8 will have this as the "From" address.│
│  Leave empty to use same "From" address as is used for user        │
│  registration other administrative notices as set at Site          │
│  information.                                                      │
│                                                                    │
│  ☐ Send approval messages                                          │
│                                                                    │
│  Acceptance e-mail subject:                                        │
│  ┌──────────────────────────────────────────────────────────────┐ │
│  │[%site] %title has been approved                                │ │
│  └──────────────────────────────────────────────────────────────┘ │
│                                                                    │
│  Acceptance e-mail:                                                │
│  ┌──────────────────────────────────────────────────────────────┐ │
│  │Your %type entry entitled "%title" has been approved by our   ▲│ │
│  │content moderator! Other visitors to %site will now be able   ▓│ │
│  │to view it.                                                   ▓│ │
│  │                                                              ▓│ │
│  │You can visit %node_url to view it yourself.                  ▓│ │
│  │                                                               │ │
│  │%note                                                         ▼│ │
│  └──────────────────────────────────────────────────────────────┘ │
│  Replacement strings are: %title, %teaser, %body, %short_date,     │
│  %medium_date, %long_date, %type, %node_url, %nid, %author_name,   │
│  %author_mail, %author_url, %site, %note                           │
└────────────────────────────────────────────────────────────────────┘
```

5. If you would like new content to be added to the moderation queue automatically, you can edit the content type and select the **In moderation queue** setting in the workflow section.

6. To view the moderation queue, select **Content management** and then **Moderated content**, from the **Administer** menu.

7. The moderation queue appears as follows:

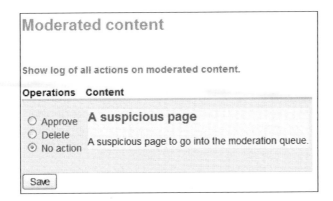

8. From this page, you can approve, delete, or defer action on any content that needs moderation. After you make your changes, click **Save** to complete your selections. You can also display a log of all the moderation actions, by clicking on **Reports** and then **Content moderation log**. The moderation log appears as follows:

Allowing users to report questionable or offensive content.

Good Eatin' Goal: Get feedback from users to learn what they find offensive so the objectionable content can be removed.

Additional modules needed: Abuse (`http://drupal.org/project/abuse`).

Basic steps

In the last task, we reviewed methods that allowed you to moderate every piece of content that is added to the site. However, this can be a time-intensive task if the proportion of content that you receive that is questionable is low. If this is the case, you can allow your users to help you to moderate the content by using the **Abuse** module, to let them report items that they find offensive.

This strategy has a couple of advantages. Firstly, you are freed from the maintenance of pre-approving all content before it is published. Secondly, it ensures that the content meets community standards, rather than placing you or your editors in charge of defining community standards.

The **Abuse** module also has a **Watchlist** component that allows you to flag content as suspicious or banned, and automatically move them into a queue for review by an administrator.

1. Begin by downloading and installing the **Abuse** and **Watchlist** modules, both of which are included in the **Abuse** installation.

2. We will begin by editing the **Watchlist** settings, which can be accessed by selecting **Site configuration** and then **Watchlist settings**, from the **Administer** menu.

Watchlist settings

[more help...]

▸ Test out watchlist word settings

▾ Watchlist word settings

These words fall in a grey area of being good or bad. Content found with these words will be flagged into the pending pile (and into a hidden pile if premoderation is allowed on the content type)

Watch list:

The watch list, one per line. Do not use empty line breaks.

▾ Filtered/banned word settings

These words will enable content to be automatically hidden from the site and, if allowed back on site, filters the banned words

Filtered/banned word list:

The banned word list, one per line. Do not use empty line breaks.

Replacement string:

****

String to replace banned words with

---

3. You can include any words that you want to, in the **Watch list** and **Filtered/banned word list**, depending on your target audience and your site's needs; just make sure that you enter one word per line. Items on the **Watch list** can be viewed while they are in the review queue, and items on the **Filtered/banned word list** will be hidden until they are reviewed.

4. You can also control which items are automatically added to the **Watch list** or banned list, based on the **Watchlist word settings** configured above.

▼ Enable moderation from the watchlist and banned list for these content types

Content gets flagged into a pending pile (users can still view item) if a match is found in the watchlist. Content gets flagged into hidden pile (hidden from users) if a match is from from the bannedlist. Users will only be validated against banned words.

☐ webform

☑ blog

☐ poll

☐ dir_listing

☐ image

☐ product

5. You can also force moderation for specific types if they are more prone to abuse.

▼ Enable pre-moderation from the watchlist and banned list for these content types

Content gets flagged regardless of abuse module setting.

☐ webform

☐ blog

☐ poll

☐ dir_listing

☑ image

6. We can now modify the **Abuse Moderation settings** by selecting **Site configuration** and then **Abuse Moderation settings**, from the **Administer** menu.

7.   The first setting controls what content types are subject to abuse reports.

Abuse Moderation settings

[more help...]

Reasons:
You can configure the list of reasons at Reason configuration settings

▾ Enable flagging for these content types

☐ webform

☑ blog

☐ poll

☐ dir_listing

☑ image

8.   The next section of controls how abuse tickets are to be handled by your moderators.

▾ Ticketing settings

☑ Abuse Assigned Moderators
Select this option if you have a pool of moderators and you wish to assign each one a certain number of tickets to work with.

Moderator queue limit:
20
This field is to set a maximum limit on the number of flagged items that will be added to the queue of a moderator

Reset assigned ticket items (Please type hour of day):
0

If you have multiple moderators for your site, you can select the **Abuse Assigned Moderators** option. If you use this, you will also need to store the maximum number of items that have been flagged for abuse that are added to the moderator's queue. If moderators live in different time zones, you can set an hour of the day at which all moderation queues are cleared, so that items do not remain in the moderation queue for an overly-long period of time.

9. Finally, you can configure the settings related to all of the items that have been flagged as abusive by a user.

Settings for all abuse content

These settings apply to all content that is allowed to be flagged into the abuse administration system

Abuse threshold: *

    3

Warning subject: *

    Abuse warning

Warning body: *

    This item has been flagged for review by an administrator. If you feel that the item does not meet site standards, please flag it for review as well.

Warning BCC:

Abuse form intro text:

The **Abuse threshold** controls how many complaints must be registered for an item before it is moved into the moderation queue. 3 is a good number to start with, but you may want to increase or decrease the threshold depending on the needs of your site.

10. You can edit the reasons for flagging an item for abuse by selecting **Site configuration**, then **Abuse Moderation** settings, and finally **Abuse Moderation reasons**, from the **Administer** menu.

Abuse Moderation reasons

[more help...]

▸ Add new reason

Current list of reasons - check items that you wish to remove

foul language

☐ Remove from of list of reasons

Edit reason

Description: The user wrote very mean things

Email content:

Please refrain from writing such mean things

All available reasons will be listed on the page using a format similar to the example above. You can add new reasons, remove reasons, or change the text for reasons from this page.

11. Before the **abuse module** is activated, you need to assign permissions to users, so that they can flag content for review.

Permission	anonymous user	authenticated user	blogger	Store Administrator
abuse module				
administer abuse reports	☐	☐	☐	☐
administer all abuse reports	☐	☐	☐	☐
configure abuse administration settings	☐	☐	☐	☐
direct flag	☐	☐	☐	☐
report abuse	☐	☐	☐	☐

12. Content that has the **abuse module** activated will have a new **Flag as offensive** link added to it, as shown in the following screenshot:

Good Eatin' Website

Submitted by admin on Thu, 07/10/2008 - 23:24

We've been working hard on our new website which has a new look and tons of new functionality. Please let us know what you think of the site by posting a comment here.

» **admin's blog**   **Login** or **register** to post comments   **Flag as offensive**

---

13. When the user clicks on the **Flag as offensive** link, he or she will be presented with a form where he or she can specify their contact information, and a reason why he or she believes that the content is offensive.

Flag

from: *

email: *

about:
Good Eatin' Website

reason: *

message:

[send] [cancel]

---

14. Administrators can review content that has been flagged as offensive by clicking on **Content management** and then **Moderate**.

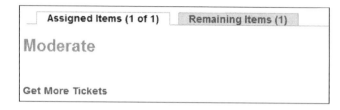

15. The administrators can click on the **Get More Tickets** link to have additional items assigned to them.

16. Once a ticket has been assigned to them, the administrator can view information about the user who submitted the content as well as the user who flagged the content, and choose what action to take for the content.

By: admin
Email:
admin@drupalbyexample.com
Age:
Offences:
　0
Warnings:
　0
　Edit Account　View Account History
allowremovewarn and allowwarn and remove
　▸ Allow content on site?
　▸ Remove content from site?
　▸ Warn and Allow
　▸ Warn and Remove

The administrator can either allow the content, or remove the content from the web site. The administrator can also optionally send a warning to the user without further action.

Upgrading to new versions of Drupal

One of the fantastic things about Drupal is that it is constantly evolving to offer new and improved functionalities. However, this requires you to regularly check for updates to Drupal and any contributed modules that are installed.

In this section, we will discuss how to find updates, test them, and install them onto your site.

There are two types of updates that you will encounter. Minor updates will correct security issues or problems found by users, and may have minimal functionality enhancements. A major update will typically have much more functionality, and may be incompatible with the previous versions.

The version number for Drupal contains two numbers separated by periods. For example, version 6.5 indicates major version 6 and minor version 5.

A custom module will begin with the version of Drupal it is compatible with, followed by a major and minor version for the module itself. If a module is compatible with all of the minor releases of a Drupal major release, the minor version will be represented by an x. For example, `version 6.x-1.5` indicates that the module is compatible with any version of Drupal 6, and that the major version of the module is 1 and its minor version is 5. A module may also indicate development versions by adding `-dev` to the end of the version, a beta version by adding `-beta1`, or a release candidate by adding `-rc1` after the version. Multiple beta and release candidates are indicated by incrementing the numbers after `beta` or `rc`, respectively.

Checking for new updates to Drupal and modules

Good Eatin' Goal: Ensure that we are using the latest versions of Drupal and the contributed modules that the site uses.

Additional modules needed: None (core).

Basic steps

Drupal 6 and later makes it easy to check for updates to Drupal and the modules that you have installed. By default, Drupal will check for updates to the system each time that cron is run.

You can check the current status of the system by selecting **Reports** and then **Available updates**, from the **Administer** menu. Drupal will also display a warning when you navigate to any administration page, if it has detected that Drupal, or some related content, is outdated.

Available updates

Here you can find information about available updates for your installed modules and themes. Note that each module or theme is part of a "project", which may or may not have the same name, and might include multiple modules or themes within it.

To extend the functionality or to change the look of your site, a number of contributed modules and themes are available.

[more help...]

Last checked: 0 sec ago   (**Check manually**)
Drupal core

Drupal 6.4	Up to date ✓

Includes: *Aggregator, Block, Blog, Color, Comment, Database logging, Filter, Help, Menu, Node, Path, Poll, System, Taxonomy, Trigger, Update status, Upload, User*

Modules

abuse 6.x-1.x-dev (2008-Aug-01)	Up to date ✓

Includes: *abuse, watchlist*

If you want to, you can click on the **Check manually** link to ensure that all modules are up-to-date.

If any modules are outdated, they will be shown as follows.

Calendar 6.x-2.0-beta3		Update available ⊗
Recommended version:	6.x-2.0-rc2 (2008-Sep-15)	Download Release notes
Includes: *Calendar*		

The display includes the version that you have currently installed, the recommended version that should be installed, a link to download a new version, and a link to the release notes for the new version. The **Release notes** will include a list of changes that have been made to the module. In the next few tasks, we will discuss upgrading your installation.

Upgrading minor releases

Good Eatin' Goal: Upgrade between minor versions.

Additional modules needed: None (core).

Basic steps

When Drupal detects that a new version of Drupal is available, it will inform you as mentioned earlier.

1. Before you download and install the new version, you should read all of the release notes for the new version, to determine if there are any potential incompatibilities with the other modules that you have installed.

2. If you do not see any potential issues based on the release notes, you can begin testing the new version yourself.

3. Before installing the new version, make a complete backup of your site including all of the files and the database.

4. You should test the new version on a non-production test site, before installing it on your live site. If you do not have a test site set up yet, you can create a test site on your local computer, in a different location on your web host, or on another web host. If you choose to have the test web site hosted at a web host, you should make sure that it is not publicly accessible to visitors. This will help to ensure that your visitors are not directed to the wrong version of your site through search engines.

5. Open the update page of your site, which is available at `http://yoursite.com/update.php`. In order to reach this page, you must be logged in using the administration account, which is the first user you created.

6. If your test site is not available to the public, you do not need to worry about putting the site into **maintenance mode**.

7. Install the module into the test version of your site by copying the files to the server.

8. Click the **Continue** button on the **Update** page.

9. Drupal will then display a list of modules where the database tables need to be updated. By default, Drupal will select the correct version to upgrade to.

Drupal database update

The version of Drupal you are updating from has been automatically detected. You can select a different version, but you should not need to.

Click Update to start the update process.

▽   Select versions

system module:
`6047`

simplenews module:
`6004`

webform module:
`No updates available`

comment module:
`No updates available`

---

10. In most cases, you will want to use the version that Drupal selects, but you can override the version selected if needed.

11. When you have selected the version you want to upgrade to, click the **Update** button.

12. Drupal will now run all of the updates and display the results with links back to your site.

13. Once the installation is complete, you should test your web site to ensure that it is still functioning correctly, and that all of the functionality related to the update is running properly.

14. Assuming that all functionality works correctly for you, and you do not detect any incompatibilities, you can use the same steps on your live site to install the updates in production. If you do detect any incompatibilities, please report the problems that you found on the Drupal site so that they can be corrected as quickly as possible. When reporting issues, make sure that you give a full description of the problem that you are having, the version it is related to, and, if appropriate, a list of the other modules installed on your site.

Upgrading to a new major release

Good Eatin' Goal: Upgrade to a new major release of Drupal.

Additional modules needed: None (core).

Basic steps

The process of upgrading Drupal to a new major release can be a non-trivial process, which you will want to undertake carefully.

1. Begin by verifying that the contributed modules you use have been upgraded to be compatible with the latest release of Drupal. This can be done by checking the project page for the module on the `Drupal.org` web site.

2. If a module has not been ported to the latest version of Drupal, you can search for a suitable replacement, wait until the module has been upgraded, or remove the functionality provided by the module from your site. It may take several months after the latest version of Drupal is released for production usage for the maintainers to port the module. You can contact the maintainer to see if they have a schedule for development, or to see if you can contribute to help cover development costs.

3. Once all of the modules that you have installed are available for update, you can begin the actual installation process. As before, you should test the installation process on a test site before doing it on the production site, to ensure that you don't encounter problems.

4. If you are upgrading a live site, put your site into maintenance mode by selecting **Site configuration** and then **Site maintenance**, from the **Administer** menu.

Change the status to **Off-line** and then click the **Save configuration** button.

5. Make a complete backup of the files and the database tables that comprise your site.

6. Disable all custom modules that you have installed. This will allow you to upgrade them later.

7. Switch to a default theme installed with the Drupal core installation.

8. Upload the new Drupal files to your site.

9. Run the upgrade page at `http://yoursite.com/update.php`, as described in the previous task.

10. Download and install the custom modules for your site.

11. Download and install your site theme(s).

12. Run the upgrade script again.

13. Back up the following files, and then remove them from your site.

    a) `install.php`

    b) `CHANGELOG.txt`

    c) `INSTALL.txt`

    d) `INSTALL.mysql.txt`

    e) `INSTALL.pgsql.txt`

    f) `LICENSE.txt`

    g) `MAINTAINERS.txt`

    h) `UPGRADE.txt`

14. Test your site to ensure that all of the functionalities are working properly.

15. If your site is working properly, you can either repeat the steps on your live site, or copy the test site to the live site.

16. If any functionality is not working properly, you can try the upgrade process again using your backup, or contact the maintainers of the functionality that is not working, so that they can help you to resolve any issues.

Summary

In this chapter, we have reviewed a number of tasks that happen behind the scenes, in order to give your visitors the best possible experience, and to ensure that your web site operates at peak performance even if you are confronted with hardware failures or other unforeseen events. We have also discussed ways of managing your content to ensure that your site is of the highest possible quality.

Although these tasks are not glamorous, they are essential to any professional web site.

In the next chapter, we will discuss ways of applying what you have learned so far to other types of businesses. We will also talk about hiring a professional to do some or all of the work for you, if you prefer not to build an entire site yourself.

11
From Restaurants to Other Businesses

Throughout this book, we have explored how to develop a-best-in-class web site for a restaurant, using Drupal. Unfortunately, there is not enough room in this book to present all of the possible functionality that you could add to a restaurant's web site. We will begin this chapter by giving you ideas for additional enhancements that you can explore on your own.

Next, we will discuss methods of applying the techniques that you learned in this book to other businesses, as most of you probably neither own a restaurant nor have clients who are restaurant owners.

Finally, we will discuss issues to be considered if you decide to outsource your site development, as well as suggestions for choosing equipment and locations for hosting your web site.

Possible enhancements to the Good Eatin' site

In this section, we will explore additional ideas for enhancing the web site, which we did not have time to cover in detail earlier in this book. For each enhancement, we will either describe how to modify the functionalities that we have already developed, or we will discuss possible modules that you can explore on your own to enhance the site.

Birthday parties

Many restaurants offer birthday parties for children especially if they have a child-friendly theme. Our web site could easily be extended to offer information about birthday parties and allow customers to reserve a time slot for their party. We could even offer birthday party hosts, and party planning functionality, which would allow them to create a guest list, have guests respond to the invitations, and track responses.

The informational pages are simply static pages that would be organized under a birthday menu. You should include information about:

- What days and times parties can be booked for
- Activities that can be done at the party
- What is included in the party package and, if there are multiple party packages, what the differences between them are
- How long parties last
- Ages that parties are appropriate for
- Printable directions for guests to use if you don't have a map on the site already

Allowing guests to register for a party could be handled using the **Public Bookings** module.

There is no dedicated module that would allow you to send invitations for a party. However, you could use the **Webform** module to create a survey that would be used to send invitations to guests and allow them to respond. We discussed using Webform in Chapter 4.

Gift certificates

Gift certificates are used by many restaurants and other types of businesses to solicit new business and to provide an additional revenue source.

Adding gift certificates is simply a matter of adding a new product to your e-commerce store, with specific amounts. You can then either send the customer a printed gift certificate or a gift card.

A fancier solution would be to automatically create a discount coupon that the customer could either use online for takeout purchases, or could print and bring the printed coupon into the store for in-store purchases. To create this type of solution, you would need to integrate Ubercart to ensure that certificates are paid for, and then generate coupon codes within Ubercart. You would also need to ensure that coupon redemption is handled on the web site to prevent customers from redeeming the coupon twice, once in the store and once online.

Employment

Most businesses are constantly looking to hire new employees. Your Drupal site can be easily extended to provide information to potential employees. Much of the information can be provided in a few static information pages.

You should include the following information:

- A description of positions that are currently available, including the duties of the position and where the employee will work, if you have multiple locations
- Who to contact to submit an application
- When the applicant needs to submit an application by, and when you expect to fill the position

You can automate the process of submitting applications using either a custom-generated content type built using CCK form, or with Webform. The Webform solution may be easier as the response will not need to be saved. However, if you would like to track applications, you may want to use a CCK node that could be extended to track the entire interview and hiring process.

If you do choose to store applicant information, make sure that it is adequately protected, to prevent the disclosure of confidential information. You may want to consider creating a separate site that is available only to employees for personnel information.

Loyalty rewards

Loyalty rewards are a great way of encouraging customers to become repeat customers, and to have them return to your store over and over again. Loyalty rewards programs typically offer free or reduced-price merchandise after a specific number or value of purchases have been made by a customer.

Although there are companies that will administer rewards programs for you, you can also administer the program yourself via your web site.

To run a rewards program, you need to:

- Create a unique tracking number for each customer or family.

- When the customer makes a purchase, their rewards balance will need to be updated to show the number of value of purchases they have made, and whether or not they are eligible for a reward.

- When a reward milestone is reached, the server should be notified, so that the customer's final bill is updated accordingly.

While these are the minimum steps for a reward program, but you can enhance your rewards by creating a newsletter for rewards customers, which reminds them of the program and encourages them to return to the store to redeem their rewards, or to take advantage of special offers available only to rewards members.

To handle a basic rewards program, you could use CCK to build a rewards program content type. Each user can then be assigned a single rewards program node. This node can be used to track both purchases and rewards. You can also allow a customer to view their own rewards information, so that they can determine when they will be eligible for another reward, and can see any rewards which they have earned but not redeemed.

You can also create a newsletter using the techniques we discussed in Chapter 6. The focus of this newsletter should be on maximizing the loyalty rewards program, although you may also want to include tips, tricks, or even jokes to keep the newsletter interesting for users.

Similar businesses

Although a restaurant is a great example for our web site and for this book, we realize that many of you don't own a restaurant. In this chapter, we will discuss how to modify the functionality that we have developed over the course of this book to meet the needs of a variety of other businesses.

Informational blogging

Many people create blogs to talk about topics that are important to them. These blogs are typically updated by a single person, although they can also be created by a team of people. A web site could contain several related blogs that are maintained by a group of people.

Drupal can certainly handle the most advanced needs of any blogging site. You can use the techniques discussed in Chapter 5 to create the foundation of your blog. Chapter 5 discussed both single-user and multi-user blogs, so you will be able to create either of these easily.

If you want to earn revenue with your blog site, there are a couple of methods you can use depending on your target audience. These are described below:

Advertising

Adding advertising to your site is one of the most popular methods of gaining revenue for an informational site. Drupal offers several modules that are designed to help you include advertisements on your site.

1. The Adsense module (`http://drupal.org/project/adsense`) assists you in displaying Google Adsense ads on your site. You will first need to create an account at Google. After installing and configuring the module, you can create Adsense blocks that will display either text or graphical advertisements that relate to the content of your site. You can track revenue on Google's web site. Payments are sent to you on a monthly basis, depending upon the amount of traffic your site receives, and the number of people that click on each advertisement.

2. If you prefer to manage your own advertisements, you can use modules like the Advertisement module (`http://drupal.org/project/ad`), which allows you to add advertisements to your site, track when each advertisement is created, and display advertisements based on the node that is displayed. There is also support for advanced functionality such as displaying ads based on the visitor's location.

Additional modules related to advertising can be found at: `http://drupal.org/project/Modules/category/55`.

Donations

Donations are another popular method of gaining revenue for a site. With donations, visitors can send you as much or as little as they want for the information provided to them by your site. If you are not looking to raise large amounts of revenue, this can be a nice option to at least cover the costs of running your site.

You can accept donations via PayPal using Ubercart. However, a simpler method is using a donation module such as **Buy Me a Beer** (`http://drupal.org/project/buymeabeer`). This module provides an easy-to-use interface for visitors to send you a donation via PayPal. You must specify an email address that accepts PayPal payments in the configuration settings for the module.

Membership

Another method of getting revenue is by selling memberships to your web site for a fee. If you decide to sell memberships, you should make sure that members are clearly aware of what they will receive for their membership, and that the members-only content is worth the fee that you are charging.

The **Ubercart Roles** module is a great way of selling memberships. This module allows you to sell access to various roles. You can then assign access to content based on the roles, so that only paid members receive access to the restricted content. If you prefer, you can have memberships expire after a specified time. This allows you to receive recurring income rather than providing lifetime access in return for a one-time payment.

Retail store

If you are running an online store, then much of the functionality described in this book will apply directly to your site. You will certainly want to provide information about your store, as well as information about the products that you sell. All of the information in Chapters 1-3 will help you to build your site. You may even want to give customers the opportunity to purchase items online for in-store pick-up, using the techniques described in Chapter 9.

Photography

A photographer can use many of the techniques described in Chapters 2 and 3 to display a gallery of images online. Downloadable pictures can be sold using Ubercart. To sell a picture, you will want to use the **File Downloads** module to restrict high quality images to only those users who have purchased them. You can also allow customers to purchase printed images that will be physically delivered to them.

Bed and breakfast

A bed and breakfast business can use the **Public Bookings** module to display when each individual room is available and when it is occupied, so that guests can select a room that they want to reserve. After they have selected a room, you can allow them to book the room using Ubercart.

You can easily provide a profile of each room, including pictures, descriptions, and even virtual tours, by using the functionality covered in Chapters 2 and 3.

Outsourcing your development and hosting

When you are ready to begin development of your web site, you will either need to purchase web site hosting, or you will need to purchase a server and have it installed at a web site hosting company. In this section, we will help you determine which route to take, and what to look for in a web host.

Although the functionality described in this book can be accomplished by most people with good computer skills, you may find that you do not have the time or desire to build the entire web site by yourself. We will also discuss how to select a firm to develop a web site for you.

Selecting a hosting company

When deciding on a company to host your web site, or to provide you with bandwidth, there are several factors that you need to consider so that you are satisfied both in the short term and over a longer time period. Because your site will last for several years, you will need to ensure that you have a plan for upgrading as traffic on your site grows, new releases of Drupal are made available, and your server ages. Although it may seem too early to think about your upgrade plans, you will be glad that you thought about them sooner rather than later.

Basic hardware needs

Because Drupal is a highly dynamic content management system, it makes frequent calls to your database and requires more processing than a simple static web site. You can reduce some of the processing requirements by using some of the caching techniques we discussed in the previous chapter. However, you will still need a more powerful server with more memory than you would need if you were creating a simple static web site.

Due to this need for increased processing power, you will want a more modern server with extra memory. In most cases, a shared hosting plan will not be a good solution because many shared hosting plans are over-sold leaving few actual resources on the server. Hosting plans that cost less than $10 per month should normally be ruled out unless you have a very small site, or are not concerned if the site experiences periodic downtimes.

If you plan to purchase a server, you should look for a server with a multiple core and, if possible, multiple processors. You should have a minimum of 1GB memory, but if you can afford it, more memory is always better. Most web sites do not require large amounts of hard drive space, and Drupal-based sites are no exception. You should be able to use 73GB hard drives unless you plan to store and serve a large number of pictures or video. You should plan on having at least two hard drives configured as a RAID array, which will automatically duplicate data from the primary drive onto the secondary drive. If your primary drive fails, you can automatically switch to the secondary drive. You may also want to consider purchasing a redundant power supply to ensure up-time even if your primary power supply fails.

You should also ensure that any server that you buy has some room for expansion, in case you find that you need to add a processor or additional memory to the site.

Fortunately, these specifications do not have to be cost-prohibitive. At the time of writing, a rack-based server with 4GB of memory, 2 processors, and dual—80 GB hard drives would cost approximately $1,200. Tower computers are typically less expensive to purchase, but can be more expensive to be hosted in a data center.

If you are running a highly-popular site, you may need to look into having a database server that is separate from your web server. You can also explore having multiple web servers that are load-balanced for performance reasons.

If you choose to purchase a virtual server, or a dedicated server from a hosting provider, make sure that you ask them what upgrade plans they have for the server (if any), how maintenance is handled, how quickly faulty components are replaced, and what the process would be if you needed to upgrade to a more powerful server in the future.

Selecting hosting

There is a wide variety of hosting plans that you can choose from. Most hosting plans include the hardware as well as hosting, for a combined price. You can also purchase hosting independently from the hardware, by purchasing the hardware and then selecting a data center to place the hardware in. Your business may also have sufficient Internet connectivity to host a server on your site.

Hosting a server at your business site is certainly the most convenient option, but you will also need the knowledge to maintain the server and the connection. An in-house connection may also be more prone to failure when compared to a data center connection that typically has multiple incoming and outgoing connections. However, having the server at your site will allow you to easily upgrade or replace the server as needed, to ensure that you are using appropriate hardware for your site.

Locating your server in a dedicated data center typically provides you with the best overall performance and reliability, since a data center will be climate-controlled to optimize server performance, will have fast and reliable connections to the Internet, and will provide sufficient clean power, with generators in case power is temporarily unavailable. However, it can be less convenient to access the server if you need to carry out physical maintenance, and you will have to give up some control over the environment.

A hosting provider that provides both hardware and hosting gives you the least amount of control over your server, because you typically cannot visit the data center or view the physical hardware. However, this type of provider will handle most or all administration tasks for you, so you do not have to worry about the day-to-day maintenance of your server.

I have used all three types of hosting, and each type has its advantages, depending on the size of your site and how busy your site will be. Smaller sites will generally choose all-in-one hosting, because performance is not as critical, initial costs are lower, and you do not need as much knowledge to get started. Larger business sites will typically purchase their own server and host it either at their own site or at a data center, depending on the connection speed at their location and how well they can secure and maintain the server.

Drupal-specific hosting plans

Several companies with all-in-one hosting plans have either servers or plans that are tailored specifically to Drupal sites. The Drupal-specific features can be in the form of improved hardware to meet the needs of busy Drupal sites, installation and maintenance of Drupal, or support teams that include people with experience creating and maintaining Drupal sites.

The Drupal site has a list of such hosts at: `http://drupal.org/hosting`. Many of these hosts provide support to the Drupal association to directly help with the ongoing development and maintenance of Drupal. This list of providers is more up-to-date than any list I could provide here.

Reviews of hosting companies

As you research web site hosts to work with, you should check the forums on Drupal.org to see if other users have tried them before, and if they have had any problems. If there are no reviews of a hosting provider, you may want to do additional research on the Internet to see what other opinions are available. Of course, negative comments should be taken with a grain of salt because most people only take the time to complain if they have a problem, and do not remember to post about great service. When in doubt, try contacting the hosting provider to see how they respond to your questions. You can also ask them for customers who may be able to give you their opinions on the service.

Experience matters

When you select an all-in-one hosting provider, you are putting a critical factor for the success of your web site into someone else's hands. After all, if your web site goes down, no one can find you, and recovery depends on the speed with which your hosting provider corrects any issues.

With that in mind, it is important to review how long a company has been in business, as a more experienced company will have dealt with a wider range of problems already, which hopefully means that they know how to avoid them in the future. A newer company may not be aware of potential issues until they arise, which could lead to additional downtime for you.

Of course, every new business needs a fair chance, so if you find a newer company that you feel will meet your needs, feel free to use them. But do make sure that you do some extra research on what plans they have to handle all of the emergencies you can think of.

Ease of access

When you set up a web site, you need to make sure that you get access to it when you need to install new releases, add new modules, and perform other maintenance tasks. If your web site is hosted in your building or in a nearby data center, you could certainly walk up to the server, log in, and perform the required maintenance. However, most of the time, you will want to transfer files to the server using FTP, and log in to the server remotely using SSH (secure shell). Make sure that your host provides access to your server using these methods.

Graphical control panels provide an alternative to SSH at some web hosts. A high-quality control panel can provide a fast method of accomplishing most administrative tasks on your site. If your host does offer a control panel, make sure that you review the functionality that it provides, when you are evaluating hosts, to ensure that it will meet your needs.

Other included features

As hosting companies try to gain new customers, they will include additional features that may or may not be of value to you. Some of the items that many host include:

1. Free domain names: This can be nice, but you may also want to purchase a domain name from a reseller, which may give you additional control over the domain settings. Having separate control over your domain can also make it easier to change hosts if this comes necessary.

2. Email accounts: In most cases, you will receive email hosting with your site hosting package. Unless you have separate email capabilities already, it would a good idea to use your host's email, or you can create a Gmail account for your site. A Gmail account allows you to access your mail from a variety of locations, and it has superb spam protection. There are both free and paid options available, depending on the size of your business. You can get more information at: `http://www.google.com/apps/intl/en/business/messaging.html`.

3. Online site builders and web site creators: Because we are using Drupal we won't need any other site builder tools.

4. SSL Certificates: If you are planning to set up an e-commerce store, you will need an SSL certificate. You could purchase one separately, but the included certificates will save you some time and money.

5. Regular backups: Some plans offer regular automated backups. You should check to see what is backed up, how often it is backed up, and what needs to be done to restore from the backup should this become necessary.

6. Support: This is a critical aspect of a hosting plan. You want to ensure that support technicians are knowledgeable and are easy to reach. Nothing is more frustrating than waiting on hold at your host for a long time, and then having the technician not being able to answer your question, or appearing to read from a script giving canned answers that don't apply to your particular problem. You should also look for hosts that provide both email- and phone-based support. You should test the support prior to signing up, to make sure that the host is responsive to questions.

Hiring a developer

Although creating a site with Drupal can be much easier than creating a site using traditional methods and programs, many people still turn to a professional developer to build their site for them. This can save time, and free you to concentrate on ensuring that your site meets your businesses needs while someone else handles the technical work.

When you select a developer, there are several issues that you should keep in mind. This section will cover each of these issues in detail.

Developer qualifications

As you select a developer to build a site for you, you will want to ensure that the developer or development firm has experience in the following areas:

- Previous experience in building Drupal-based sites
- Experience in building Drupal modules, if you need to have custom functionality developed
- Experience in working with MySQL
- Experience with the hardware and operating system that you plan to deploy your site on
- Experience in tuning Drupal to meet the performance needs of your site
- Experience in running projects similar to the scope and complexity of your project

A developer should also be easy to work with, and you should be able to communicate easily with him or her using the medium of your choice. For example, if you prefer to discuss the project on the phone, it makes no sense to select a developer who will only communicate via email.

Graphic design qualifications

A graphic designer can be placed in charge of developing the look and feel of your site. The graphic designer may work with the developer, or he or she may be independent, providing only the finished images to the developer, who will integrate the images into the web site theme.

Selecting a graphic designer can be an intensely personal process, because site design is a very subjective work. A good designer will take your suggestions and transform them into a work of art better than you imagined. However, success is not guaranteed as each designer tends to have a particular style that he or she is good at. Before hiring a graphic designer, you should carefully review the designer's portfolio to ensure that you like the designs that he or she has previously created. You should also contact any references that he or she provides, to ensure that his or her prior customers were satisfied.

You also need to ensure that the developer has worked on Drupal-based web sites before, to confirm that they understand how to build a design that can be used easily with a variety of content, and to ensure that they can provide the correct information to successfully theme each block and custom view that you are creating.

Finally, you need to determine if the designer will be responsible for building the theme for the site, or if they will only create one or more images that will be used by the developer to create the theme. If your developer is building the theme, you need to ensure that they are comfortable with building Drupal themes.

Finding a developer on Drupal.org

A great place to begin looking for a developer to build your site is the Drupal web site. The Drupal site has a forum where developers can post their availability or respond to job postings.

You can access the forum at: `http://drupal.org/paid-services`.

As a minimum, before you post a request for a proposal, you should make sure that you have fully defined what you want done, and have an idea of how much you are willing to pay for the work.

By putting a limit on how much you want to pay, you can decide if the developer estimates are in line with your budget. If the quotes come in higher than you can afford, you will need to trim functionality to meet your budget. If all of the estimates are within your budget, you have the luxury of selecting a developer based solely on the quality of the proposal.

The more complete your request for a proposal is, the better the response from the consultant will be. So make sure that you have a complete outline of what you need to do. Here are some topics that you may want to include in your request:

- The proposed structure of the site.
- Functionality that you need to implement on your site.
- A complete description of any custom functionality that you want to have developed.
- A description of what you want the site to look like. If you have an existing site you want to mimic, providing that information will help. If you don't have an existing site, try picking out between three and five themes on the `Drupal.org` site that you like, and tell the developer what you do or don't like about each one.
- A description of what hardware the web site will run on, if you have that information.
- An estimate of the number of visitors who will use the site per month, and how many concurrent users there will be on the site at peak times.
- A list of any deadlines that the developer needs to meet.
- Any testing the developer will need to do on his or her own.

- Information about the resources that will be available to the developer to complete the project, including testing resources, business resources, and project management resources.

- If functionality can be added in phases, a description of each milestone should be included.

- Payment terms, including whether or not you prefer a fixed cost quote, or a cost based on the actual time spent on the project.

Although many project proposals will not include all of these elements, you should try to provide as many as possible in order to help the developer create a complete and accurate proposal for you.

After your proposal is ready, you can submit it on the `Drupal.org` site. You can also review some of the development groups that are listed on the Drupal site and contact them directly to request a quote.

As developers review your project, they will most likely need to ask you additional questions to clarify specific points in your project. Make sure that you answer any questions as quickly and as thoroughly as possible.

When you evaluate a developer, you should talk with him or her in person, or on the telephone, to ensure that he or she has a thorough understanding of your project, and to ensure that you can work well with him or her. You will also want to check samples of his or her work, and discuss his or her work with any references that he or she can provide.

Summary

In this chapter, we have explored different ways of modifying the techniques used in this book to apply them to your site. For those readers who want to set up a web site, but don't want to do all the work themselves, we also discussed tips for outsourcing the development of thee web site to another company.

If you choose to build your own site, I wish you many hours of enjoyment as you build and enhance your site. The wonderful thing about Drupal is that you can make your site as simple or as complex as you want. You certainly do not need to build a site as complex as the Good Eatin' site. You can also start with a simple site and graduall evolve into a complex site over time, letting your confidence grow with each step.

If you choose to outsource development, the knowledge that you have gained by reading this book will help you to effectively communicate the goals of your web site to the company doing the development work. This will in turn reduce the cost of building your web site, reduce or eliminate rework, and help the developer in creating a site that best meets your needs. You will also understand the possibilities that Drupal offers, giving you new ideas for how your web site can promote your business. After the initial development is complete, you may even want to build new pages or edit existing pages using the techniques described in this book.

Of course, Drupal is always evolving and improving, which gives you the chance to take advantage of the latest web site technologies to give your customers the best possible experience. To keep up-to-date with Drupal, make sure that you visit `drupal.org` frequently.

Index

[PACKT] PUBLISHING

Thank you for buying
Drupal 6 Site Builder Solutions

Packt Open Source Project Royalties

When we sell a book written on an Open Source project, we pay a royalty directly to that project. Therefore by purchasing Drupal 6 Site Builder Solutions, Packt will have given some of the money received to the Drupal project.

In the long term, we see ourselves and you—customers and readers of our books—as part of the Open Source ecosystem, providing sustainable revenue for the projects we publish on. Our aim at Packt is to establish publishing royalties as an essential part of the service and support a business model that sustains Open Source.

If you're working with an Open Source project that you would like us to publish on, and subsequently pay royalties to, please get in touch with us.

Writing for Packt

We welcome all inquiries from people who are interested in authoring. Book proposals should be sent to author@packtpub.com. If your book idea is still at an early stage and you would like to discuss it first before writing a formal book proposal, contact us; one of our commissioning editors will get in touch with you.

We're not just looking for published authors; if you have strong technical skills but no writing experience, our experienced editors can help you develop a writing career, or simply get some additional reward for your expertise.

About Packt Publishing

Packt, pronounced 'packed', published its first book "Mastering phpMyAdmin for Effective MySQL Management" in April 2004 and subsequently continued to specialize in publishing highly focused books on specific technologies and solutions.

Our books and publications share the experiences of your fellow IT professionals in adapting and customizing today's systems, applications, and frameworks. Our solution-based books give you the knowledge and power to customize the software and technologies you're using to get the job done. Packt books are more specific and less general than the IT books you have seen in the past. Our unique business model allows us to bring you more focused information, giving you more of what you need to know, and less of what you don't.

Packt is a modern, yet unique publishing company, which focuses on producing quality, cutting-edge books for communities of developers, administrators, and newbies alike. For more information, please visit our website: www.PacktPub.com.

Building Powerful and Robust Websites with Drupal 6

ISBN: 978-1-847192-97-4   Paperback: 362 pages

Build your own professional blog, forum, portal or community website with Drupal 6

1. Set up, configure, and deploy Drupal 6

2. Harness Drupal's world-class Content Management System

3. Design and implement your website's look and feel

4. Easily add exciting and powerful features

5. Promote, manage, and maintain your live website

Drupal 6 Themes

ISBN: 978-1-847195-66-1   Paperback: 291 pages

Create new themes for your Drupal 6 site with clean layout and powerful CSS styling

1. Learn to create new Drupal 6 themes

2. No experience of Drupal theming required

3. Techniques and tools for creating and modifying themes

4. A complete guide to the system's themable elements

Please check **www.PacktPub.com** for information on our titles

3088485

Made in the USA